Computer Corpus Lexicography

EDINBURGH TEXTBOOKS IN EMPIRICAL LINGUISTICS

CORPUS LINGUISTICS
by Tony McEnery and Andrew Wilson

LANGUAGE AND COMPUTERS
A PRACTICAL INTRODUCTION TO THE COMPUTER ANALYSIS OF LANGUAGE
by Geoff Barnbrook

STATISTICS FOR CORPUS LINGUISTICS
by Michael Oakes

COMPUTER CORPUS LEXICOGRAPHY
by Vincent B. Y. Ooi

If you would like information on forthcoming titles in this series, please contact
Edinburgh University Press, 22 George Square, Edinburgh EH8 9LF

EDINBURGH TEXTBOOKS IN EMPIRICAL LINGUISTICS

Series Editors: Tony McEnery and Andrew Wilson

Computer Corpus Lexicography

Vincent B. Y. Ooi

EDINBURGH UNIVERSITY PRESS

Transferred to digital print 2009

Edinburgh University Press
22 George Square, Edinburgh EH8 9LF

Typeset in 11/13pt Bembo by
Koinonia, Manchester
and printed and bound in Great Britain by
CPI Antony Rowe, Chippenham and Eastbourne

A CIP record for this book is available from the British Library

ISBN 0 7486 0996 2 (cased)
ISBN 0 7486 0815 X (paperback)

Contents

Acknowledgements

The main input for this book arose out of research done at both the National University of Singapore and Lancaster University. In the course of carrying out my research, I have been fortunate to have had the opportunity of interacting with a number of leading researchers (either in terms of having studied with them or correspondence via electronic mail) on the subject of computers and the lexicon, of whom the following merit special mention: Professor Geoffrey Leech, Professor John Sinclair, Dr Jonathan Webster, Professor Adam Makkai, Mr Roger Garside, Dr Richard Sharman, Mr John McNaught, Professor Richard Hudson, Ms Sue Atkins, Mr Richard Piepenbrock, Professor Ray Jackendoff, Dr John Self, and Dr Roger Evans.

The data and corpora cited in this book have been taken from various sources. The PROLEX corpus and the Singapore ICE corpus represent data drawn from research projects carried out at the National University of Singapore: I wish to thank Associate Professor Ban Kah Choon, Head of the Department of English Language and Literature, NUS, for permission to draw from both corpora in this book. Part of the inspiration, as it were, for Chapter 3 came from a series of video-conferencing sessions conducted by Professor John Sinclair between August and October 1996 for my courses on Computational Linguistics and Lexicology and Lexicography: these video-conferencing session also involved, at the same time, Internet access to the Bank of English corpus at Birmingham University. I am grateful to Mr Jeremy Clear for permission to use the data drawn from the Bank of English corpus created by COBUILD at Birmingham University, and I hasten to add that whatever factual errors made in reporting on the COBUILD enterprise are mine alone. Part of Chapter 4 appeared in the proceedings of the 21st LACUS Forum; thanks are due to the Linguistic Association of Canada and the United States for allowing me to incorporate the essay into this chapter.

I wish to record my many thanks to the series editors, Dr Tony McEnery and Dr Andrew Wilson, for their editorial guidance, patience, and understanding which has seen this book through. Similar thanks are due to Ms Jackie Jones and her staff at Edinburgh University Press, and to Ms Mairi Robinson for her excellent copy editing.

Finally, I am indebted to my family, friends, colleagues, and students for providing me with their moral support and various types of assistance.

Abbreviations

AI	Artificial Intelligence
AL	Associative Lexicon
AP	Associated Press Corpus
CELEX	Centre for Lexical Information at Nijmegen
CL1	Computational Linguistics
CL2	Computational Lexicography (and Lexicology)
CL3	(Computer) Corpus Linguistics
CLAWS	Constituent-Likelihood Automatic Word-tagging System
COBUILD	Collins-Birmingham University International Language Database
DATR	The lexical representation language developed by Evans and Gazdar (1990)
ICAME	International Computer Archive of Modern and Medieval English
ICE	International Corpus of English
LDB/LKB	Lexical data/knowledge base
LDOCE	Longman Dictionary of Contemporary English
LFA	Lexical Frame Analysis: the framework that I use in Chap 4
MRD	Machine-readable dictionary
MRT	Machine-readable text
NLP	Natural Language Processing
OALD	Oxford Advanced Learner's Dictionary
PATR	(or 'PATR-II'): the formalism described in Shieber (1986)
PROCOMPARE	A corpus of business English templates
PROLEX	The PRO(fessional) LEX(is) Project
PROLOG	The AI language PRO(gramming) LOG(ic)
reuse_e	The first sense of reusability, i.e. reusing existing lexical resources
reuse_m	The second sense of reusability, i.e. achieving multifunctionality
SGML	Standard Generalized Markup Language
TEI	Text Encoding Initiative

What is Computer Corpus Lexicography?

1.0 INTRODUCTION

Ever since the well-known dictum that 'in the beginning was the word', the word has always been basic to human understanding and communication. In turn, facts about the word are recorded in a dictionary, whose making has been undertaken for centuries by what Samuel Johnson calls a 'harmless drudge', the lexicographer. Nowadays, 'dictionary-making' takes on a number of new meanings, especially with the computer which offers its vast resources of storage, retrieval, analysis, dissemination and exchange of data as well as increased sophistication in database design and linguistic research: partly from such a development, the contribution to the dictionary-making process now prominently includes (among others) linguists, language engineers, and computer scientists. Linguistic research on the theory and nature of the word is concerned with the nature of the lexicon. Such linguistic principles form the basis of **lexicology**, which has as its aim the analysis of the lexicon. **Lexicography**, popularly known as dictionary-making, draws on such a set of linguistic principles and is concerned with the description of the lexicon.

   This book therefore introduces you to these two related (and to a large extent inseparable) disciplines of lexicology and lexicography, with a focus on the computer for both lexicon-building and dictionary-making. I call this programme of research **computer corpus lexicography**,[1] which represents a convergence of interest from the viewpoints of Computational Linguistics (henceforth CL1), Computational Lexicography (henceforth CL2), and Computer Corpus Linguistics (henceforth CL3). In practice, CL1 has always sought to specify lexicons which are formal (i.e. explicit to the computer) and rich enough for the building of natural language processing systems. However, such lexicons may not necessarily be 'user-friendly' or suitable for human consumption. CL2 is used to refer to either using the computer to achieve the goal of fully automating lexicographic tasks or utilising existing machine-readable versions of commercial dictionaries into a format explicit enough for computational linguistic systems. CL3, of which this book complements the other works in the Edinburgh series on empirical linguistics (e.g. McEnery and Wilson 1996), focuses on the principles and practice of compiling bodies of (largely electronic) texts of actual language in use. From these three perspectives, the convergence of interest is on the use of natural language text for one or more of the following: (1) lexicon extraction and building, (2) lexicon-based language modelling, (3) computational storage of the lexicon, (4) the employment of richer lexicons for natural language processing systems, and (5) defining standards for lexical exchange and reusability, so that individual efforts can be maximised. Such issues will be considered in this book.

Besides the lexicographer then, the linguist's contribution to the dictionary-making process can be subdivided into, at least, three roles. Firstly, the theoretical linguist can extend the notion of his/her theoretical dictionary, the lexicon. Secondly, the computational linguist can extend the notion of a lexicon by storing it in the computational lexical structure known as the lexical data/knowledge base. Thirdly, the corpus linguist can extend the notion of the lexicon by basing its description on an appropriate analysis of textual instances. But why should the linguist take on such agendas? For the theoretical linguist, a richer lexicon represents the creation of new knowledge which can be used and disseminated by the lexicographer in various ways. Also, contemporary linguistic theories are now emphasising an ever-greater reliance on the lexicon: indeed, the lexicon may be viewed as the central repository of linguistic knowledge. For the computational linguist, the lexicon is the 'bottleneck' of natural language processing systems, so research into richer lexical descriptions is needed. This includes attempting to manipulate machine-readable versions of printed dictionaries and transforming them into computational lexicons. Also, storing the dictionary in a lexical data/knowledge base allows the search for lexical information beyond the perspective of a mere printed dictionary, as well as allowing the creation of various lexicons, as and when needed. For the corpus linguist, the increasing reliance by dictionary-makers on corpora as the authoritative source of their linguistic evidence shows that lexicographic description on 'real' language in use provides a complement to the traditional reliance on introspective lexical knowledge. While manipulating machine-readable dictionaries is a feasible computational option, we now realise that the descriptive accuracy of lexical data is also dependent on machine-readable texts, of which the corpus offers itself as a rich lexical resource.

The book draws its examples from English and is organised broadly into two themes: **lexical theory** and **lexical practice**. By lexical theory is meant the construction of a linguistic framework for the analysis of a corpus-informed lexicon. By lexical practice, I mean the application of such a framework to a corpus (or corpora) for the description and extraction of a corpus-informed lexicon.

Linguistics, computer science, lexicography: this book hopes to show, in its own small way, that the relation between computers and dictionaries – as indeed, computers and corpus lexical analysis – through a convergence of these various perspectives becomes an ever-closer one, which invests 'dictionary-making' with a new significance.

1.1 DEVELOPING NOTIONS OF THE LEXICON

I would now like to ask the basic question of what the **lexicon** is by tracing some ways in which its nature and function has been characterised in the literature.

From early days when the lexicon was equated merely as 'a dictionary, a book teaching [only] the signification of words' (Johnson 1755), the lexicon is nowadays generally equated as 'the vocabulary of a language, especially in dictionary form [which is] also called **lexis**' (Crystal 1995: 454), offering various types of linguistic information. Strictly speaking, a useful distinction may be made between the lexicon as 'an object defined by linguistic theory' and the dictionary which presents 'certain information drawn from the lexicon in a stylised way' (Grimes 1988: 167). Grimes goes on to describe the lexicon as 'simply the totality of all the information there is about words and word-like objects in a natural language; it registers items and their properties in contrast to the **grammar**, which registers combinations of items and their properties' (Grimes 1988: 168). Similarly, Bennett et al. (1986: 26) make a distinction between a grammar (i.e. 'a set of rules for the formation of meaningful and well-formed sentences') and a lexicon (i.e. 'a set of words and expressions whose use is governed by those rules').

Grimes' definition for the lexicon is interesting since it raises the question of whether a 'theory-neutral' lexicon (see Section 2.8) is possible to create, there being not one linguistic theory, but numerous linguistic theories – converging as well as diverging – which abound in the literature. His definition is also justifiably vague as to what a lexicon should contain, since individual lexicons will have their own specification, depending on the purpose for which they were built. A more recent definition by Mel'cuk (1992: 332) similarly views the lexicon (or dictionary) as 'a specific list of **lexical units** of a language, arranged in a specific way and supplied with specific information, the whole being designed for a specific purpose'.

Theoretically, the relation between the lexicon and other levels of linguistic structure has been a subject of contention. In particular, the lexicon has to be discussed vis-à-vis its relation to the grammar, since what precisely constitutes grammatical and lexical facts respectively continues to be a matter of debate. In tracing the cause, so to speak, for this state of affairs, we may say that in early days the lexicon was treated as a peripheral component, as illustrated by Bloomfield's statement that 'the lexicon is really an appendix of the grammar, a list of basic irregularities', whereas a grammar was treated as 'the meaningful arrangement of forms of a language' (Bloomfield, 1933: 274).

The lexicon was conceptualised as an independent component in linguistic theory by Noam Chomsky, one of the most influential linguists of this century, with the publication of Chomsky (1965). However, in Chomsky's early characterisation of the nature and function of the lexicon, lexical facts were not only said to be a different type from general facts, but the lexicon was still viewed as a 'wastebin' into which irregular items went: 'regular variations are not matters for the lexicon, which should contain only idiosyncratic items' (Chomsky and Halle 1968: 12).

With regard to the grammar, Chomsky more recently no longer equates **grammar** with the speaker's grammar: the term is instead used as 'a description or theory of a language, an object constructed by a linguist' (Chomsky 1986: 19). While it would now appear that Chomsky equates the term with the linguist's grammar, it is undeniable that the Chomskyan linguist still characterises a native speaker's idiolect or mental knowledge of the language, assuming that this occurs in a homogeneous speaker-hearer community: there is thus a focus on the **I-language** ('internalised language') or **linguistic competence**. On the other hand, the **E-language** ('externalised language') or **linguistic performance** may be regarded as everyday speech and writing: newspapers, magazines, televised speeches and dialogues etc. The grammar of the E-language may be regarded as equivalent to Bloomfield's notion of grammar. For Chomsky, the E-language has a 'theoretical status that is harder to characterise', being full of 'noise' (false starts, speech fillers, performance errors etc.), and so it is only the I-language that may be equated with the broad notion of language. This equation of the I-language with language, to the exclusion of the E-language, is a debatable and indeed false notion for many other persons. Instead, many people consider firstly, that there is no such thing as a totally homogeneous speaker-hearer community and, secondly, that Chomsky has exaggerated the gap between competence and performance. While much more discussion is possible on these two important theoretical notions, it suffices to conclude that Chomsky (1986, 1995) continues to argue for a focus on the I-language as the object of linguistic study.

The present book (with its use of corpora) is, of course, one which focuses on the E-language (in the sense that it looks at observable data as the primary type of data) and so any lexical study which derives information from a corpus might have a theoretical status 'hard to justify', in Chomskyan terms. Nevertheless, the last few years have witnessed a resurgence of interest in the so-called E-language: since the methodology of using a corpus is well-established nowadays (see McEnery and Wilson 1996), there is no need to labour this point. Further, with regard to the seemingly competing method-ologies of the I-language and the E-language, Leech (1991b: 74) is right to point out that 'the all-sufficient corpus of the post-Bloomfieldian linguist and the all-sufficient intuitions of the generative linguist ... is essentially a false opposition.' Leech argues for a mediation of these two diametrically-opposite positions and characterises the use of a corpus in linguistic study 'as a question of corpus *plus* intuition, rather than of corpus *or* intuition' (Leech 1991b: 74). Thus, by extension, any opposition postulated between the lexicon of the I-language and that of the E-language would appear to be a false opposition.

Recast in these terms, the relation between the lexicons of the E- and the I-language may be formulated in terms of, say, an **Associative Lexicon** of the type postulated by Makkai (1980, 1986):

> An Associative Lexicon (henceforth AL) is an information retrieval system that represents in visual and audible form the knowledge native speakers possess about the lexis of their language. The human brain is, naturally, the primary 'information retrieval system' housing our ability to associate lexemes with one another. Any artificial system we may build must, therefore, try to do justice to what there is in human sociopsychological reality. The natural ALs we carry in our heads are dialectically and sociolinguistically limited in addition to being subject to growth and shrinkage due to learning and forgetting. The AL, then [as described] differs from natural ALs insofar as it will also represent the cumulative knowledge of most available geographic and sociological dialects of English indicating, as it were, that members of various speech communities have the capability of learning from one another either by memorisation or by immigration. The AL here outlined is not to be likened to the 'ideal hearer-speaker in the homogenous [sic, "homogeneous"] society', because such people do not exist.
>
> (Makkai 1980: 125)

The 'cumulative knowledge' of the AL parallels Leech's notion of **corporate lexical competence** which is 'greater than the lexical competence of any one of its users. This pool of lexical information is what is embodied in the printed dictionary' (Leech 1981: 205).

The difference between a printed dictionary and an AL, however, is that conventional dictionaries tend, by and large, to ignore the associative groupings of lexemes to form natural semantic nets around concretely observable and abstract (non-observable) entities.[2] Conventional dictionaries also rely traditionally on alphabetisation by which they endeavour to present a totality of the available lexis in the form of a list while ignoring frequency of usage, exact range of dialectal habitat, the speaker's sociological status etc. Conventional printed dictionaries tend to submit to this psychologically quite unmotivated tyranny of the alphabet, leaving the user uninformed as to a term's typologically-based frequency and collocational range. On the other hand, because Makkai's AL is envisaged not to be printed but computerised, this problem of the 'tyranny of the alphabet' is resolved: a computerised lexicon offers various non-alphabetic paths of access to the word according to various linguistic (e.g. phonetic, grammatical, and semantic) features of classification, as well as the word's associative or semantic interconnections with other words. Hence, the present book will emphasise the importance of storing the lexicon in a computationally tractable format.

Storing the lexicon in this format allows for flexibility in its retrieval. It also reduces the number of problems associated with its organisation. In this book, the notion of **lexical entry** (as represented roughly by each bold entry in a dictionary) is retained, but its boundaries ought to be shaded. Shading the boundaries of the lexical entry accords well with Hudson's (1988: 299; 1995) suggestion for a conception of the lexicon which is 'much more like a network or relational database', instead of being restricted – like mainstream linguistic theories – to the 'crude and inflexible' notion of the lexical entry. Hudson stresses that a lexicon is much more than just a list of lexical entries, and that 'entries are ordered on more than one dimension – a phonological ordering shows phonological relatedness ... a semantic ordering shows semantic relatedness ... and so on' (Hudson, 299).

1.1.1 The trend towards lexicalism

As the preceding section has indicated, early Chomskyan thinking recognised the lexicon as an individual component of the grammar, although not a very important one. Interestingly enough, the start of **lexicalism**, i.e. the tendency to shift linguistic explanation from facts about constructions to facts about words, may be said to have started with Chomsky (1970), where transformational rules (within the grammar) were now said to be unsuitable for explaining the relations between some kinds of partially analogous structures, e.g. in sentences like *They destroyed Pompeii* and *their destruction of Pompeii*. Chomsky formulated the Lexicalist Hypothesis which suggested that, in the example just cited, the lexical information for *destroy* should include subcategorisation features which allow for an object NP (noun phrase). The lexicon then specifies either the nominal form (if *destroy* is the head of an NP) or the verbal form (if *destroy* is a VP). Therefore, the relation between *destroy* and *destruction* was explained not by means of the transformational component within Chomsky's grammar but rather in terms of the lexicon.

Taking up the suggestion in Chomsky (1970), Jackendoff (1975) describes some of the redundancy rules that the lexicon would have with regard to the mental representations of such word structures. In his more recent description of the lexicon, Jackendoff (1992a, 1992b, 1995) sees the word as a correspondence rule between the three levels of representation: phonological structure (PS), syntactic structure (SS), and conceptual structure (CS). There is no explicit lexical component, but the word is a <PS, SS, CS> triple that licenses correspondence of these structures; a sentence/clause may be analysed just as a <PS, SS, CS> triple. Similarly, Pike and Pike's (1983: 109) notion of the lexical manifesting substance centrally binds the triple hierarchies of phonology, grammar, and reference.

What is also particularly significant in Jackendoff's grammar here is that the terms **semantic structure** and **conceptual structure**, as in Jackendoff (1983: 94), 'denote the same level of representation'. Thus, Jackendoff points out that the structures of language and cognition are not dissimilar (until proven otherwise). Figure 1.1 diagrammatically gives an overview of his grammar.

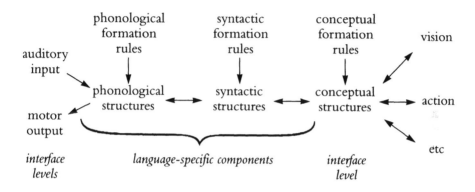

Figure 1.1 Overall organisation of the information structure involved in language: from Jackendoff (1995: 138)

If this idea is extended to its extreme, there does not seem to be any distinction between 'semantic' and 'encyclopedic' knowledge, because the *form* in which semantic and encyclopedic knowledge are represented is the same, although words package this knowledge in a certain way.

Also, if Jackendoff's theory is indicative of contemporary mainstream research, there is an increasing tendency to emphasise the similarities and continuities between linguistic and non-linguistic knowledge, and minimise the distinction between the lexicon and the rest of the grammar. This position accords well with Lamb (1973: 80) where 'the linguistic network and the cognitive network are two parts of one large relational network'. Hudson also argues that, for 'mental representations of word structures', 'the linguistic network is just part of a larger network, without any clear differences between the linguistic and non-linguistic beyond the fact that one is about words and the other is not' (Hudson 1984: 6).

With regard to this 'linguistic network', lexicalism (for example in the work of Hudson) has moved to a more thoroughgoing shift from the grammar to the lexicon. However, it is but one of the parallel trends noticeable in linguistics during the 1980s. According to Hudson, the other trends include the following:

- **wholism**: the tendency to minimise the distinction between the lexicon and the rest of the grammar;
- **trans-constructionism**: the tendency to reduce the number of rules that are specific to just one construction;
- **poly-constructionism**: the tendency to increase the number of particular constructions that are recognised in a grammar;
- **relationism**: the tendency to refer explicitly to grammatical relations, and even to treat these, rather than constituent structure, as primary;
- **mono-stratalism**: the tendency to reject the transformational idea that a sentence's syntactic structure cannot be shown in a single structural representation;
- **cognitivism**: the tendency to emphasise the similarities and continuities between linguistic and non-linguistic knowledge;
- **implementationism**: the tendency to implement grammars in terms of computer programs.

(Hudson 1990: 3)

Hudson claims that Word Grammar (WG), his model of language, reflects each of these trends. However, where the lexicalist and (w)holist trends are concerned, Hudson is right to observe that 'one of the weaknesses of the lexicalist movement has been its general failure to define precisely what the lexicon is, and how it differs from the rest of the grammar' (Hudson, 1990: 5). He goes on to reinterpret lexicalism as an approach to grammar in which words are basic and the boundary around the lexicon plays no part, as postulated in his WG. In this view, the word assumes central importance because it is universally recognised as at least one of the units that grammars describe, and generally recognised as the boundary between morphology (inside the word) and syntax (relation between words), each of which allows rather different processes. For Hudson, the word is the unit where internal structure is most arbitrary, relative to meaning, so it is the unit where memory plays the biggest part. In this conception, taken to the extreme, there should not be any work left over to be done by any other unit once everything is described of the word (Hudson, personal communication).

Estival (1991: 488) also notes the trend towards lexicalism by a number of current syntactic frameworks, such as Bresnan's (1982) Lexical Functional Grammar, Gazdar et al.'s (1985) Generalised Phrase Structure Grammar, and Pollard and Sag's (1987) Head-driven Phrase Structure Grammar: 'more and more syntactic information which used to be encoded in the rules of the grammar is now considered to be part of the lexical entries themselves, or to be derivable by lexical rules'.[3]

1.1.2 The word vs the clause as the most basic unit in linguistics

The question of what goes into the lexical entry is therefore one which involves the role of the lexicon vis-à-vis the grammar in an overall conception of the linguistic system.

In this section, I reformulate this issue with regard to having either the 'clause' (which is roughly equivalent to the 'sentence') or the 'word' as the more basic unit in linguistics, hence by extension underlining the centrality of each respective component. Two linguistic theories stand out in this respect.

Halliday's Functional Grammar (FG) is designed for the understanding and evaluation of the text (Halliday, 1985 and 1994: xv). For this purpose, Halliday takes the **clause**, being the unit of grammar, as the most basic in his theory of language. The clause is a functional unit with a triple construction of meaning: it functions simultaneously for

1. construing a model of experience ('experiential' metafunction) and logical relations ('logical' metafunction), thus reflecting **ideational** meaning;
2. enacting social relationships, thus reflecting **personal** meaning;
3. creating relevance to context, thus reflecting **textual** meaning.

(Halliday, 1994: 36)

In FG, these three forms of meaning are the components of the semantic system. Halliday's perspective on meaning – which he names 'the metafunctional hypothesis' – is also compared to language as **field, wave**, and **particle**. The textual meaning, expressed by what is put first (the Theme); by what is phonologically prominent; and by conjunctions and relatives which if present must occur in initial position, forms a 'wave'-like pattern of periodicity that is traced by peaks and prominence and boundary markers. The interpersonal meaning is 'field'-like, because it is expressed by the intonation contour; by the 'mood' block, which may be repeated as a tag at the end; and by expressions of modality which may recur throughout the clause. Experiential meaning, which is part of the ideational meaning, is 'particle'-like because it gives us our sense of the building blocks of language (Halliday, 1985: 169). Despite taking the clause as the most basic unit, FG is a lexicogrammar which, as its name suggests, comprises both lexical and grammatical components. More recently, in writing about the advantages of interrogating the corpus, Halliday has explicitly maintained that the lexicogrammar is 'inherently probabilistic' (Halliday 1991, 1992). In addition, although a lexicogrammar is regarded as consisting of lexis, syntax, and morphology – with syntax and morphology grouped as 'grammar' – Halliday thinks it would not be appropriate to suggest that lexis and grammar are entirely different from each other: a lexicogrammar is seen as 'a unified phenomenon, a single level of "wording", of which lexis is the "most delicate" resolution' (Halliday 1991: 32). Lexis and grammar form a continuum of which open-ended choices at one end are treated as constituting lexis and closed-ended ones are most appropriately treated as grammar.

To elaborate, for Halliday, 'lexis' and 'grammar' are names of complementary perspectives, 'each explaining different aspects of a single complex phenomenon' (Halliday 1985: 32). This may be said to be one instance of the (w)holist trend mentioned in Section 1.1.1. Nevertheless, Halliday does choose the clause as the most basic unit for his expressed purpose of saying 'useful' things about the text, and regards it as 'perhaps the most fundamental category in the whole of linguistics, as well as being critical to the **unity** of spoken and written language' (1985: 67).

The alternative perspective – or more probably a complementary one – to the clause is the assumption that the **word** (lexeme) is the most basic unit in linguistics, a position exemplified by Hudson (1984, 1990) in his Word Grammar (WG). Hudson sees his position on the word as psychologically the most plausible fundamental unit in linguistics, and asserts that his view is compatible with Halliday's conception of lexis as 'most delicate' grammar, instead of lexis being regarded as a separate kind of linguistic patterning from the syntax. In WG, the analysis of a sentence consists of an analysis of each word. As Hudson is concerned about mirroring the structure of the speaker/ hearer's knowledge, WG regards language as consisting entirely of **declarative** knowledge, expressed as propositions. A WG proposition includes the following parameters: predicates, arguments, quantification, retrieval and inference. In terms of predicates, or 'types of propositions', Hudson (1984: 8) recognises five types of propositions:

> composition (part–whole relations)
> model (instance:model relations)
> companion (word:word relations)
> referent (word:referent relations)
> utterance event (word:context relations)

These parameters, which help integrate grammatical and lexical knowledge, are reanalysed by Hudson (1990: 16) to include 'is, has, precedes, follows, isa' in order to define the relations between the arguments. Hudson acknowledges his notation has changed, but the relations remain the same: 'the list of permitted predicates has fluctuated wildly, and yet there has been very little change in the relations being expressed' (Hudson, 17). In computationally implementing his grammar, Hudson reduces all these predicates to just one, 'is', in keeping with the 'slot:filler' or 'attribute-value' notation system (see Section 1.3).

I have thus dwelt at length on the long-standing question of which unit in linguistics is the more basic, because this is theoretically important in the practice of analysing texts, in particular textual corpora, for this book. In this book, I follow the practice of viewing the word as the most basic unit, but analysing it in relation to other items at the level of clause.

1.2 LEXICAL CONTENT

If the lexicon is conceived in the above manner, with an increased role, then the question of what linguistic information it should contain becomes important.

1.2.1 Characterisations of lexical content

In practice, what information the lexicon should contain depends on the purpose for which the lexicon is built. However, general statements are useful because they give us an idea of how the lexicon is conceived by the respective linguistic theory.

Thus, the following characterisations of the lexicon are general statements on what the lexicon should contain, and are by no means exhaustive. Chomsky (1986: 86) suggests that 'the lexicon presents, for each lexical item, its (abstract) phonological form and whatever semantic properties are associated with it. Among these will be the "selectional properties" of heads of constructions: nouns, verbs, adjectives, and particles (prepositions or postpositions, depending on how the head-complement parameters are set in the language)'. Chomsky (1995: 130) still maintains that 'the lexicon is a set of lexical elements, each an articulated system of features. It must specify, for each element, the phonetic, semantic, and syntactic properties that are idiosyncratic to it, but nothing more.' Gazdar and Mellish (1989: 104) go beyond defining it as 'minimally a list of words that associates each word with its syntactic properties' to specifying that its properties include its '(gross) syntactic category – for example, whether the word is a verb or a noun. In addition, depending on the sophistication of the overall grammar, the lexicon will contain information as to the subcategory of the word (such as whether a particular verb is transitive or intransitive), other syntactic properties (such as the gender of a noun in a language that makes gender distinctions), and perhaps also morphological and semantic information.'

In the case of verbs, Atkins and Levin (1991) specify the following fields of information:

- Semantic class, aktionsart,[4] and arguments
- Selectional restrictions on the arguments
- Subcategorisation
- Morphologically-related nouns, adjectives, and verbs
- Related extended uses
- Related idiomatic uses
- Collocates
- Domain labels
- Pragmatic force
- Corpus citations exemplifying each feature

(Atkins and Levin 1991: 242)

In turn, Fillmore (1968), for instance, is credited as being among the first in providing a general set of semantic roles associated with the word, particularly for the verb which can take such arguments as **Actor, Goal**, and **Recipient**. The idea of these semantic cases, like those for the frame, is a general notion, and has been applied variously since Fillmore's influential paper. However, while verb semantics is well-treated in the field, Pustejovsky (1991: 410; 1995) is right to point out that 'the lexicon is not just verbs', and in his theory posits a set of four semantic roles (called the **qualia structure**) to handle the semantic information carried by nouns and adjectives: **constitutive,** the first role, specifies the relation between the lexical item and its constituent parts; **formal**, the second role, distinguishes the lexical item within a larger domain; **telic**, the third role, specifies the purpose and function of the lexical item; and **agentive**, the fourth role, specifies 'whatever brings [the lexical item] about' (Pustejovsky 1991: 418).

This qualia structure is, in turn, only one of the four levels in Pustejovky's theory of mapping the lexicon to the syntax. These four levels of representation may be listed as:

1. **Argument Structure**: The behavior of a word as a function, with its arity specified. This is the predicate argument structure for a word, which indicates how it maps to syntactic expressions.
2. **Event Structure**: Identification of the particular event type...or a word or phrase: e.g. as state [S], process [P], or transition [T].
3. **Qualia Structure**: The essential attributes of an object as defined by the lexical item.
4. **Inheritance Structure**: How the word is globally related to other concepts in the lexicon.

                                        (adapted from Pustejovsky 1991: 419)

Since the lexicon is not just about verbs and nouns, it would be interesting also to note further developments in the field related to other word classes and types in the lexicon.

1.2.2 Hudson's All-Inclusive Lexicon

In general, we may say that the conception of a richer lexicon leads to a combination and integration of phonological, morphological, collocational, syntactic, semantic, and pragmatic information in various ways. In discussing these types of linguistic information, Hudson (1988, 1995) provides a checklist for an 'All-Inclusive Lexicon': this all-inclusive lexicon would blur the distinction between the lexicon and the grammar, reflecting the trends towards lexicalism (as mentioned in the preceding section). Figure 1.2 reproduces his checklist of information which could be considered for inclusion in such a lexicon:

1. *Phonology*
- Underlying segment structure; or several such structures if allomorphs are stored rather than computed;
- prosodic patterns of word (to the extent that there are no rules for computing these) – i.e. mainly word-stress or tone.

2. *Morphology*
- Structure in terms of morphemes or alternating phonological structures (e.g. Semitic languages);
- irregular morphological structures linked to particular morpho-syntactic features (i.e. irregular inflections);
- partial similarities to other words (in the case of derived words or compounds);
- cliticising properties (i.e. whether or not the word concerned may be used as a clitic or as host of a clitic).

3. *Syntax*
- General word-class (e.g. 'verb');
- sub-class (e.g. 'auxiliary');
- obligatory morpho-syntactic features (e.g. *beware*);
- valency :
  - deviant position of dependent (e.g. *someone* etc);
  - deviant position of head (e.g. *enough*);
  - class of dependent (e.g. object of *discuss* is a noun);
  - class of head (e.g. head of *very* is an ad-word);
  - morpho-syntactic features of dependent (e.g. objective of *folgen* is dative);
  - morpho-syntactic features of head (?);
  - lexical identity of dependent (e.g. high-degree-modifier of *drunk* is *blind*);
  - lexical identity of head (e.g. head of past participle *sein* is *sein*; neutral prepositional head of *foot* is *on*);
  - semantic identity of dependent (e.g. dependent of *herd* refers to a set of cows);
  - semantic identity of head (e.g. head of *each* refers to a distributed event);
  - semantic identity of dependent if optional and absent (e.g. *He shaved* = 'He shaved himself').

4. *Semantics*
- Name of entity referred to (=X) by a word W;
- identity of X (e.g. referent of *me* is speaker);
- more general entities of which X is an instance (e.g. if W = *apple*, X is an apple);
- semantic valency of X (i.e. entities to which it is related by semantic roles such as 'agent');
- entities which are inherent to X (e.g. purpose of 'assassinate');
- entities which are given only as defaults (e.g. 'theme' of 'drink' is alcohol);
- entities which must be defined by anaphora (e.g. 'excluded' of 'other', 'known' of intransitive 'know');
- how semantic roles are linked to syntactic dependents of W (e.g. goal of *reach* is defined by direct object).

5. *Context*
● Restrictions relating to immediate social structure (e.g. power/solidarity markers);
● restrictions relating to style (e.g. 'formal', 'slang');
● restrictions relating to larger social structure (e.g. speaker classification);
● restrictions relating to discourse structures (e.g. topic-change markers).

6. *Spelling*
● Normal orthography;
● standard abbreviations or ideographs;
● inflectional irregularities in spelling.

7. *Etymology and language*
● The language to which the word belongs (in a bilingual dictionary);
● the language from which it is 'borrowed';
● the word on which it is 'based';
● the date when it was 'borrowed'.

8. *Usage*
● Frequency and familiarity;
● age of acquisition;
● particular occasions on which the word was used;
● clichés containing the word;
● taboos.

Figure 1.2 Hudson's 'All-Inclusive' Lexicon (from Hudson, 1988: 311–12, 1995: 50–1)

As with Makkai's AL, the rationale for the range of information in this list is that

> any attempt to model psychological reality must therefore take account of this broad range of knowledge-types; but so must any lexicographer whose purpose is to make accessible all the kinds of knowledge which a typical native speaker has (and which is needed if typical native speech is to be simulated either by a non-native or by a machine).
>
> (Hudson 1988: 310)

Moreover, in Hudson's lexicon, there does not seem to a clear dividing line between linguistic (word) knowledge and encyclopedic (world) knowledge. This position is supported by White (1991: 149) who suggests that, while lexical and world knowledge must be distinguished ('lest we lapse into an unen-lightened determinism of human institutions'), we are unable to discretely separate lexical (linguistic) and world knowledge.

1.2.3 The TEI Lexicon[5]
Similar concerns have been voiced regarding what should go into the lexicon.

In the quest for standardisation, the Computational Lexicon Working Group of the Text Encoding Initiative began, in August 1991, to conduct a survey of currently existing (NLP) lexicons to help the TEI in their overall goal of producing standards for interchanging electronic documents of various types. The group aims 'to produce standards for interchanging data stored in lexicons i.e. lexical databases intended for use by natural language processing systems of all sorts'. Specifically, the Lexicon Working Group was set up to propose standards for interchanging data stored in lexicons, i.e. lexical databases intended for use by NLP systems. At the time of writing, a more adequate TEI specification of the lexicon, its form and content, for common standards enabling the interchange of lexical data is being made (see Ide and Veronis 1995, and Section 2.5). Notwithstanding this, we can obtain an approximate understanding of what should go into the TEI lexicon by looking at the various types of lexical information that a TEI-sponsored survey asked for some years ago. These types of information are listed in Figure 1.3:

---

1. Nouns:
- entity nouns – *apple, book*, etc.
- relational nouns – *speed, age, height, father, brother*, etc.
- abstract nouns – *courage, love, altruism*, etc.
- mass nouns – *wine, sand*, etc.
- proper names – *John, Europe, IBM*, etc.
- complement-taking properties: e.g. "factive" nouns like *story*, "transitive" nouns, etc.

2. Pronouns *(I, he, she, it,* etc.) and bound anaphors (*myself, himself, herself, each other*, etc.)

3. Verbs:
a wide variety of valency classes:
- intransitive
- transitive
- ditransitive
- clausal complement taking
- infinitival complement taking (raising and control)
- 'small-clause' taking verbs including naked infinitives etc.
- an indication of variants of a basic valency class (e.g. whether a transitive verb passivises, whether an indirect object-taking verb allows "Dative movement", etc.)
- in a language like German, the nominal complements of a verb may appear in different Cases (e.g. *helfen* takes a dative object while *sehen* takes an accusative object): how such information is represented should also be shown.

4. Modals and auxiliaries

5. Prepositions:
- (any) indication of subclasses of prepositions, e.g. "case-marking" prepositions vs. semantical contentful;
- whether English particles are represented as a subset of prepositions.

6. Adjectives:
- complement-taking properties; e.g. *proud of, likely to*, etc.
- semantic classes of adjectives distinguished: e.g. scalar vs. bi-polar, intersective vs. subsective, etc.
- the position in which an adjective can appear (pre-nominal, post-nominal, predicate position, etc.)

7. ***Determiners and other similar nominal modifiers*** (e.g. articles, quantifiers, demonstratives, etc.). Also, whether polarity, monotonicity, etc. are represented.

8. ***Multi-word lexical entries***

9. ***Inflected categories of noun, verb, and adjective:*** how irregular forms, inflectional paradigm, and other morphological information are stored.

Figure 1.3 Lexical content: extracted from the Computational Lexicon Survey (sponsored by the Computational Working Group of the Text Encoding Initative, September 1991)

From Figs 1.2 and 1.3, it is also clear that different word classes vary in their specification of linguistic content and so merit different treatment: in this respect, words are not, as it were, born equal.

1.3 LEXICAL FORM
While the content and specification of each word class might be different, nevertheless, it is important to provide a uniform means for representing word and world knowledge. One such way is to utilise frames. Indeed, for Barsalou (1992: 21), 'frames provide the fundamental representation of knowledge in human cognition.' What then is a frame?

The **frame** is used by Minsky (1975) to refer to 'a data structure for representing a stereotyped situation.' The frame is able to represent the attributes of a particular object or concept more descriptively than is possible by just using rules. The frame consists of a number of slots (or 'attributes'), each of which may contain a value ('filler') or be left blank. In other words, a frame basically uses a slot:filler or attribute:value[6] notation.

Applied to language, the slot:filler / frame:value notation forms the basis of Metzing's definition of a **lexical frame** as 'a device to represent lexical items in terms of speaker-dependent constructs ("lexical representations")' (Metzing, 1981: 325). This definition is not dissimilar to Fillmore's (1977) reference to 'the specific lexico-grammatical provisions in a given language for naming and describing the categories and relations found in schemata' (Fillmore 1977: 127). Following Fillmore,

A frame is invoked when the interpreter, in trying to make sense of a text segment, is able to assign it an interpretation by situating its content in a pattern that is known independently of the text. A frame is evoked by the text if some linguistic form or pattern is conventionally associated with the frame in question. For example, the sentence *We never open our presents until the morning* makes no mention of Christmas, yet interpreters who share certain cultural experiences, would immediately … invoke a Christmas context; replace the simple noun *presents* with *Christmas presents* and we have introduced a word which evokes that same context.

(Fillmore 1985: 232)

In turn, conceptual **schemata** may be defined as frameworks 'linked together in the categorisation of actions, institutions, and objects … as well as any of the various repertories of categories found in contrast sets, prototype objects, and so on' (Fillmore, 127). Linguistic frameworks or schemata commonly use a slot:filler approach; in frame semantics, for instance, the slots could correspond to linguistic cases (e.g. 'Agent', 'Patient', 'Addressee', etc. – see Fillmore 1968) and the fillers would be the actual values instantiating the slots respectively. A related Fillmorean notion is **text model**, which can be thought of as 'the assembly of schemata created by the interpreter, justified by the interpreter's knowledge of the frames in the text, which models some set of possible complex scenes' (Fillmore, 127). In the present book, a lexical frame is therefore taken to be a linguistic attempt to bring these notions together in terms of the word as the central unit of language.[7]

Linguistic information may be encoded as an attribute with an associated value.

[Arg1 Val1]
[Arg2 Val2]
… …..
[Argn Valn]

This notion of attribute:value can be built upon in a linguistically non-trivial manner for encoding the information in a lexical entry, wherever one's linguistic predilections may lie.

In practice, what can a lexical frame look like? Hudson's (1984) types of propositions (see Section 1.1.2) can be illustrated for the verb *pop* (as in the clause *The balloon popped*) in the left column, with a prose translation in the right column as a guide to the reader.

composition(*pop*):	$p_1 + p_2 + p_3$,	*Pop* consists of three phonemes
model(p1):	/p/	of which the first is an instance of /p/,
model(p2):	/o/	the second is an instance of /o/,
model(p3):	/p/	and the third is another instance of /p.
model(*pop*):	verb	*Pop* is an instance of a verb.
companion(verb):	c,	Verbs (e.g. *pop*) take a companion which precedes them.

referent(*pop*):	pop★	*Pop* refers to pop★, which is an instance
model(pop★):	event,	of an event, and involves a 'changer',
		namely the referent of the companion *c*.

Figure 1.4: The representation of the verb *pop*, from Hudson (1984: 9)

Webster (1986), who (like Metzing) points to the potentiality of frame theory as a uniform means for representing word and world knowledge, represents this in the following computational format:

[pop [composition	[p1	[model [/p/]]]
	[p2	[model [/o/]]]
	[p3	[model [/p/]]]]
[model	[verb	[companion [<[c]]]]
[referent		[pop★ [model [event]]
		[changer [c★]]]]]

Figure 1.5: The representation of the verb *pop*, from Webster (1986), in relation to Hudson (1984: 9)

Also, according to Metzing, a lexical frame should fulfil the following requirements:

1. it should correspond intuitively/empirically to the knowledge of a natural language speaker;
2. it should provide a formally satisfactory basis for the definition of terms
   (Metzing, 1981: 325)

By 1., I interpret a lexical frame to mean Makkai's concern with the Associative Lexicon, as well as similar calls by other linguists such as Jackendoff and Hudson, as we have seen. The notion of socio-psychological reality has been touched upon in this chapter, and recurs throughout the book. By 2., I interpret a lexical frame to be useful in terms of using a grammatical representation both explicit and 'theory-neutral'; in addition, the frame should fulfil recent concerns with multifunctionality and reusability.

Frame theory accords well with the view of language (as expressed by linguists such as Richard Hudson) as mainly declarative, not procedural. Following Shieber (1986: 7), the term **declarative** is concerned with 'the association between strings and informational elements in terms of what associations are permissible, not how they are computed.' For instance, a declarative view of language is that any clause can consist of, say, 5 elements: S(ubject), V(erb), O(bject), C(omplement), A(dverbial). A **procedural** view of language, by contrast, would also require which elements are to be processed first. For instance, a simplistic view of a procedural approach would be something like the following: 'On encountering a clause, start isolating the V element first based on its occurrence in the lexicon; note the subcategorisation information for the verb; then isolate the S element which usually occurs to the left of the V element and is the argument that the V subcategorises for; then see whether the verb takes a C or an O; assign either C or O (or both) accordingly; then see whether there are any remaining prepositional phrases, adverbial phrases, or noun phrases which will correspond to the A element.' These two basic distinctions correspond to the distinction in computer programming between procedural languages (such as C++ and Pascal) and declarative languages (such as the programming language PROLOG). While a useful distinction may be made between these two paradigms, it should also be noted that both declarative and procedural approaches are more often than not present in any substantial computer program.

1.4 CONCLUSION AND ORGANISATION OF THIS BOOK

This chapter has tried to answer the question: Do we need to divide grammar and lexis? There appears to be less of such a need; instead there is a trend towards lexicalism, where the notion of a word is expanded and enriched to include more types of linguistic information vis-à-vis the grammar. If a richer lexicon is implemented in computer-based systems, the general belief and agreement is that it will help resolve the 'bottleneck' underlying computer systems built for solving problems related to language. This chapter has also discussed some issues relating to the form and content that such a lexicon should take: it suggests the notion of a lexical frame as both a viable computational and conceptual (including sociopsychologically real) structure which can be used to unify the uneven types of linguistic information for the various parts of the lexicon.

Chapter 2 takes us into a brief survey into how the lexicon has been treated in each of the related sub-fields of CL1, CL2, and CL3: this leads to a greater understanding of the efforts made by various people in coding the lexicon. Also, the emergence of a convergence of interest in being able to specify lexicons that can be mutually beneficial and exchanged is discussed in this chapter.

Chapter 3 begins a more detailed exploration into what it means to 'derive', as it were, lexicons from corpora. It first explores the notion of what it means to use a corpus as a lexical resource, which involves issues of choice, size, and type of corpus data. It explores the basic notion of a concordance as a first means of lexical acquisition. Also, in examining a concordance listing, however casually, the reader is actually constructing various frames of expectations regarding the behaviour of the word. But the reader can do more than just render an informal ocular scan: the chapter sketches a linguistic framework of expectations postulated by a well-known linguist for the systematic sifting of corpus lexical evidence.

While the tenets presented in Chapter 3 would currently be easier for humans rather than machines to carry out, Chapter 4 discusses relevant issues in getting the machine to reach the ideal objective of deriving a lexicon fully automatically from the corpus. It first considers the formal relationship (if any) between a lexicon and a corpus: tying in strands from the discussion in the foregoing chapters, it offers a diagrammatic representation of the tasks involved in utilising various lexical resources, especially the corpus. It then considers how a lexicon may be 'learned' from real text, of which 3 methods present themselves: manual, semi-automatic, and automatic. For the immediate future, the most successful method seems to be the use of semi-automatic means for deriving a lexicon from a corpus. The chapter ends with an outline of a lexical framework, the LFA.

Chapter 5 will deal with the issue of the computational storage and format of the lexicon. It focuses on the notion of both lexical and knowledge bases, of which some actual databases/knowledge bases in practice will be illustrated. Invariably, the chapter also deals with the notion of formalism, which means the encoding of information in a manner explicit enough for the computer. Also, with the increasing use of the Internet and the World Wide Web, Appendix B contains a list of some of these sites for lexical research.

As an instantiation of the principles offered in the other chapters, Chapter 6 offers a case study based on two corpora of business English. It details the application of the LFA framework to specimen lexical entries culled from these corpora.

Chapter 7 is the concluding chapter.

1.5 STUDY QUESTIONS
1. Is it possible to provide a satisfactory definition of a **word**?
2. Look up the following terms in a linguistics dictionary: **lexical entry, lexeme,** and **lemma**. Do they mean the same thing?
3. (i) Examine some older British and American English Dictionaries (late nineteenth century and early twentieth century) for the definition of *mackerel* and *laurel*. Is there a difference between the British and American versions in their treatment of these words?
   (ii) 1995 is perhaps better known as the 'Year of English Learner Dictionaries', since there were no fewer than five learner dictionaries edited by Crowther (1995), Higgleton and Seaton (1995), Procter (1995), Sinclair (1995), and Summers (1995) respectively. Examine these dictionaries to see how both word and world knowledge are incorporated.
4. Take the same 10 words (be sure that all the word classes are covered: noun, verb, adjective, adverb) from each of the dictionaries listed in 3 (ii), and compare and contrast them in terms of the following parameters:
   (a) Definitions and examples used (Are they all corpus-based?)
   (b) Grammar codes/Style/Usage
   (c) Cross references

(d) Derivative words

(e) Pronunciation

(f) Antonyms and Synonyms

(g) Pictures (How does this relate to Question 3 (ii))?

5. Comment on the statement that 'the price we pay for the easy location of the lexical unit is that words that derivationally or at least semantically belong together are put together in different places.'

6. If you have access to the 'Wheel of Fortune' programme on television,

(i) systematically collect the expressions used on the programme over a period of 8 weeks. What are the respective percentages for single words, compounds, idioms, names, cliches, titles, and quotes?

(ii) From your answer to (i), would you say that these expressions are a marginal part of our use of language?

1.6 FURTHER READING

For introductions to other aspects of lexicography not mentioned in this book, read Jackson (1988) and Carter (1987). In addition, Zgusta (ed.) (1980) contains articles on issues which are still relevant today: dictionaries and the description of the norm, dictionaries and the structure of language, dictionaries and the computer, and dictionaries and culture. Read also McCawley's (1986) seminal article on how linguists might contribute to the process of dictionary-making. For the relation between lexicon and grammar, read Hasan (1987) and Gleason (1975). Stubbs (1993) also sketches aspects of the Firthian tradition which has influenced such eminent linguists as Michael Halliday and John Sinclair.

NOTES

1. Why not title this book **Corpus Lexicography** instead? It is true that the corpus is always stored electronically nowadays, and it is inconceivable that anyone would want to build a large corpus without putting it into the computer. However, Leech (1992a) points out that the term was used long before the computer came about (see Section 2.3). Also, my use of the title 'computer corpus lexicography' is to distinguish it from Atkins' term 'corpus lexicography' (see Section 2.3.1) to denote the use of lexis in CL3, as it is practised. I use the term 'computer corpus lexicography' to subsume the enterprise of using the lexicon for CL3, as well as incorporating insights from both CL2 and CL1.

2. In this respect, Meijs (1992b) cites some psycholinguistic evidence which suggests that 'a language user's mental lexicon is not, or not primarily, organised ... as a long list of isolated elements.' Further, 'the mental lexicon forms a coherent, tightly-knit whole, whose elements are somehow intricately related to one another along a number of different dimensions: phonological, morphological, orthographical, etc. One of the most basic organising dimensions, however, is no doubt the semantic-conceptual one, as witness word-association and semantic priming tests: words activate, "call up", other words that are related to them in meaning' (Meijs 1992b: 130–131). See also Aitchison (1987, 1994) which is an attempt to describe the mental lexicon.

3. Klein (1988) gives a useful summary of such frameworks, and Sproat (1991) relates the lexicon to its use in formal grammar.

4. 'Aktionsart' refers to lexical aspect: see, for instance, Alonge (1992: 197) for a more detailed explanation.

5. The list of linguistic items presented here can only be tentative; Ide and Veronis (1995) make it clear that work is being undertaken to make (what is termed in this book) the 'TEI' lexicon more comprehensive.

6. Ingria et al. (1992: 345) trace the first use of the attribute:value structure to Martin Kay, who formalised

the linguistic notion of features in what is now called feature structures. Kay also introduced the idea of using unification for manipulating the syntactic structures of natural languages. See Knight (1992: 1633–4), as well as Kay (1984a).

7. Fillmore (1985: 223) says his **word frame** is motivated by specific unified frameworks of knowledge holding word groups together. Fillmore also mentions the equivalent terms used by various people, such as **frame** (Minsky 1975), Winograd (1975); **schema** (Rumelhart 1975); **script** (Schank and Abelson 1977); **global pattern** (Beaugrande and Dressler 1981) etc. As Fillmore says, these terms 'are used in a fairly wide variety of ways, and some scholars use several of them, distinguishing among them according to whether they are static or dynamic, according to the kinds of inference making they support, etc.'

The lexicon in Computational Linguistics (CL1), Computational Lexicography (CL2), and Corpus Linguistics (CL3)

2.0 INTRODUCTION

Perhaps the most appropriate way to begin this chapter is to echo Grishman (1986: 1) who warns that 'to attempt a unified survey of a field [i.e. computational linguistics] where there is sharp disagreement even about basic approaches may seem foolhardy'. Nevertheless, prior to any consideration of the lexicon in this field, I shall first discuss what various writers have meant by Computational Linguistics (CL1) and then go on to outline the form, content, and quantity of lexical items used in (early) CL1 systems. In turn, I discuss the notions of Computational Lexicography (CL2) and Corpus Linguistics (CL3) and what they entail for the lexicon.[1]

2.1 WHAT IS COMPUTATIONAL LINGUISTICS (CL1)?

It is a truism to say that what exactly counts as 'computational linguistics' is controversial for two main reasons. Firstly, the term 'computational' attached to the headword 'linguistics' implies that any activity involving an analysis of language using the computer has a claim to being, in some sense, **computational linguistics**: this would include that which constructs programs for the understanding and generation of natural language, and that which would use the computer in a less demanding way. Secondly, and more importantly, the confusion over the use of this term is due to its evolving nature over the years.

Gazdar and Mellish (1989: 3) avoid any definition of the term and treat it as somewhat similar, if not equivalent, to **natural language processing.** They negatively define it as 'no longer involving the use of computers to derive indexes and concordances from computer-readable texts' (which, for them, should probably come under the rubric of 'literary and linguistic computing'). I agree with Butler (1992: viii), however, that CL1 need not treat indexing and concordancing techniques as primitive tools unworthy for inclusion within its ambit; rather such tools – whatever their limitations – should form an integral part of CL1 systems for textual analysis, especially so when the enterprises of

CL1, CL2, and CL3 can be seen to be converging (see Section 2.4). In fact, a cursory review of the articles during the past ten years in the journal *Computational Linguistics* (the journal of the Association for Computational Linguistics) and the proceedings of the various international biennial computational linguistics conferences *COLING* (see COLING–90, 92, 94, 96) would suggest that these three types of activities are coming together.

Grishman (1986: 4) treats CL1 as 'the study of computer systems for understanding and generating natural language.' The stress here may be put on 'understanding', with the implication that its objective is equivalent to that for natural language understanding in Artificial Intelligence. Another, not dissimilar, definition regards CL1 as the result of the 'marriage' between linguistics and computer science, concerned with the processing of natural language, a rubric covering 'the understanding and synthesis of speech, and the analysis and generation of written texts' (Bennett et al., 1986: 8).

For Karlgren (1990: 97), the key concepts associated with the term CL1 are 'computation, not computer, and linguistics, not language processing.' This seems to go against the grain nowadays in failing to treat the label 'computational linguistics' as more or less synonymous with that of natural language processing. Both are part of the same interdisciplinary field, but are seen from the complementary points of view of the two different disciplines of computer science and linguistics. From this perspective, we may try to make sense of Karlgren's definition by seeing CL1 as the computing of natural language seen from the point of view of linguistics, while NLP is the computing of natural language seen from the point of view of computer science. With these names comes a difference of emphasis predictable from the disciplines in question. For example, NLP will be more concerned with natural language front ends which interface other systems, whereas CL1 will be more concerned with purely linguistic tasks such as parsing or testing grammars. Since these are merely differences of emphasis, however, the distinction between these two terms need no longer be contentious, and Gazdar and Mellish are right to use both terms interchangeably.

This view is not dissimilar to that of Ballard and Jones (1992: 203), who distinguish between the linguistic and engineering aspects when they say 'research in computational linguistics … is concerned with the application of a computational paradigm to the scientific study of human language and the engineering of systems that process or analyse written or spoken language'. For them, 'natural language processing' is an interchangeable term dealing especially with the 'engineering side of the discipline'. Similarly, Ramsay (1991: 29) makes a distinction between what he calls the **engineering approach** and the **cognitive science approach**, within the enterprise of Artificial Intelligence (AI). For him too, the term NLP is used for the engineering viewpoint whereas he more or less equates the term CL1 with the cognitive-science viewpoint. By this, he means that cognitive science is very much concerned with the same phenomena as traditional linguistics, but differs mainly in its 'degree of precision', and 'the constraint that theories must pay attention to the possibility of being used in programs' (Ramsay, 29). The goal of the cognitive-science approach is to design systems not primarily to outperform humans but to find the evidence reflecting on how humans do ('intelligent') tasks, that is to say, to see how well the systems fit what we know about human cognitive structures and processes.

Karlgren's motivation for distinguishing 'linguistics' from 'language process-ing' may be seen in his assertion that 'all agree that the scope [of computational linguistics] does not extend to studies, however good, about computation applied to language material unless some linguistic insight is at issue or about computer support for linguistics unless the computational procedure has some non-trivial linguistic aspect'. This may be seen as an extension of the cognitive science approach.

Complementing this observation, the engineering approach in NLP nowadays also includes statistical processing of language provided for by information-theoretic models of language (e.g. bigram or trigram models) involving huge quantities of data but minimal linguistics be included as part of the CL1 rubric.

The discussion on what might or might not constitute *de jure* CL1 inevitably leads to the recognition that researchers in CL1 may at present be grouped, *de facto*, into two camps: the 'self-organising' and the 'knowledge-based'. 'The former attempts to use the statistical regularities to be found in mass text as a key to analysing and processing it; while the latter brings in the results of linguistic theory and logic as the foundation for its models of language' (Atkins et al. 1992: 12). But the situation seems to be changing with an ever-increasing convergence of these two seemingly diametrically opposite positions.

The characterisation of CL1 as one using the 'knowledge-based' approach within the AI enterprise is not without its disadvantages, since a consensual definition of AI has not been achieved. However, even if the whole AI enterprise should stop completely, CL1 would still exist by being associated with such projects as implementing and testing linguistic theories. As Hudson (1990: 9–10) notes, the tendency nowadays in linguistics is towards the construction of models and theories that are computationally implementable, because it is only through the computer that complex grammatical theories can be tested for their overall coherence.

Finally, Karlgren (1990: 97) also stresses that machine language learning of natural language is very much part of the CL1 enterprise in order to 'get a relevant model for human linguistic competence'. In this context, neural computing for learning language in an unsupervised manner is emerging as an important method in CL1.

2.1.1 The lexicon in CL1

The above sketch of what CL1 entails leads to the next point: that CL1 systems (for, say, parsing) has tended, as in earlier linguistic treatment of the lexicon, to view the lexicon as a peripheral component: Gazdar and Mellish (1989: 257) observe that, 'in practice, many (existing) NLP systems treat the lexicon as a necessary evil that is of little theoretical interest and which is implemented by a collection of relatively unprincipled programs'. Furthermore, a workshop held in 1987 reported that the average number of lexemes in these systems tended to be 25 words (Ritchie 1987: 234). Nowadays, the increasing importance of the lexicon is seen in the evolution from the traditional task of constructing computational components for the automatic generation and analysis of natural language sentences in isolation to the more recent task of constructing components suitable for the treatment of large, naturally-occurring texts. As an indispensable component of an NLP system, the significant improvement of the lexicon is generally regarded as a crucial means which enables the NLP system to deal with real-world applications: Amsler (1989: 12) for instance claims that 'natural language systems cannot *understand* text for which they do not possess the lexicon' – Amsler's point is that such understanding can take place only if the lexicon is rich enough. Indeed, Amsler's conception of the lexicon for CL1 is that it 'serves not only as the basis for the recognition vocabulary of any text-processing system, but as the indexed repository of the vast array of additional syntactic, semantic, and pragmatic information upon which text-processing algorithms are based' (Amsler 1982: 660).

The design, content, and specification of the lexicon in any CL1 system is invariably tied to the purpose for which that CL1 system has been constructed, to the influence of prevailing theories, and to current requirements for computational tractability. Because of this, in this section, I do no more than outline some developments in the lexical component of Machine Translation (MT) systems (because MT [arguably] is the oldest CL1 enterprise) to illustrate how the lexicon has been treated in such systems. I then consider a case in which lexicalism has undergone a thoroughgoing shift from the grammar to the lexicon.

The first MT dictionaries (in the 1940s) were little more than word lists in which words were stored in a simple, often alphabetical, order, with source language words on one side and the target language translation(s) on the other (Papegaiij 1986: 66): in other words, the idea was to translate words in the source text, and then reorder the output so it fitted the word-order rules of the target language. The systems that resulted from this simple-minded approach appeared to be almost worse than useless, largely because of the degree of lexical ambiguity of a non-trivial subset of the vocabulary of a natural language. Trying to deal with lexical ambiguity by including translations of each possible interpretation of each word led to 'the generation of text which contained so many options that it was virtually meaningless' (Ramsay 1991: 30). When syntactic parsing became the centre of interest, word lists acquired a form more like traditional dictionaries: each word was listed with its possible syntactic functions and – as syntactic techniques progressed – often detailed syntactic information such as the kind of syntactic structures it could form, what exceptions it posed to certain rules, etc. MT systems based on syntax only, however, had disappointing results because 'what was discovered was that to translate a sentence one had to *understand* at least as much of its *meaning* as of its structure' (Papegaiij et al. 1986: 32). The structure of a sentence was of little use on its own when its meaning could not be analysed. But understanding implies *knowledge*: a knowledge of the world which computers seemed to lack completely. MT soon declined in the 1960s but revived again in the 1970s with the development of knowledge-based AI applications.

The addition of semantic information – intended to represent the meaning of the words in a formalised notation – was the final step towards turning the earlier word lists into fully-developed dictionaries. By now it was realised that the amount of semantic knowledge that needed to be entered was far larger than had initially been thought necessary. The increasing complexity of the data involved has led to the notion of the Lexical Knowledge Bank (also 'LKB', see Chapter 5) which is essential to the type of MT known as 'lexicon-driven' MT, which is primarily guided not by a global grammar but by the system's knowledge about individual words. Lexicon-driven MT is made possible by the exponential increase in the processing and storage capability of present-day systems.[2]

The Semantic Word Expert System (SWESIL) of the Distributed Language Translation Project that Papegaiij et al. (1986) carried out is a case in point. The core of the system is its Lexical Knowledge Bank, a structured database which is meant to contain such types of information as real-world concepts, selection rules, valencies, combination rules, syntactic information, morphological information, and world knowledge.

The need for such a sophisticated lexical database, one which is needed for an MT system to deliver high quality translation, is noted by Knowles (1982: 149), who points out that

> however powerful and sophisticated a particular set of parsing algorithms may be, the successful analysis of a text into a correct meaning representation is only possible if a commensurably 'powerful' and sophisticated lexical database is wedded to the dynamic modules of an MT system.

The LKB makes for a new kind of dictionary with its posited extension from primarily morpho-syntactic to formalised semantic and 'word knowledge' information, together with powerful and flexible storage, access and data entry techniques derived from AI expert systems technology. What seems particularly irrelevant in such a dictionary is the traditional divide between linguistic and encyclopedic knowledge (see Amsler 1989).

Nowadays, a more modest specification of the lexicon for natural language processing (of written texts) would 'provide information on a range of syntactic matters including at least part of speech, subcategorisation possibilities, case, finiteness, number, person, gender or noun class, aspect, mood, reflexiveness, and WH-ness' (Gazdar and Mellish, 1989: 256–257). For the majority of languages where there is regular inflectional morphology, the lexicon, to avoid large-scale redundancy, must list word roots or stems, together with sufficient morphological and syntactic information for the regular forms of words to be deduced. This in turn means that the lexicon should also make explicit provision for irregular forms. For Gazdar and Mellish, if the parser is to resolve ambiguity more effectively, then the lexicon must include semantic inform-ation about the words that it contains (or defines). To this latter requirement, pragmatic information (the behaviour of the word in context), it seems to me, should be added to the lexicon as a more comprehensive specification to reach the goal of resolving lexical ambiguity: this pragmatic information would be of the type indicated in Makkai's Associative Lexicon (see Section 1.1). Thus, the lexicon should contain morphological, syntactic, semantic, and pragmatic information and, for applications involving speech, would also contain phonological information.

An idea which takes the conflation of word knowledge and world knowledge to its extreme is Steven Small's **Word Expert Parser** (WEP).[3] As a semantic parsing program, WEP is 'an early AI model of natural language understanding to make a serious attempt at handling multiple senses of the word in its vocabulary' (Adriaens and Small 1987: 13).[4] Words are seen as **experts** – little program-like entities – that have to be activated and, once activated, will search their context for information and clues to guide the way they continue processing. By viewing the word, as the central unit of language, in this manner, WEP aims to achieve lexical ambiguity resolution as an essential step towards natural language understanding. In Small's view of language, the dictionary ceases to be a static listing of facts and rules, and becomes a storage place for thousands of little programs waiting to be activated. Knowledge of the world is seen not as a separate source of information, but as an integral part of the word's behaviour. This leads to the construction of a Word-Expert Dictionary which is a combination of lexicon, encyclopedia, and language parser.

Predictably, the requirement of richly informed lexicons (especially Small's) leads to the construction of *small* lexicons because the hand-crafting of such lexicons is an overwhelmingly labour-intensive task. Hence, there is a need to acquire lexical knowledge more automatically: this issue is treated in Chapter 4.

In summary, this section has attempted to outline the development of the lexicon involving the appropriate form, content, and quantity of lexical items in (some) CL1 systems. Since early systems tended to be sentence-based and the lexicon was needed in so far as it helped in the parsing of the sentence, the size of lexicons tended to be small. Building lexicons by hand is an immensely difficult task, especially when one requires large numbers of lexemes (but see Section 4.3). With the recognition that CL1 needed to move from 'toy' systems to those for the analysis of 'real' texts, this meant that a large computational lexicon was needed. Thus, CL1 began exploring the use of MRDs (since they were the obvious first source of lexical information) as the main lexical resource for the acquisition of large lexicons.

2.2 WHAT IS COMPUTATIONAL LEXICOGRAPHY (CL2)?

The immediate relation of CL2 to CL1 is that 'dictionaries are a certain kind of expert system', since 'they contain knowledge either about the general vocabulary of a language, or about the terminology of a specific field' (Lenders 1991: 48). Also, in NLP, the requirement for rich lexicons to enhance the system has led to the term **computational lexicography** being used to refer to the enterprise of exploiting machine-readable versions of published dictionaries (MRDs) as potential sources of lexical information for use by automated natural language processing systems, i.e. developing lexicons for machine use (Boguraev and Briscoe, 1989: 2). Boguraev and Briscoe argue that the term extends to such an enterprise because 'although strictly speaking [we] are not in the business of dictionary construction, it is certain that the lexicons which are derived from MRDs for use by machine will be very different from conventional published dictionaries, both in terms of how they organise and how they represent information.' Boguraev and Briscoe would also extend the term to the enterprise of using computational techniques in the development of dictionary databases for human use.

A more general use of the term refers to the automation of dictionary construction using as much help from the computer as possible. In this sense, Bennett et al. (1986: 26) define computational lexicography simply as referring to 'the automation of lexicographic tasks'. This is understood in the context of their definition of other related terms. A language is seen as consisting of a grammar (i.e. 'a set of rules for the formation of meaningful and well-formed sentences') and a lexicon (i.e. 'a set of words and expressions whose use is governed by those rules'). In addition, the lexicon is an open-ended set, and its members subject to change in both form and content. Further, they see a distinction between

> Lexicology and Lexicography, where Lexicology is the scientific study of the lexicon and aims to discover the principles underlying its behaviour and use. While the analysis of the lexicon is the goal of lexicology, its description is the domain of lexicography, the complex process of compiling dictionaries. Lexicography is thus concerned with the description of a range of observable phenomena (the lexicon or vocabulary of a language community) which it defines by drawing on a set of linguistic principles (lexicology). The product of this process, the dictionary, is an

arbitrary collection of words, together with information on their meaning, spelling, etc. and, in the case of multilingual dictionaries, their equivalents in other languages.

(Bennett et al., 1986: 4)

In the present book, there is no need to make such an absolute distinction between the two enterprises of **computational lexicology** and **computational lexicography**, each of which refers in a general sense to the enterprise of CL2. While the term 'computational lexicography' seems to be the more popular term (see, for instance, Boguraev and Briscoe 1989), the term 'computational lexicology' came into popular use with Amsler (1982): Amsler defines **computational lexicology** generally as 'the application of computers to the study of the lexicon.' In so doing, he also rightly predicted (as we will see in Section 2.4 and Chapter 4) the importance of using both knowledge-based and statistical approaches to the lexical analysis of texts: this involves applying 'computational linguistic (morphological and syntactic parsing) and information science techniques (cluster analysis, cooccurrence relationships, frequency counts) to gather and present the raw text to human lexicographers or experts for their assimilation and restructuring into formal analyses of terminology' (Amsler 1982: 661).

In brief, there seem to be three goals, not necessarily separable, for CL2: 1. the techniques of automating dictionary construction: computational lexicographic tools are needed for creating, maintaining, and developing lexicons as well as for the transfer of lexical information etc.; 2. the development of lexicon construction for machine use; and 3. the development of lexicon construction for human use.

To elaborate on these three goals, I would like to sketch some theoretical issues in CL2 before moving on to a specific consideration of three well-known dictionaries as exemplifying the development of lexical computing.

2.2.1 Human consumption vs machine-use

McNaught (1988: 20) rightly observes that publishers tend to use the computer in some way to store their dictionaries in a form geared towards **human consumption**, and not for **machine-use**.

Traditionally, an MRD ('machine-readable dictionary') may be seen essentially as a typesetting tape which stores a dictionary. As a product of thousands of man hours, the MRD is undoubtedly an expensive publishing investment, and a rich lexical resource. For this reason, an underlying assumption in NLP (until recently, at least) has been that it would be better to modify and convert an existing MRD into a database capable of machine exploitation, rather than to collect lexical data from scratch (say, from a corpus).

However, this objective of exploiting a publisher's MRD seems to work against the tendency for such an MRD to be primarily organised for human use in various ways, some of which include the following, as pointed by McNaught (1988: 21–23):

- An MRD relies heavily on the user's background linguistic and com-
  mon-sense knowledge to retrieve and comprehend the information it
  contains, so a human is not overly concerned when, say, circularity of
  definition occurs;
- It more often than not makes use of a human's reaction to visual attributes (bold face, italics, etc.) implicitly to convey semantic information and help in the interpretation of sub-sections of an entry;
- It is presented in an informal fashion and tends to be organised as a list
  of lexical entries sorted alphabetically by headword. Makkai (1980:
  127; 1986) therefore quite appropriately observes that 'the psychologically quite unmotivated tyranny of the alphabet' has made people
  accustomed to looking up words in a dictionary: however, such
  heterogeneous alphabetical inventory (HABIT) dictionaries, as
  Makkai points out, are so firmly enshrined for centuries that they are
  here to stay.

On the other hand, a dictionary for machine use has to be explicit by
containing a formal description of lexical data, and has to be as systematic and
flexible as possible. Such flexibility includes being able to compare or generalise
across lexical entries, so that making the orthographic form of the headword
the only means to a particular entry might work against this enterprise.

Another point which can be marshalled regarding the human consumption
of a dictionary is that a dictionary tends not to be sufficiently detailed,
especially in syntactic information, and persists in using 'inferior' grammar
codes. 'It can be argued, however that, as the general public does not receive a
formal linguistic training, there is little point in including sophisticated codings
or classifications (e.g. case frames for verbs) in a standard dictionary'
(McNaught 1988: 23). However, the next question then becomes one of asking
how useful the considerable efforts put into the adaptation of the MRD to a
natural language processing system really are, given that such coding might not
be sufficiently detailed for NLP purposes.

In the light of the foregoing comments, it is notable that the first edition of
LDOCE (Procter 1978) is the example of an MRD which has proved most
adaptable to the needs of NLP, because of its relatively detailed subcategorisations
of major word classes (particularly verbs). However, this rich coding of syntactic
features was simplified in the second edition of LDOCE (Summers 1987)
because it was felt to be too difficult for most of the dictionary's potential users.

Another point to note about MRDs is that internal inconsistencies tend to
creep into them, given the fact that a team of lexicographers works on the
dictionary and so differences in training among members of the team are
bound to be reflected in the result (McNaught 1988: 21).

Leaving aside these points, the reliance of modern NLP systems on a formal
expression of linguistic (and lexical) knowledge means that the system
concerned would have to alter in order to assimilate the unformalised knowledge

that can be found in many aspects of MRDs. Alternatively, some intermediate
system which takes as input unformalised knowledge and produces a
formalised version for input into the NLP system proper would have to be
invented. An instance of the latter is described in the collection of papers edited
by Boguraev and Briscoe (1989), where the MRD tape of the LDOCE
dictionary is utilised for this purpose: this is outlined in the next section.

2.2.2 The lexicon in CL2

There appears to be some disagreement regarding exactly when CL2 may be
said to have started. Lender (1991: 46) claims that 'automatic lexicography
began during the sixties', while Meijs (1992a: 140) asserts that 'the connection
between computers and dictionaries first arose in the 1970s, when ... the
production and typesetting of dictionaries ... came to include a computerised
stage, i.e. a stage in which all or most of the contents was available in so-called
"machine-readable form"'. Whichever account is more accurate, there is no
doubt that a crucial phase in CL2 concerns the role of automation in the
development of a series of dictionaries for the advanced learner.

Since the basic motivation for lexicography is the building of dictionaries to
meet the needs of its target audience, the type of information needed by the
advanced learner is one of unusual explicitness. As claimed by Evens (1988: 10),
'the kinds of explicit information needed by advanced learners is precisely the
kind of information needed by natural language processing programs'. Evens
also asserts that information-retrieval systems need relational thesauri to add
index terms to queries, natural-language front ends and text-understanding
programs need verb-pattern information and verb forms for parsing, text-
generation systems need even more lexical data to generate coherent text, and
machine-translation systems need lexical databases for both languages and a set
of transfer relations to record bilingual correspondences. In terms of human
use, it is important for such information as verb patterns to be stored in a lexical
database, rather than on printed paper, so that 1. the learner can be provided
with the means to access such information easily, given his or her need to consult
such patterns frequently; and 2. the lexicographer can use the database 'both as
a tool and a source for information in dictionary building' (Evens 1988: 10).

According to Meijs (1992a: 145–6), such dictionaries include the *Oxford
Advanced Learner's Dictionary*, OALD (Cowie (ed.) 1989, Crowther (ed.) 1995),
as 'the first strictly computer-readable MRD', the *Longman Dictionary of Contemporary English*, LDOCE (Procter (ed.) 1978, Summers (ed.) 1987, Summers
(ed.) 1995), as 'the first computer-assisted MRD', and the *Collins-Birmingham
University International Language Database*, COBUILD (Sinclair (ed.) 1987,
Sinclair (ed.) 1995), as 'the first computer-designed MRD.'

In terms of helping the advanced learner, the OALD stands out from a lot of
other dictionaries in providing assistance for the mastery of all possible verb
arguments. Now in its 5th edition,[5] it identifies approximately 50 verb comple-

ment patterns in verb entries, gives a full explanation of affixes and of irregular verb forms and plurals and lists thousands of phrases and idioms. For Meijs (1992a: 144), the OALD tape is an MRD in the strict sense of the term because the computer involvement includes machine-readability merely as one of the stages in its production i.e. the computer does not play any role in the actual lexicographic preparation of the dictionary. Perhaps this is a factor to explain why a disadvantage of the OALD tape is its being in 'the form of unstructured lines of text, interspersed with number codes for font changes, etc., which makes it rather difficult to identify the different kinds of information' (Meijs, 144).

By contrast to the OALD, LDOCE (Procter (ed.) 1978) has involved the computer more actively: 'computer programs were used to check overall consistency, for instance, to make sure that only words from the controlled vocabulary were employed in the definitions' (Meijs 1992a: 144). Various other factors help make LDOCE especially suitable for CL2. Firstly, LDOCE has an extensive set of its own verb patterns and adjective categories.[6] Secondly, LDOCE uses approximately 2000 basic words 'selected by a thorough study of a number of frequency and pedagogic lists of English' (Procter, 1978: ix) for its defining vocabulary. Another factor is its word-sense information (contained in its machine-readable form, but not in the printed version). This information is structured in the form of 'subject' and 'box' codes which encode such semantic notions as register, semantic type of object, and cross-references: such an encoding makes LDOCE 'unique amongst MRDs in providing a formal representation of some aspects of meaning' (Boguraev and Briscoe 1989: 17).

The first edition of COBUILD represents an advanced learner's dictionary that is derived from a corpus of approximately 7.3 million words of mainly general British English (see Krishnamurthy 1987: 77; Sinclair (ed.) 1987). COBUILD represents a major development in CL2 in that it is based on huge amounts of computer corpus data and so can claim to make use of nothing but 'real' examples. Further, the derived database is especially detailed because of the large number of programs written to extract information from the corpus, construct database entries, and access database information. What makes COBUILD especially remarkable is that the compilation process for COBUILD utilised the computer in all the four traditional lexicographic stages of data-collecting, entry-selection, entry construction and entry-arrangement (Krishnamurthy, 62).

An interesting innovation for the printed version of the COBUILD dictionary is an 'Extra Column' (see Sinclair 1987b: 110) at the side of each lexical entry, which provides the advanced learner with two sets of inform-ation: 'formal'/'grammatical' and 'semantic'. The advantage of having the Extra Column is that it provides 'a link between the broad generalities of grammar and the individualities of particular words' (Sinclair, 114). Formal features in the Extra Column relate to syntax, collocations, morphology, etymology, and phonology; semantic features include uniqueness of referent and real-world knowledge, lexical sets, connotation and allusion, translation equivalence, discourse/clause functions, and pragmatics (see Moon 1987). In terms of the grammar which formed the basis of the training for the lexicographers involved, the starting point used was Sinclair's own surface grammar of English (see Sinclair 1972), which is not dissimilar to an earlier version of Halliday's (1985, 1994) grammar known as the Scale-and-Category model.

The set of criteria used for the analysis of meaning in COBUILD echoes the specification of the lexicon in Section 2.1.1 in terms of the four basic parameters: morphology, syntax, semantics, and pragmatics (phonology in the case of speech). I shall elaborate on this specification in Chapter 4.

Apart from their significance in the history of lexical computing, I have dwelt at length on these three MRDs (in particular, the COBUILD) because of a further development in lexical computing. It is claimed that the English lexical database of the Centre for Lexical Information (CELEX) at Nijmegen is a merger of certain types of information of the three dictionaries mentioned. More will be said regarding this database in Chapter 5. What is important to note at this point is that the development of COBUILD has meant that CL2 has evolved to using the corpus as an important, in fact essential, resource for the construction of dictionaries. Indeed, it is significant to note that the latest editions of the COBUILD (Sinclair (ed.) 1995), OALD (Crowther (ed.) 1995), and the LDOCE (Summers (ed.) 1995) dictionaries all base their main linguistic evidence on corpora. Other more recent dictionaries including the CIDE (Procter (ed.) 1995) and the TCEED (Higgleton and Seaton (eds) 1995) also use corpus evidence. Thus, appropriately enough, we turn next to the enterprise of corpus linguistics for the treatment of the lexicon.

2.3 WHAT IS CORPUS LINGUISTICS (CL3)?

Perhaps **corpus linguistics** is not quite the right term to characterise CL3: Leech (1992a: 106) points out that **computer corpus linguistics** would be the more appropriate term since, long before the advent of the computer, linguists and grammarians had already been gathering corpora for the study of language. In the present context, corpus linguistics is used in the sense of CCL, although I have preferred to keep to the abbreviation CL3, because 'corpus linguistics' is still the term which the field is associated with.

A recent definition of corpus linguistics as 'the study of language on the basis of text corpora' (Aijmer and Altenberg, 1991: 1) might be amended to the following: **corpus linguistics** is a field of study that 'involves the study of language on the basis of textual or acoustic corpora, almost always involving the computer in some phase of storage, processing, and analysis of this data' (Ooi 1994a: 2). **Textual corpora** usually refers to the written aspect, while **speech** or **acoustic corpora** (see Atkins et al. 1992: 1) refers to CL3 research into spoken language, with application to speech technology. In both cases, it is doubtful whether any 'corpus linguistics' project nowadays would be carried out without some use of the computer as the basis. Since the computer is involved, CL3 is concerned not only with the analysis (and interpretation) of language but also with computational techniques and methodology for the analysis of these texts (McEnery and Wilson 1996; Garside et al. (eds) 1987). Indeed, Leech suggests that corpus linguistics refers 'not to a domain of study, but rather to a methodological basis for pursuing linguistic research' (Leech 1992a: 105), one which is amenable to any branch of linguistics by the process of using machine-readable corpora and associated computational techniques as the basis for linguistic investigation. According to Leech (1992a: 107), the typical focus of attention in computer corpus linguistics is a focus on 1. linguistic performance, rather than competence; 2. linguistic description, rather than linguistic universals, 3. quantitative, as well as qualitative models of language, and 4. a more empiricist, rather than a rationalist view of scientific inquiry.

For the foreseeable future, CL3 projects will tend to be concerned with analysing and processing vast amounts of (textual) data, simply because large quantities of text are needed in order to build probabilistic systems for natural language processing. In the 1960s, 'large' meant the collection of a million or so words of text.[7] In the future, this is likely to mean hundreds and thousands of millions of words (see Section 3.4). However, the stress on size or quantity for a corpus does not necessarily mean that all types of computer corpora gathered must be large, since there are some genres of texts restricted in scope and size. For instance, a corpus of Old English texts can never be of the order of a hundred million words, simply because it is restricted to the set of texts which have survived from the Old English period. Leech (1991a: 10–12) therefore also warns that 'to focus merely on size … [in defining something as worthy of the enterprise of corpus linguistics] … is naive', although he is in favour, of course, of having large corpora. So, a definition which defines corpus linguistics as 'the branch of linguistics that is concerned with the study of language use by means of large text corpora' (Oostdijk 1991: preface) not only begs the question of what is 'large', but also neglects the inclusion of the computer by which the word 'large' has been made possible (through the expansion of hardware storage) and applicable (through considerable success in using probabilistic methods of analysis).

It has been suggested that the guiding principle involved in calling some collection of machine-readable texts a corpus is that it is 'designed or required for a particular "**representative**"[8] function' (Leech 1991: 11). A corpus can be designed to serve as a resource for general purposes, or for a more specialised function such as being a resource which is representative of a particular sub-language (roughly equivalent to a language genre). Atkins et al. (1992: 1) distinguish four types of text collection, which in brief may be reproduced as follows:

> **Archive:** a repository of readable electronic texts not linked in any coordinated way, e.g. the Oxford Text Archive

Electronic text library (or ETL, French *textothèque*): a collection of electronic texts in standardised format with certain conventions relating to content, etc., but without rigorous selectional constraints.

Corpus: a subset of an ETL, built according to explicit design criteria for a specific purpose, e.g. the Corpus Révolutionnaire (Bibliothèque Beaubourg, Paris), the Cobuild Corpus, the Longman/Lancaster corpus, the Oxford Pilot corpus.

Subcorpus: a subset of a corpus, either a static component of a complex corpus or a dynamic selection from a corpus during on-line analysis.

The notion of representativeness for the corpus as a lexical resource will be treated in Section 3.2.

2.3.1 The lexicon in CL3

Like CL1, many CL3 systems have in the past treated the lexicon as an incidental component (see Section 2.1.1), since the methodology in CL3 has thus far been the quantificational analysis of language that uses corpora as the basis from which to induce stochastic models of language (e.g. Garside et al. 1987, Sharman 1989a, 1989b, 1990). However, as Ingria et al. put it,

> the term **language model** ... [while being] typically associated with notions like probabilistic part-of-speech taggers ... and parsers ... has a substantial lexical component to it. A tagger assigns syntactic categories to lexical items; thus the output of such a program can be used to annotate a word list with part-of-speech labels. Similarly, the very existence of a parse tree would enable further enhancement of items in a word list by adding, eg, subcategorization information. It is just a matter of emphasis whether essentially the same operational mechanisms are applied for language analysis per se, or for language processing with a view of [*sic*] further integration of (aspects of) the output into a permanent lexical structure. In this vein, more recent, and explicitly of lexical acquisition nature, work [*sic*] includes, for instance, frequency based elicitation of word distribution patterns, concordance-driven definition of context and word behavior, extracting and representing word collocations, acquisition of lexical semantics of verbs from sentence frames, and even derivation of transfer lexicons for machine translation ...
>
> (Ingria et al., 1992: 360–61)

Such a view of language analysis and processing involves a methodology for the derivation of lexical/lexicographic information from corpus processing and the storage of this information in a 'permanent lexical structure', a suitable lexical database (see Chapters 4 and 5).

Thus, while there might not be any necessary direct relation between an LDB/LKB (which stores the lexicon) and a corpus (the object of CL3 research), the advent of the COBUILD dictionary has given rise, in part, to the issue of deriving large computational lexicons from corpora/unrestricted text as an alternative or supplement to the MRD (see Sections 3.2 and 4.2). In this respect, Sinclair (1985) and Atkins (1987, 1991) argue for a methodology, as evidenced by the one used in the COBUILD project, for measuring hard evidence of the lexical behaviour of words since this will (arguably) result in a more representative, coherent, and consistent output than a lexicon produced from conventional means (such as dictionaries produced by 'armchair lexicography' or crafted just on the basis of a CL1 linguist's intuition.) This enterprise Atkins calls **corpus lexicography**. By advocating such a methodology, Atkins is of course not ignoring the fact that for 250 years (at least), dictionaries have been based on textual examples (citations), such as Samuel Johnson's well-known dictionary: Atkins calls for a more holistic approach, especially at a time when corpus-based methods to lexicography have begun to emerge, partly because of the COBUILD dictionary approach.

Similarly, this methodology may be extended to one which uses text corpora, as a complement to dictionaries, for lexical knowledge acquisition. To recapitulate (see Section 2.2.1), the inadequacy of the MRD for the enterprise of lexical knowledge acquisition includes 'the omission [rather than commission] of explicit statements of essential linguistic facts ... lack of systematicity in the compiling in one single dictionary ... [and] ambiguities within entries and incompatible compiling across dictionaries' (Atkins, 1991: 168). A further justification for using text corpora rather than MRDs for lexical knowledge acquisition is the matter of keeping up with language as it evolves, so 'the analysis of words, from decisions concerning the make-up of the word list to the specific content of individual entries, should be carried out entirely on the basis of a large representative [current] corpus, both of spoken and written text' (Ingria et al. 1992: 361).

This last requirement raises a number of issues which are methodologically challenging for the use of a corpus as an on-line lexical resource, and will be returned to in the next chapter.

2.4 THE INTERDEPENDENCE AND CONVERGENCE OF CL1, CL2, AND CL3

It is now no longer possible nor desirable to consider CL1, CL2, and CL3 as being isolated from one another. For instance, in the case of CL1, I mentioned in Section 2.1 the division of the field broadly into two groups with different methodologies: 'self-organising' and 'knowledge-based'. However, adherents of both these approaches can learn from each by means of the CL3 enterprise. As Atkins et al. (1992: 14) point out, the self-organising camp can 'act on the output of grammatically based analysis' which would lead to the means of analysing the semantic analysis, or content, of texts. The knowledge-based camp, in turn, now recognises the value of corpora, 'primarily to assess the level of coverage achieved by processes that they have designed *a priori*.' Further, the resurgence in the use of probabilistic methods for use in CL1 systems presupposes the use of large corpora, which is what current CL3 systems adopt. In CL2 and CL3, the emergence of corpus lexicography means that it is no longer unusual for large corpora to be compiled by lexicographers for the analysis of the behaviour of words. At the same time, in CL3, the formalised approach characteristic of the knowledge-based camp in CL1 is gaining increasing pace.

The trends that I have outlined above have recently been similarly formulated by Ide (1992:67) who sees an overlap between what she calls **humanities computing** and **computational linguistics**. The overlap comes in the focus on the analysis of texts using the computer. Using the abbreviatory terms I have formulated, the dissimilarity between CL1 and the other two enterprises (CL2 and CL3) has come about because of different circumstances. Ide (1992) notes that, in humanities computing (presumably CL2 and CL3), the analysis has traditionally involved such things as the analysis of style, content, and theme. In addition, there is a concern for providing better access to textual materials through the use of concordances and other retrieval tools. For analyses of style and content, humanities computing has needed information such as the part of speech for each word in the text, in order to determine the syntactic constituents of sentences. In the analysis of content, there is a need for such datasets as semantically related words, and all the morphological forms in which such words appear in a text. Furthermore, information is needed for semantic properties (animate etc.) and the roles (e.g., agent, object) words and phrases play in various sentences in a text. CL1 has also needed such types of information. But it has been unfortunate that these two enterprises have been working almost entirely independently of each other. For Ide, the independence resulted because both enterprises worked with entirely independent methodologies. Humanities computing tended to be concerned with what Martin Kay calls 'remarkable' language, as contrast the 'unremarkable' language with which CL1 is concerned (Ide 1992: 66). According to Ide, CL1 has always wanted to handle 'straightforward' language first, before coping with things as complex as metaphor and irony. Humanities computing was concerned with broad features of style and content – general patterns across texts that indicated trends and frequent patterns or usage, while CL1 struggled to come up with a deep and complete representation of the syntax and full meaning of a handful of sentences. Thus humanities computing used statistical methods to find the probable and the characteristic, while CL1 relied on linguistic theory. At the same time, the attention in humanities computing was on the amassing of corpora of texts, the notion of genre, and the use of such basic resources as word lists (CL3). In CL1, the focus predomin-antly used to be on the parsing and interpretation of the sentence, with peripheral attention paid to the construction of large-sized lexicons and the analysis of texts.

Ide rightly observes that both humanities computing and CL1 have encountered common problems. Humanities computing has found that such analyses as style and theme cannot be done successfully without in-depth information on syntax and semantics. In CL1, while linguistic theories predict the possible, information about the improbable and uncharacteristic properties of language is needed in order to make more progress in handling language by machine. So, there is an increasing tendency for each to be interested in what the other has to offer: humanities computing is becoming interested in CL1 methodology and formalism while CL1 is applying statistical methods to large corpora in order to gather information about general properties of language use, and has begun to use tools from humanities computing such as concordances and word lists.

The comparisons made by Ide (1992) are not dissimilar to those of Church and Mercer (1994: 15) in their summary of the rationalist and empiricist approaches to natural language processing and how these two approaches are converging.

2.5 THE TEI FOR THE EMERGENCE OF TEXTUAL AND LEXICAL STANDARDS

The common focus on the use of the computer to analyse **texts** by CL1, CL2, and CL3 has led to the establishment of the Text Encoding Initiative (TEI), which had its origins in the autumn of 1987 and is sponsored jointly by the Association for Computers in the Humanities, the Association for Literary and Linguistic Computing, and the Association for Computational Linguistics (see Ide and Sperberg-McQueen (1995), and Section 1.2.3). The TEI has as its task the production of a set of guidelines to facilitate both the interchange of existing encoded texts and the creation of newly encoded texts. The guidelines are meant to specify both the types of features that should be encoded and also the way these features should be encoded, as well as to suggest ways of describing the resulting encoding scheme and its relationship with pre-existing schemes. The development of such text-encoding standards opens up the possibility of encoding extra layers of information: this means entire categories of information which can be searched for automatically.

It is claimed that the TEI project will result in such advantages as the following:

1. Standardised descriptive-structural markup, by means of the Standard Generalized Markup Language (SGML, see Burnard 1995), offers strategic advantages over procedural document markup by separating text structure and content from textual appearance.
2. Such generic encoding forms the basis for a wide range of document interchange and text processing operations common to scholarly publishing, database management, and office automation.
3. TEI/SGML encoding renders textual data accessible both to traditional (paper) printing demands and to electronic search and retrieval – across an arbitrarily wide range of computing architectures and applications packages.

4. TEI encoding supports language-specific text processing within multilingual text, and hence opens up the multilingual dimension of research documents and databases.

While the range of information in any one lexicon depends on the purpose for which it has been built and need not be exhaustive, the list of lexical information proposed by the TEI Guidelines should contain all the possible types of information that can be considered for inclusion in a computational lexicon and should be a more exhaustive list than Hudson's (see Section 1.3.1). As people continue to agree on the standard, the latest TEI Guidelines on this issue can be obtained from their World Wide Web home page (see Appendix B): currently, the TEI Guidelines contain the base tag set for encoding human-oriented monolingual and polyglot dictionaries.

It is also helpful to be aware that, although the TEI is the only attempt known deliberately to propose a common standard for the sponsored fields, there are other related attempts to identify and promote the reusability of information in such various sources as MRDs, lexicons, and corpora. These include the following projects, the first five of which are based in the European community: ESPRIT ACQUILEX, EUROTRA-7, GENELEX, MULTILEX, the EUROPEAN CORPORA NETWORK, and the CONSORTIUM FOR LEXICAL RESEARCH AT NEW MEXICO (see Armstrong-Warwick 1995, Atkins et al. 1992: 12–13, Copestake 1992, Copestake et al. 1993, Heid and McNaught 1991, and Section 2.7). The European Commission has also launched three projects coordinated by the Istituto di Linguistica Computazionale (Institute of Computational Linguistics) at the University of Pisa: the EAGLES, RELATOR, and PAROLE projects. These projects aim to create, manage, specify standards, and distribute such linguistic resources as lexicons.

2.6 THE NOTION OF THE REUSABILITY OF LEXICAL RESOURCES

As a result of a focus on the notion of 'standards' in lexical data (as evidenced by Ide and Veronis 1995), there is a great interest in the 're-use' of lexical information.

The term **reusability** can be interpreted in two basic ways, which I call **reuse_e** (for reusing **e**xisting lexical resources) and **reuse_m** (for achieving **m**ultifunctionality):[9]

(1) The term 'reusable linguistic knowledge resource' refers to a resource which can be used again in another application or in another usage situation other than its original one. Examples include: a machine-readable version of a dictionary for human users which is subsequently also used in a computer program and a dictionary produced for a machine translation system which is subsequently used for a man-machine interface.

(2) The term 'reusable linguistic knowledge resource' also refers to a resource which is initially deliberately constructed in such a way that it
can be used in several applications or usage situations. Example: a lexicon constructed in such a way that it can be shared by several NLP
applications, or in several products of a company.

(Heid and McNaught, 1991: 35)

Thus, in interpreting the notion of 'reusability', Heid and McNaught appropriately make the distinction between 1. using again what already exists, for
another purpose other than the one initially conceived (i.e. **reuse_e**), and 2.
producing multiply usable (i.e. multifunctional) resources (i.e. **reuse_m**). We
may see text – an existing resource – as being reused in order to 'populate' the
lexicon (as a linguistic notion) which is stored in the lexical data/knowledge
base (as a computational structure). Multifunctionality is oriented towards such
applications as the construction of a lexical data/knowledge base.

The two senses of the term 'reusability' are similarly formulated by Calzolari
and Zampolli (1991: 281). The first (**reuse_e**) involves the notion of reusing
lexical information implicitly or explicitly present in what they call 'pre-
existing lexical resources' (such as machine-readable dictionaries, terminological
databases, and textual corpora) as an aid to the construction of a lexical
knowledge base. The second interpretation of 'reusability' (**reuse_m**) involves
the notion of constructing multifunctional resources (such as an LKB) in order
to allow different NLP systems (different theoretical frameworks having
different applications) and human users such as lexicographers and linguists to
extract – with appropriate interfaces – relevant lexical information. This is
understood in the context of their assertion that computerised lexicons have
evolved from the creation of Machine Readable Dictionaries (MRDs) in the
seventies through Lexical Databases (LDBs) in the early eighties and Lexical
Knowledge Bases (LKBs) in the late eighties to currently, proposals for 'the
creation of a vast "reservoir" of linguistic knowledge, in the form of reusable
linguistic descriptions that are as complete as possible, structured as in a large
LKB or in various kinds of interconnected linguistic bases (grammatical,
lexical, textual, or knowledge bases)' (Calzolari and Zampolli, 1991: 280).
According to Calzolari and Zampolli, computational lexical research is now at
a point where it is considering the multifunctionality of such a LKB. In other
words, for them the LKB should 1. function as a central repository, and 2. be
large enough and reusable in different contexts for different purposes in order
to avoid a duplication of effort from each of the three perspectives outlined.

Of course, such a complete LKB has yet to manifest itself, and the construction of such a multifunctional resource is a challenge facing not only CL1, but
also CL2, and CL3. There has also been Martin Kay's proposal to build a
'dictionary server' which is 'a computer with a large dictionary in its file system'
(Kay 1984b: 461). This server would be on-line for various access needs: Kay
presumably means that the server would facilitate the creation of any 'virtual
lexicon' targeted to the specific needs.[10]

2.7 THE CORE-REUSABLE MULTIFUNCTIONAL LEXICON

The prospect of developing such an LDB/LKB highlighted by the agenda in the preceding section involves a prior consideration of tasks such as the development of computational tools which would help in building up, maintaining, exchanging and using computational lexicons. In this connection, this is realised by three ongoing efforts: the Consortium for Lexical Research, the Centre for Lexical Information at Nijmegen, and the Eurotra-7 proposal to construct a core-reusable lexicon system.

A first step for the sharing of 'precompetitive' lexical resources has been the setting up of the Consortium for Lexical Research in New Mexico State University, which aims to facilitate this type of research by making available to the NLP community resources ranging from lexical database management tools to morphological analysers (see Appendix B).

Similarly, the objective of the CELEX project (see Section 5.8) is to provide on-line accessible lexical information because of the demand for such information in applications as various as 'natural-language-like interfaces in man-machine communication, new approaches to (semi)-automatic translation, and the interest in getting more detailed insights into the structure of lexica': the CELEX project is meant to 'offer computerised, multilingual, multifunctional, lexical databases' to institutions (CELEX 1986: 1).

In terms of multifunctionality, the Eurotra-7 report contains a proposal to construct a reusable lexicon system whose specifications include the following:

Core system:
- Formal descriptive specifications;
- Representational specifications;
- Exemplary reusable resources;
- Compilers and interpreters for the derivation of application specific dictionaries from the reusable resource and vice versa;
- Tools for semi-automatic acquisition of linguistic knowledge from SGMLencoded dictionary material;
- Interactive data entry and dictionary management tools;

Extensions:
- Tools for the extraction of linguistic information from text corpora prepared in a suitable form for NLP (support tools for lexical acquisition);
- Other types of lexical acquisition and term acquisition tools;
- Applications of a reusable lexical or terminological resource in tools for the language professionals

(Heid and McNaught 1991: 107)

This may be schematically represented in Figure 2.1 as:

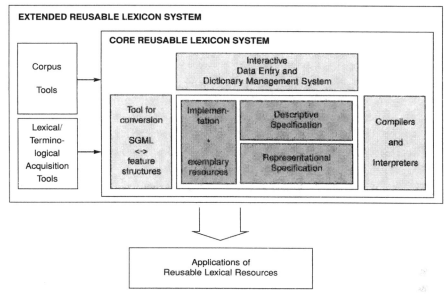

Figure 2.1 Towards a reusable lexicon system – core, extensions and applications: from Heid and McNaught (1991: 108)

If cooperation in lexical research leads to such an integrated environment where lexicons can be easily constructed and reused, it would reduce reduplicative efforts among researchers. For the immediate moment, however, we have to deal with questions of varying form, content, and computational format.

2.8 THE POLYTHEORETICAL LEXICON

The idea that it might be possible to agree on the content of the lexical item in the TEI guidelines (Section 2.5) leads to the prospect of achieving the **polytheoretical lexicon**, which would be multifunctional with respect to different linguistic theories and have the advantage of being usable by different NLP programs. Work towards such a lexicon might lead to 'a better understanding of the subsets of data successfully handled in different frameworks and to a more precise characterisation of those points on which we agree and disagree' (Kegl 1989: 27).

At first sight, this notion of achieving the polytheoretical lexicon might seem a contradiction in terms. Firstly, although various linguistic theories have been, and will be, vying for the title of being the most generalisable linguistic model, it is unlikely that any theory will emerge undisputed. Secondly, different linguistic theories may well describe the same facts, but they use different devices and possibly different basic underlying concepts, thus arriving sometimes at quite diverging generalisations. Thirdly, the controversy lies in specifying when a particular framework is 'theory-neutral' or not. For instance, it is difficult to decide whether Pustejovsky's theory of Qualia Structure (as in Section 1.2.1) is 'neutral' – indeed, arguably, whether any theory (by virtue of being a theory) can be regarded as neutral.

Nevertheless, it might be possible that (irrespective of the linguistic theory concerned) there are minimum facts about language which different theories can agree upon. Such instances include 'categorial description of lexeme words (verb vs. noun vs. adjective etc), order and adjacency (i.e. some element is to the left or right of another), morphological ('surface') or otherwise observable facts, such as the opposition in some languages between singular and plural, tenses, etc' (Heid and McNaught 1991: 21). And even if the exact order of any of these categories remains controversial, the consensual point is that these facts have to be recorded in any lexicon of general application. Therefore, Quirk et al. (1985), by virtue of their (arguably) neutral metalanguage for linguistic description, might be useful as a starting point for the description of such categories. This might go some way towards meeting Heid and McNaught's (1991: 23) agenda that what is needed for the sharing and exchange of lexical descriptions is a description of linguistic phenomena in terms of the relevant 'minimal observable' facts.[11]

The usual situation, as Heid and McNaught point out, is that of a **partial overlap** between any two linguistic approaches: 'linguists may agree, for example, on the fact that "objects" are arguments of verbs, have a certain behaviour under passivisation, but they may disagree about "objects" having "case" or being only noun phrases or also infinitivals and/or sentential complements' (Heid and McNaught, 23).

Finally, a first step towards the implementation of a theory-neutral lexicon might be the intermediate format of the Alvey lexicon (see Grover et al. 1988, Carroll and Grover 1989, and also Ritchie et al. 1987): in terms of content, the lexicon approximates the type of minimal information indicated in this section.

2.9 CONCLUSION

This chapter on the issues surrounding the form and content of the lexicon concerns its increasing role in both linguistic theory and the building of computational systems for *representing, analysing,* and ultimately *understanding* natural language – a concern shared by CL1, CL2, and CL3 alike. This chapter has sought to outline the notions of CL1, CL2, and CL3 and the treatment of the lexicon in these enterprises. The trend towards lexicalism by an increasing emphasis on the centrality of the lexicon has been examined from these three perspectives. Given the various efforts discussed in this chapter, the prospect of the standardisation and the sharing of lexical resources does not seem too far off. Also, unlike the times when rationalist (or Chomskyan) linguistics reigned supreme, all three enterprises now focus on the notion of the text (representing the 'E-language', still disparaged by Chomsky (1995) who postulates whether E-languages do really exist!) and empirically derive a (reusable) lexicon from it. Of course, the investigation of natural language texts does not necessarily mean the encouragement of an atheoretical enterprise, a charge often levelled at corpus linguistics by die-hard Chomskyans. On the contrary, Chapters 3 and 4 will discuss two theoretical frameworks for the handling of text, from a lexical perspective. .

2.10 STUDY QUESTIONS

1. If you have access to the Internet and the World Wide Web, use a browser such as Netscape to log on to relevant sites, such as those maintained by the Oxford Text Archive, the Consortium for Lexical Research, and the Special Interest Group on the Lexicon (see Appendix B). Try to access lexicons which are available: what are the form and content of these lexicons?
2. From your examination of the lexicons in (1) , can you now see why the lexicon is widely regarded as the 'bottleneck' of a natural language processing system?

2.11 FURTHER READING

Atkins and Zampolli (1994 (eds)) contains many good papers which deal with current issues raised in this chapter. Also, Walker et al. (1995 (eds)) contains papers which, although actually written some time ago, have been published only fairly recently; nevertheless, these papers are still relevant to current lexical research.

Machine learning has been emerging as a field of research in CL1 during the course of the last few years. Daelemans and Powers (1992) contains the proceedings of the first machine-learning workshop. A number of such papers investigating various aspects of neural computing in CL1 have been written: see, for instance, Daelemans and Powers (1992), and the COLING proceedings in recent years. Neural computing is being used to address such areas as speech recognition and machine learning; the idea is to train these networks to perform operations which require associative recognition.

For a more detailed overview of MT, see Lewis (1992), and Hutchins and Somers (1992). For an overview of NLP and its components, see Sparck-Jones (1992), Shieber (1992), and Flickinger (1992).

De Beaugrande and Dressler (1981) give in-depth treatment of the notion of 'text' and the enterprise of textual linguistics. For an introduction to the notions of reusing texts, encoding standards, and descriptive markup, see Ide and Veronis (1995 (eds)) as well as Burnard (1992, 1995).

NOTES

1. For some people, it might be a little irregular to treat what I've characterised as CL1 and CL3 (and even CL2) separately, since corpora have been incorporated into the enterprise of CL1. However, these trends are still slow to come by: thus, the Association for Computational Linguistics (ACL), the Association for Literary and Linguistic Computing (ALLC), and the International Computer Archive of Modern and Medieval English (ICAME) have demonstrably separate objectives and agendas. Many common insights can be gleaned from these three enterprises.
2. An announcement by Bonnie Dorr for a Conference on 'Building Lexicons for Machine Translation' (AAAI-93 Spring Symposium Series, 23–25 March 1993) puts the need for considering the lexicon in

the following manner:'The lexicon plays a central role in any machine translation (MT) system, regardless of the theoretical foundations upon which the system is based. However, it is only recently that MT researchers have begun to focus more specifically on issues that concern the lexicon, e.g., the automatic construction of multi-lingual semantic representations. Large dictionaries are important in any natural language application, but the problem is especially difficult for MT because of cross-linguistic divergences and mismatches that arise from the perspective of the lexicon. Furthermore, scaling up dictionaries is an essential requirement for MT that can no longer be dismissed.'

3. c.f. the 'All-Inclusive Lexicon' in Section 1.2.2: Richard Hudson's conception of an all-inclusive lexicon contains only the declarative aspect, unlike Small's WEP which requires procedural knowledge also.

4. WEP goes back as early as 1980, in Small's PhD thesis *Word Expert Parsing: A Theory of Distributed Word-Based Natural Language Understanding*, Department of Computer Science, University of Maryland.

5. A. S. Hornby was chiefly responsible for the OALD, and saw it through the first three editions (1948, 1963, and 1974 respectively). The third edition was coedited with A. P. Cowie and A. C. Gimson. More recently, an encyclopedic edition based on the 4th edition has come out, lending support to the current view which does not treat word and world knowledge as distinct entities that are totally unrelated to each other: see Crowther (1992). In his foreword, Crowther says that this encyclopedic edition 'grew out of a realization that there is a need among foreign learners of English at an advanced level ... for a dictionary that gives full and detailed information on English lexis, grammar and usage within a controlled defining vocabulary, but at the same time offers wider reference coverage than other such dictionaries currently available.' Many encyclopedic entries - especially those of a literary, geographical, and biographic nature – are included here.

6. Akkerman (1989) gives a comparison between the OALD and LDOCE grammar coding systems.

7. Examples are the Brown and LOB corpora. See Kucera and Francis (1967) for the Brown Corpus and Johansson et al. (1978) for the LOB Corpus.

8. The term **representative** as applied to a corpus is problematic. See Summers (1993, 1995) and Biber (1993) for a detailed treatment. See also Section 3.2.

9. Like Heid and McNaught, Walker et al. (1995: 15) interpret the notion of 'reusability' in terms of 'reusable-1' and 'reusable-2', which I have reformulated to 'reusable-e' and 'reusable-m' respectively.

10. Kay (1984b) also calls for the 'courage and foresight to invest in lexicographic data bases of radical design'.

11. Heid and McNaught also specify that this will mean the inclusion of rules which relate the differences between these different systems. This latter objective might be an objective worth considering when resources are available.

Corpus evidence and lexicon-based language modelling

3.0 INTRODUCTION

In this chapter, we will explore what it means to use the corpus as a complement to the dictionary as a lexical resource, including the choice, size, and representativeness of corpus data. In other words, we will explore what it means to derive lexicons from corpora by exploring both the nature of the corpus as lexicographic or lexical evidence and the means by which this evidence can be gleaned. Such 'means' include, firstly, the basic tool of lexicographers and linguists alike for word evidence, the concordancer, and secondly, a linguistic framework postulated by John Sinclair for the systematic sifting of corpus data as linguistic evidence. The concordancer as a tool has more or less been adequately dealt with elsewhere (see, for instance, McEnery and Wilson 1996; Barnbrook 1996; and Appendix B for the relevant World-Wide Web sites detailing the use of such concordancers). Since this is the case, we will focus on the linguistic implications of the evidence reflected in the concordance rather than the actual operations of the concordancer. Also, while the notion of a concordance is a relatively simple one, the gleaning of linguistic evidence in the manner that Sinclair postulates has not been more thoroughly discussed, and will be dealt with in this chapter.

3.1 TYPES OF LEXICOGRAPHIC AND LEXICAL EVIDENCE

How is lexical (for the formulation of linguistic theory) or lexicographic (for dictionary-making) evidence derived? An obvious way is first to consult and rely on a dictionary. In turn, a dictionary bases its evidence on one or more of 3 methods of gathering evidence: **lexical introspection**; **casual citation**, and **corpus**.

The first method, **lexical introspection**, has been in existence for as long as there have been lexicographers, and indeed, language. If we rely on this method alone, perhaps a dictionary is only as good as its lexicographer(s), since what constitutes an acceptable usage or definition depends on whether it accords with the lexicographer's intuitions and judgement. Since the average person's own mental lexicon is firstly, finite and secondly, static and unchanged (i.e. in need of updating) it is probably not sufficient to rely on only one person's linguistic intuitions. But, of course, the lexicographer worth his or her salt tends to have a more well-informed lexicon – perhaps larger but certainly more updated – than the average person in recording current or contemporary usage. The reliance on such lexical intuitions alone in the making of dictionaries is often called 'armchair' lexicography.

The second method of lexicographic and lexical evidence, **casual citation**, is offered when the lexical behaviour of one's family members, friends, or strangers is observed and recorded. It is often casually noticed, which raises two questions: 1. Did the observer note the particular feature out of context? and 2. Does the observer's circle of people constitute a random sampling which represents the behaviour of the society in which he or she live in? If, in the first case, the observer casually noted that the word *error* was used more than *mistake* (for expressions like *computer error*, rather than the much less well-known *?computer mistake*), the observer may not be right to reach the conclusion that the former occurs more than the latter in the English language, without considering the context in which the word *error* occurs. As in the second case, if the observer often spends time with a group of computer boffins who talk of nothing except computers, a frequent use and thus occurrence of the expression *computer error* might lead to the skewed conclusion that the English language prefers *error* to *mistake*. While this example might seem a little far-fetched to some people, it is not inconceivable that there are people who base their lexical or lexicographic evidence mainly on the behaviour of the people they come into contact with.

On the other hand, **corpus** methods offered by, say, the 1995 edition of the LDOCE dictionary (see Summers (ed.) 1995) show how different the picture can be from the one just sketched. It is *mistake*, not *error*, that occurs more in speech; in writing, both words tend to be equal in their frequency of usage. *Error* tends to refer to particular mistakes made. In order to reach this view, dictionaries like the LDOCE rely heavily on corpus evidence nowadays. The essential difference between corpus and citational data is that, although both are instances of observed data, only the corpus is systematically gathered for a particular purpose, and is coherently organised for this purpose. Further, the criterion for distinguishing between an **archive** and a corpus is also one of systematicity. In a workshop on corpus resources, Leech (1990: 5) makes the following point:

> A 'corpus' should be distinguished from an 'archive', the latter being a repository of available language materials, and the former being a systematic selection and collection of material for given purposes. A corpus draws upon the resources of an archive, and therefore both are important. The systematic compilation of a structured corpus, however, is the primary objective.

Extending my definition of a corpus in Section 2.3, we may say that the corpus, if representative, will indicate the collective intuitions of a relevant group of people using the word or linguistic expression under study. Thus, if one wanted to see whether writers of computer manuals tend to use the expression *computer error* in preference to *computer mistake*, then obviously one should use a corpus of computer manuals and not cookbook recipes as evidence. If this corpus is sufficiently contemporary and maximally representative of the writings of computer manual writers, then the evidence offered should be indicative of current patterns of usage among this group of people.

Is a corpus always necessary for lexical and grammatical evidence? The full verb phrase in English, which consists of the structure modal + *have*-perfective + *be*-progressive + *be*-passive (as in the phrases *might have been being built* and *had been being interviewed*), is described in corpus-oriented grammar books (e.g. Quirk et al. 1985). The question then becomes one of asking how often this structure occurs in contemporary English corpora. A few years ago, I sent an electronic message to the corpus linguistics network (see Appendix B) to seek their assistance in searching for such a structure in existing English corpora. The results[1] came back in less than a day: in their trawl, this type of phrase rarely occurs; the majority of verb phrases containing auxiliary verbs are limited to two or, less commonly, three elements (as in *might have built* or *might have been built*). In any half billion words searched, it is probably safe to say that the full verb phrase structure occurs once or twice, or not at all. What conclusion(s) can then be drawn regarding the corpus enterprise (of which the die-hard Chomskyan uses this structure not only to show that there are grammatical structures that rarely occur in any corpus but perhaps also to cast aspersions on the value of the corpus-based approach)? No one (either Chomskyan or non-Chomskyan) denies the grammatical correctness of the full verb phrase structure but, given its rare occurrence, the reader can draw one of the following conclusions: 1. The rare occurrence of the full verb phrase structure shows that the appropriate language corpus which would show its contexts of occurrence, has not yet been compiled, stored electronically, and made available for electronic search; or 2. The rare occurrence of the full verb phrase structure shows that corpus linguistics is inadequate in capturing language phenomena, and thus corpus linguistics is not worth studying; or 3. The full verb phrase structure is a rare form anyway, so this is, of course, precisely what the searched corpora indicate: that the full verb phrase structure is a marked feature which is hardly in current usage. The first and third options are well borne out: an informed corpus should show only the typical and central tendencies of language, and an examination of several representative corpora should be taken as adequate evidence. What is also remarkable is the ability to use the computer for searching through millions of electronic words in such a short time, something which would not have been possible twenty years ago.

A different example concerns the terms *handphone, mobile phone,* and *cellular phone*. In my mental lexicon, I originally thought that *handphone* was a 'core' English item, if by this we mean that it is transparent mainly to both educated British and American speakers of English, and so is perceived as 'standard' usage. Also, of the three lexical items mentioned, *handphone* appears to be the one most used in my circle of friends and acquaintances, and indeed in formal and informal situations in both Singapore and Malaysia. However, I was astonished to find that such a 'strongly core English' term was not listed in the more recent editions of the CIDE, COBUILD, LDOCE, OALD, and TCEED learners' dictionaries, as well as the Oxford English Dictionary on CD-ROM; on the other hand, the terms *mobile phone* and *cellular phone* are variously listed in these dictionaries as being typical of British and American usage respectively. This preliminary conclusion was supported by other central pieces of evidence. Firstly, a 'native' English informant carried out a survey in Leeds on the term *handphone* and found that this term was not very comprehensible among her respondents: after all, a *telephone* was something you carry in the hand! Secondly, the various corpora I had access to at the time bore out this fact as well: out of 323 million words in the COBUILD 'Bank of English' (see Section 3.4), there are 2479 occurrences of *mobile phone(s)*, 447 occurrences of *cellular phone(s)* respectively corresponding to British and American usage (since the COBUILD Bank of English is predominantly British in nature) and only 1 occurrence of *hand phone* (as two words, instead of one) as indicated in the following sentence: *And they were still smarting from the Air Supply concert at which the lead singer threatened to deck the chap in the front row if he made one more call on his hand phone.* It is interesting to note that this sentence in which *hand phone* occurs is taken from the Australian newspaper component of the Bank of English, which therefore indicates that this word is not transparent to either educated British or American speakers.

However, even in a million-word corpus such as the Singapore ICE corpus, the word *handphone(s)* occurs 7 times, as Figure 3.1 shows:

Singapore ICE corpus: spoken component

```
1. … time of any telephone in its class the[handphone]] fits easily into a shirt pocket.
2. …    (David Keller) JO: But your        [[handphones]] do not come cheap
3.. … customers consideration for cellular [[handphones]] PSL: The cellular
4. …set to increase Whether prices for     [[handphones]] will go up will depend
```

Singapore ICE corpus: written component

```
1. …old unemployed man, used pagers and     [[handphones]] to contact his distributors.
2. …,    capable of intercepting signals from[handphones]], walkie-talkies and possibly
3. ..    more drug suspects had been using   [[handphones]] and pagers to set up deals.
```

Figure 3.1 Concordance listing of *handphone(s)*, from the Singapore ICE corpus, generated using *MonoConc for Windows* (see Appendix B)

I thus updated my own mental lexicon and came to the following conclusion: *handphone* is a term more suited for intranational or regional varieties of English. This example also indicates the need to build various regional corpora of English (such as a Singaporean-Malaysian 'Bank of English') in order to make detailed comparisons of how English functions world-wide: in this respect, the ICE project (see Greenbaum (ed.) 1996; Greenbaum and Nelson 1996) is a major international effort in this direction.

In concluding this section, the three basic methods of obtaining data that have been sketched correspond roughly to the traditional distinction between 'observed' and 'elicited' data. The linguist may either introspect into his or her own mental lexicon or 'elicit' what constitutes the mental lexicon of an informant, but both the linguist's lexicon and that of the informant are not directly observable. 'Observed' data refers to both 'casual citational' and 'corpus' data: the crucial difference between these two is that corpus data is said to be systematically and coherently organised.

Corpus- 'based' linguistics	Corpus- 'driven' linguistics
– a corpus is used to validate, check, and improve linguistic observations that have already been made; the corpus-based linguist does not feel 'threatened' by corpus data at all	– a corpus is of prime importance in bringing out new ideas for the examination of data
– the linguist does not question received theoretical positions or well-established descriptive categories; instead, his position to language structure is already well-formed.	– the linguist believes that the kind of evidence emerging from corpora may be difficult to reconcile with established positions in the discipline, and he leaves open the possibility of the need for a radical change in linguistic theory in order to cope with the evidence
– the corpus is used to help extend and improve linguistic description	– evidence from the corpus is paramount, therefore the linguist makes as few assumptions as possible about the nature of the theoretical and descriptive categories
An example of a relevant question: "Is *whom* still used in English, and if so how?	An example of a relevant question: "Is the distinction between grammar and lexis necessary?"

Figure 3.2 Corpus-based vs Corpus-driven linguistics: from Sinclair (1996b)

It is important to note that a reliance on corpus data does not mean a denial of the other two methods for the gathering of lexicographic or lexical evidence. Far from exclusiveness, it is often necessary to utilise all three methods for the gleaning of such evidence adequately.

We may further postulate that any lexical enterprise using corpus data may be characterised into either the **corpus-based** or **corpus-driven** approaches, both of which are equally respectable. These two basic positions are summarised in Figure 3.2.

Extending the characterisation by Sinclair, the distinction between the 'corpus-based' and 'corpus-driven' approaches may be seen to correspond to the 'top-down' and 'bottom-up' approaches to the analysis of lexical data. Roughly speaking, a top-down approach begins with some theory, which is then applied to the data for confirmation, extension, or rejection of the theory; a bottom-up approach begins with some data, whose analysis leads to the formulation of the theory. In practice, a mixed bottom-up and top-down approach is often necessary.

3.2 THE CORPUS AS A LEXICAL RESOURCE: THE ISSUE OF REPRESENTATIVENESS

Challenging the supremacy of dictionaries as the only viable lexical resource, Heid and McNaught (1991: 59) observe that the corpus should be considered as an alternative for the construction of lexicons, especially those suited for natural language processing systems. Primarily, this is because idiosyncrasies exist in most available MRDs, as mentioned earlier (see Sections 2.2.1 and 2.3.1). For instance, idiosyncrasies and inconsistencies inevitably occur in MRDs because these are compiled by a team of lexicographers each with his/her own predispositions. Similarly, Jacobs (1991: 39) observes that 'the fact that dictionaries do not contain much of the information needed for natural language processing should not be a surprise, because these reference sources have evolved for other purposes'.

However, the use of the corpus as the alternative to MRDs is not without its problems. Basically, there are two main issues associated with the use of the corpus as a lexical resource, including how there might be a 'standard' methodology of

1. corpus building
2. corpus utilisation

which correspond to the distinction respectively between the use of the 'most appropriate corpus' to use and the 'most appropriate techniques' for processing the corpus. A corpus selected wrongly or inadequately runs the risk of generating not only 'noise' in the information acquired but not offering any information at all. The use of the wrong or inappropriate computational technique runs the risk of generating false or incomplete results.

Therefore the first methodology, 1., achieves importance since the validity of a corpus as a source for lexical descriptions depends on how 'representative' or 'well-balanced' it is for (the variety of) the language it purports to represent: **representativeness** may be defined as referring to 'the extent to which a sample [text] includes the full range of variability in a population' (Biber 1993: 243). Since the descriptive adequacy of a corpus underlies the descriptive adequacy of the corpus-derived lexicon, I agree with Summers (1993: 186) that 'unless the corpus is representative, it is *ipso facto* unreliable as a means of acquiring lexical knowledge.' A 'true' corpus, Summers adds, is one which 'reveals most about the general core of the language when it can be thought to be representative, to a reliable degree, of a broad range of document types'. Furthermore, Summers (1996: 262) suggests that one of the most important reasons for having a representative corpus is that it facilitates the generation of reliable frequency statistics: however, she warns that 'different corpora will present the lexicographer with different frequencies for words and repeated strings', so that there is a need to moderate raw statistics with 'intelligence and common sense'.

A related notion to a representative corpus is a **balanced corpus** which Atkins et al. (1992: 6) define as 'a corpus so finely tuned that it offers a manage-ably small-scale model of the linguistic material which the corpus builders wish to study.' Although Atkins et al. do not claim to provide a methodology for 'balancing' a corpus, the guidelines they offer for corpus design are a step towards achieving this objective.

Currently, representativeness is a notion taken as 'an act of faith' (Leech 1991a: 27), but continuing efforts are being made to establish an objective basis for it. For instance, Biber (1993) sets out a range of principles for achieving representativeness. For Biber, the criterion of variability for determining representativeness basically consists of two main parameters of acquiring texts (otherwise known as textual acquisition): genre/register, and text type. **Genre** is a situationally defined text category (e.g. fiction, sports broadcasts, pyschology articles); **text type** is a linguistically defined category (e.g. the distribution of first person pronouns to past tense verbs, 'wh' relative clauses, prepositions etc.). For Biber, the first type takes precedence over the second, since the first is based on criteria external to the corpus which need to be determined in advance on theoretical grounds. In other words, 'registers are based on the different situations, purposes, and functions of text in a speech community, and these can be identifed [*sic* = 'identified'] prior to the construction of a corpus' (Biber, 245); in contrast, 'identification of the salient text type distinctions in a language requires a representative corpus of texts for analysis; there is no a priori way to identify linguistically defined types'. To elaborate, the task of compiling texts should take into account, firstly, the identification of the situational parameters that distinguish among texts in a language or culture, and secondly, the identifi-cation of the range of important linguistic features that will be analysed in the corpus. Moreover, in deciding on the representativeness of a particular corpus, it is helpful to distinguish a general-purpose corpus from one designed for a more specialised function, that is to say, representativeness as an objective is made in relation to a given 'sampling frame', which may be defined in narrow or broad terms, in relation to either general language or a sub-variety (genre/register) of it (Biber 1993).

The process of compiling a representative corpus does not, however, seem to be linear. Rather, it seems to function more in a cyclical manner, involving the following stages:

> A pilot corpus should be compiled first, representing a relatively broad range of variation but also representing a depth in some registers and texts. Grammatical tagging should be carried out on these texts, as a basis for empirical investigations. Then empirical research should be carried out on this pilot corpus to confirm or modify the various design parameters. Parts of this cycle could be carried out in an almost continuous fashion, with new texts being analyzed as they become available, but there should also be discrete stages of extensive empirical investigation and revision of the corpus design.
>
> (Biber 1993: 256)

In terms of 'empirical investigation', Biber suggests the use of statistical techniques such as factor and cluster analyses for the analysis of linguistic variation: both of these have been used by Biber to identify text types in English (see also Section 6.1).

A further discussion on the issue of representativeness is found in Sebba (1991), who cites the work of two German linguists. The first is Rieger (1979), who comes to the paradoxical conclusion that 'a sample with respect to the features under consideration can only be characterised as representative when so much is known about the universe from which it comes that the construction of this sample is no longer necessary' (Sebba 1991: 22). Because such a sample will be impossible to obtain, Sebba turns to Bungarten (1979) who proposes that a corpus should be merely 'exemplary', rather than 'representative', thus legitimising the use of existing corpora. To elaborate, Bungarten seems to support the existing enterprise of Corpus Linguistics (or CL3) which gathers data for linguistic description and analysis. Moreover, Bungarten also observes that 'the more narrowly defined the domain of a corpus and the more precisely its potential or actual performance phenomena are already analysed and described, the more representative it will be and the more reliable will be the statements based on it' (Sebba, 23): this lends support to the sublanguage approach to corpus processing, which this present book advocates (see Chapter 6).

In the case of corpus utilisation, there is perhaps less of a 'standard' methodology, which in this book will be taken to mean the construction and use of corpus tools sufficiently robust for corpus-driven lexical acquisition. In this connection, Church et al. (1991: 115) complain, presumably of CL3, that 'the computational tools available for studying machine-readable corpora are at present still rather primitive'. By this they mean basically that there is a lack of interactive software which would facilitate the human enterprise of lexical analysis. They point out that the main tool in CL2, the concordance program (which is basically a keyword-in-context index with the facility of extending the context), is still very labour-intensive and would work well 'only if there are no more than a few dozen concordance lines for a word, and just two or three main sense divisions' (Church et al., 1991: 16). This is because 'the unaided human mind simply cannot discover all the significant patterns, let alone group them and rank them in order of importance' (Church et al., 16), so the lexicographer would be prone to errors of omission: however, corpus annotation (tagging, skeleton parsing, etc. – see Section 4.4) helps to overcome this problem by enabling concordances to be more linguistically selective. Similarly, in the writing of grammars and especially in the design of disambiguation rules, CL1 suffers like concordance analysis from lack of linguistic sensitivity, especially where the resolution of lexical ambiguity is involved. If the tools were better, many more sources of constraint could be modelled by CL1: 'For example, a parser really ought to be able to take advantage of the fact that *eating food* and *drinking water* are much more plausible that [*sic* = "than"] *eating water* and *drinking food*, but it is currently just too labor-intensive to deal with facts such as these' (Church et al., 119).

3.3 CORPUS SIZE AND THE 'BANK OF ENGLISH'

Once a corpus is believed to be representative, the question of sampling size may (controversially) be considered more or less resolved. As Biber (1993: 243) says:

> Typically researchers focus on sample size as the most important consideration in achieving representativeness: how many texts must be included in the corpus, and how many words per text sample. Books on sampling theory, however, emphasise that sample size is not the most important consideration in selecting a representative sample; rather, a thorough definition of the target population and decisions concerning the method of sampling are prior considerations.

Nevertheless, while this principle is an important one, it would not be applicable for an approach such as the Collins COBUILD enterprise which emphasises the continuing construction and analysis of a **monitor corpus** (see Sinclair (ed.) 1987), a continuing effort at the collection of newer texts. This method is used to monitor the occurrence of new words or the change in word senses, as well as extending the scope of the language sampled. A corpus, like a dictionary, is a mere snapshot of the language at a certain point in time, and therefore may need to be continually updated for changing and new patterns of usage.

For such an enterprise, size is a most important consideration. Indeed, Sinclair (1996b) shows that, even with phrases involving frequent words, each additional word in a phrase 'requires an order of magnitude raised in the corpus to secure enough instances.' Roughly speaking, if 1 million words is sufficient for showing the patterns of an ordinary single word (e.g. *fit*), then 10 million words will be needed for showing new patterns of selection in, say, a phrasal verb (e.g. *fit into*), and 100 million words for a three-word phrase (e.g. *fit into place*). A very large corpus is needed for significant phraseological patterns (including very frequent collocations and idiomatic expressions) to appear, and is therefore important to isolate meaningful patterns from random ones.

Such a corpus for us to have recourse to is the COBUILD 'Bank of English', which grew from 20 million words in 1987, 211 million words in 1995, to currently 323 million words (perhaps the largest single English-language database in the world). This corpus consists of the following texts, as seen in Figure 3.1:

indy	19452295	BR Independent broadsheet newspaper
oznews	33378314	Australian newspapers
brephem	4721964	BR ephemera
brmags	30137896	BR popular magazines
brspok	20181050	BR informal transcribed talk
usephem	1255655	US ephemera
bbc	18522600	BR BBC World Service radio
guard	24261095	BR Guardian broadsheet newspaper
newsci	6087440	BR New Scientist magazine
npr	22259602	US National Public Radio
brbooks	42127619	BR miscellaneous books
usbooks	32656385	US miscellaneous books
usnews	8578632	US newspapers
econ	12125208	BR Economist financial magazine
times	20950497	BR Times broadsheet newspaper
today	26606537	BR Today tabloid newspaper

Figure 3.3 The COBUILD 'Bank of English',[2] from Sinclair (1996b). The numbers are expressed as millions of words (note: BR=British; US=United States of America). In all, there are 16 categories

The corpus comprises evidence from mainly British (c. 225 million words) and American (c. 65 million words) sources, and also Australian newspapers (c. 33 million words). The texts range widely from spoken to written, from newspapers and books to transcribed talk; the Bank of English is organised to provide (as far as possible) representative, current spoken and written language by native speakers from around the world.[3]

3.4 THE SEARCH FOR UNITS OF MEANING

An extensive corpus such as the Bank of English lends itself readily to the study of general language patterns from a lexical perspective. A language pattern, following Sinclair (1995), is one in which the item occurs at least twice in the corpus; an item which occurs only once (i.e. hapax legomenon) is much less interesting to study: 'for language, unlike many other areas of research, only events that recur are worth assessing the significance of; no matter how unusual, a single occurrence is unremarkable in the first instance'. Moreover, just as in life where freedom and determinism are two principles whose apparent conflict leads to a rich continuum, language follows what Sinclair (1995) calls the **open-choice principle** and the **idiom principle**. Most language use lies between these two principles. As Sinclair says:

> Tending towards open choice is what we can dub the *terminological tendency*, which is the tendency for a word to have a fixed meaning in reference to the world, so that anyone wanting to name its referent would have little option but to use it, especially if the relationship works in both directions. Another tendency – almost the opposite – is the natural variation of language, so that very little indeed can be regarded as fixed. Tending towards idiomaticity is the *phraseological tendency*, where words tend to go together and make meanings by their combinations. Here is collocation, and other features of idiomaticity.

Thus, for Sinclair, words tend to be grouped into larger meaningful units through linkages such as collocation. 'Idioms' and 'fixed phrases' are familiar concepts but are perhaps wrongly thought to be sporadic in text, and incidental to its structure; instead, Sinclair suggests that these patterns are much more central and structural than has been originally thought; they form an upper layer of lexical structure above the word. Such patterns therefore range along a continuum from

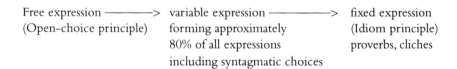

Free expression ——>	variable expression ——>	fixed expression
(Open-choice principle)	forming approximately 80% of all expressions including syntagmatic choices	(Idiom principle) proverbs, cliches

The principles of linguistic determinism and choice accord well with the linguist J R Firth's (1957: 11) dictum that 'you shall know a word by the company it keeps'. Such knowledge of the behaviour of word can be gleaned via a concordance listing, especially in a Keyword-in-Context (KWIC) format, where the recurrence of the lexical item under study is matched by the recurrence of significant lexical items to the left and right spans of the item.

Let us first take the phrase *true feelings* for illustration of how a word might be known by the company it keeps. The following (edited and shortened)

concordance listing for *true feelings*, together with its frequency of occurrence
in the various categories in the Bank of English, is seen in Fig. 3.4:

Corpus	Total Number of Occurrences	Average Number per Million Words
usbooks	43	1.3/million
brmags	36	1.2/million
brbooks	40	0.9/million
oznews	26	0.8/million
today	20	0.8/million
indy	5	0.3/million
times	5	0.2/million
bbc	4	0.2/million
guard	5	0.2/million
npr	4	0.2/million
newsci	1	0.2/million
brspok	0	0.0/million
usnews	0	0.0/million
econ	0	0.0/million
usephem	0	0.0/million
brephem	0	0.0/million

```
        but abruptness betrayed their true feelings. Were they disappointed to have
         account of history and the true feelings of people. Q: How would you
        her formal policy and her true feelings. It is Mrs Thatcher's negative
       they have revealed their true feelings about the federation by blocking
              he had to express his true feelings. <p> In January, two months after
     to the rise of tensions and true feelings to be hidden.Meanwhile, Carrie is
     <p> Alvarez, who tempers her true feelings for the business at hand, is
         women tried to hide their true feelings. <p> A chemical imbalance
  it very difficult to write my true feelings about the events of a Test match,"
        the boot in expressing his true feelings about Australian cricket. <p> I
     few challengers voiced their true feelings even after the latest boardroom
  who is constantly masking his true feelings while being drawn into a web of
    past while Mark confides his true feelings to Lucy. <p> When the winner of
         and does not reflect the true feelings of the rank and file police with
         and does not reflect the true feelings of the rank and file police with
   to her mother to express his true feelings for her daughter, now dead. <p>
   to her mother to express his true feelings for her daughter, now dead. <p>
           in love with her; <p> her true feelings for me were unclear. <p> It was
            to offer journalists her true feelings rather than go through the motions
this opportunity to express my true feelings about inequity being the biggest
   not being able to show their true feelings or their concerns or their fears,"
   afternoon they showed their true feelings when they were invited to
     Pearen) but can't reveal his true feelings because of his guise. <p> Even if
  my teeth, grimly hiding my true feelings, and talk about , moving house,
        words cannot express my true feelings, let me just say # Shalom chaver'.
        words cannot express my true feelings, let me just say # Shalom, chaver.
         began dissecting their true feelings about Powell, and what his non run
```

```
         Palace loo to take away his true feelings. <p> I thought you had to do
      were sufficient to bring the true feelings of the members concerned to the
      tell lies to disguise their true feelings or they talk for the pure pleasure
   for many of the characters' true feelings # feelings which are cleverly
            myself to acknowledge my true feelings - maybe because having a
   s more of us in there, of our true feelings, rather than just ranting on about
   tough with their own needs and true feelings full stop, being so anxious to
   charmer will never reveal his true feelings; he has to appear hard, macho and
   me - why?" you may prompt the true feelings behind the anger to come out and
   have been unable to share your true feelings with him. As a result, it now
           incapable of experiencing true feelings. And not just as a man, but even
   problems or insights into your true feelings. <p> <h> THE SILVA 'GLASS OF
      you were forced to hide your true feelings during childhood and became self-
      be time for you to show your true feelings, and stop pretending you're happy
      not be keenly aware of your true feelings until later, when you're on your
      it comes to revealing their true feelings. Why hold back and miss out on so
   <p> Your month ahead: The true feelings and emotions of your partner will
      close wants to know your true feelings. And things will improve immensely
   less open about showing their true feelings and noticeably less polite than
   when I'm able to reveal my true feelings. <p> Can we win? Yes, but we have
   cakes magically flavoured with true feelings. Taste it and see. <p> <c> PHOTO
          seething, hiding their true feelings in adolescent petulance? <p> I
   so careful about expressing my true feelings and told them things that were
      up and soothing down the true feelings, hopes and demands of an oppressed
   we appease others, deny our true feelings and conform. I suspected the
   you cannot communicate your true feelings means you put out stress hormones
          shows no regard for the true feelings and their needs. The blatant
      the ability to express our true feelings and creativity because we are
      Cancerian lover to reveal true feelings so trust and love can blossom. You
   It's hard to express your true feelings early in August, but later on all
   response when you express your true feelings. Take a good look at your money
      and happy hero reveals his true feelings for his friend Willie Polhaven
   you play games to hide your true feelings, nobody every wins. By Lesley
   but have now followed their true feelings. I think one day I too will have
   it much easier to express your true feelings. You now have benevolent Jupiter
   have little regard for their true feelings about topics they know intimately,
   you'll be inclined to hide you true feelings behind a mask of aloofness this
   the lovers who conceal their true feelings behind barbed witticisms at each
   dreams can help indicate your true feelings at the moment-take heed of them
```

Figure 3.4 Edited concordance listing of *true feelings*, from 323 million words in the Bank of English

Of the 189 instances of the phrase in the Bank of English, *true feelings* seems more commonly used in books, magazines and newspaper columns. As Sinclair (1995) says, the phrase *true feelings* consists of a core lexical item (i.e. *feelings*) and a collocation (i.e. *true*). At N-1 position, immediately before the collocation, 'there is a strong colligation with either a possessive adjective such as "*my, his, your, the*" or some other indication of possession. At N-2 position, such words as "*express, show, reveal, share, admit, show, follow*" reveal a 'clear semantic preference for "expression" – usually a verb.' At N-3 position and beyond, there is a semantic prosody, or attitude, of 'reluctance', as in *"cannot (express), not being able to show"* etc.

Another concordance listing from the Bank of English obtains for the verb
brook (see Figure 3.5):

```
President Assad will be in no mood to brook any more. Treachery, however
        of the country. And the army will brook no weakening of its power. In 1988,
unenthusiastic for Delorism, will not brook Britain's petulant isolation from
              pound; 100m. <p> David did not brook a lot of meetings and paper and
     these Eisensteinian workers will brook absolutely no shirking. <p>
 her stout bosom - a woman who would brook no nonsense. She ran a catering
     secret at all stages, and the judges brook no appeal from the disappointed or
          the woman who wears this would brook no arguments and would relegate you
politicians from Wayne Goss down will brook no argument about this. <p> Anyone,
     but it seems that Blainey cannot brook any criticism of the history of
   his coaches and his swimmers which brook no shirking, no settling second
Lew, spelling out in words that could brook no ambiguity that he had to go as
insistent about the # tasks that will brook no delay # but there is a need for
        that society would not always brook such nonsense. They had only to
fantastic. They fear no mocking, they brook no brickbats and from the moment
      out-that Mrs. Thatcher would not brook the thought of a husband and wife
  s absolutely useless. We will not brook any decision by any court from
again shown its determination not to brook any challenge to its authority. It
minded determination of the Tigers to brook no opposition in the Tamil areas of
Yitzhak Shamir has said Israel will brook no interference concerning the
about the ANC, about its inability to brook any criticism or opposition. Like
another indication that SLORC cannot brook any objections or protests against
sales overseas, British Gas does not brook comparison with giants of the oil
   keeping wicket, then that should brook no argument. <p> I think people
   Mrs Plomley won't say. Nor will she brook any criticism of Sue Lawley, except
of those fiercely radical rabbis who brook no argument with their written
editorially or managerially. We won't brook any interference." But there is
       Surely the team's performances brook no argument on that score. <p> And
   store by his Irish flock and won't brook defiance, further riling men who
when Mr Suharto said Indonesia would brook no interference in internal
   numbering Belgium's Enzo Scifo, will brook little sympathy if they fail in the
in superhuman terms, people who would brook no opposition and who, in the
of gooseberry fruit was so fine as to brook no equal. May I, to such dreamers,
 evidence is conclusive and the facts brook no denial," the official Xinhua
anger in her companion's veins would brook no control, and Sarah Ellis had
    Warn them that, on this one, we'll brook no interference. And if, by some
had an urgent appointment which would brook no delay. <p> HMS <f> Ilara <f> had
          o it <f> at once <f> She would brook no argument or opposition and on
        put upon", but did not readily brook interference. <o> His # Ere, who d'
armed with an attitude that will not brook defeat. The opening scene of the
and those influenced by its rays will brook no denial in seizing their
        needs or wants. Artemis-type women brook no nonsense from their menfolk, as
a leap. But Fisher's determination to brook no opposition meant that defective
Tibet was in its isolation." He would brook no delay, calling for informal free
of the motherland # The peoples will brook no interference", warned another
      who thought the party would not brook continued participation in the
   crafted prose which seemed to brook no interruption. Moreover, his
   patience was at an end and he would brook no argument. He had never been in
and Niyazov far too authoritarian to brook any opposition, however muted.
 time with him up, however, she would brook no pleas of 'just one more game",
        allegiance to, and refusal to brook criticism of, their icon. Having to
   of perfection that scarcely could brook human visitation. Doric columns,
```

```
       again, it was in a voice that didn't brook resistance. You just told me that
    of action for herself, one that would brook no interference. <p> Pallas and
       thin enough to make it clear they'd brook no interference # and his jaw was
   and intolerant teachers, as they will brook no # mispronunciation or mis-
   enemies within Germany that he would brook no opposition. Calling upon his
              authenticity? Anthea: It doesn't brook any messing around. There is no
                 most likely, that she did not brook self-indulgence, laziness, or
                 most likely, that she did not brook self-indulgence, laziness, or
                 artistic freedom and who need brook no interference from moneymen. The
          the control of men who soon would brook no opposition to their policies."
    at the table of any visitor who would brook their awful presence.17 <p> As the
       gay men who were clearly unwilling to brook any restrictions on their evening's
                 no such examinations. He would brook no opposition to his plan. He was
    Department. The Constitution does not brook riddles, solved or unsolved. <p>
          of mediocre academics who don't brook disagreement with their world view.
    become a state of mind that does not brook contradiction. Yet a few modest
              or what have you) and they will brook no delay. <p> This feat has never
    laughter. Meanwhile, Eritrea's rulers brook no interference from their de jure
          Francois Mitterrand, vowing to brook no interference from France's
    Left in the care of those who would brook no contradiction, feminism became
       has made it plain that he will not brook obstruction of his 'reconstruction'
       first term was up. Mr Riordan will brook nothing that threatens to take cops
    by attack, the Judges' Council will brook no criticism. Its memo proclaims
```

Figure 3.5 Edited concordance listing of the verb *brook*, from 323 million words in the Bank of English

An examination of *brook* as a verb shows that it tends to occur with a negative (in the form of *no, n't, cannot*) in positions N-1, N+1, N-2, or N-3: these negatives are inherent in the expression of the verb. Further to the left, colligation occurs with modal verbs, mainly expressed by *will* and *would*, supported by *'ll* and *'d*. At N+2, there is a semantic preference of 'intrusion' realised by a strong collocation of *interference* and prominence given to *delay* and *opposition*. Where N-1 is negative, the emphatic *any* often comes at N+1. Moving further to the left, there is a semantic prosody which can be expressed by a 'reported threat by authority', as evidenced by the Agentive role of an authority figure who (e.g. *Mr Suharto* and *Francois Mitterrand*) or which (e.g. *the Constitution, a state of mind*) refuses to brook any intrusion. '*Brook* is always negative; it expresses intolerance, not tolerance; the intolerance is of intrusive behaviour by another' (Sinclair 1995).

Thus, Sinclair's careful inspection of various concordance listings (which, besides *true feelings* and *brook*, includes such other expressions as *bright future* and *veritable*) leads him to postulate the following syntactic cooccurrence operating for a (compound) lexical item:

semantic prosody + semantic preference + colligation + collocation + CORE

lexical item

For Sinclair (1995), 'the speaker/writer [first] selects a prosody … [which is then] applied to a semantic preference … which [in turn] controls the collocational and colligational patterns.' A **collocation** refers to a word or more which strongly tends to co-occur with the core lexical item: Sinclair (1991: 170), while defining it generally as the 'occurrence of two or more words within a short space of each other in a text', also uses it primarily to mean only the lexical co-occurrence of words. A **colligation**, following Firth (1957), refers to the co-occurrence of grammatical choices. A **semantic preference** concerns the meaning of the string of words concerned, but is not put to use in a viable communication without the **semantic prosody**, which 'expresses something close to the "function" of the item – it shows how the rest of the item is to be interpreted functionally' (Sinclair 1995). The semantic prosody is attitudinal, and on the pragmatic side of the semantics/pragmatics continuum; it links meaning to purpose. To elaborate, following Louw (1993: 157), a semantic prosody is 'a consistent aura of meaning with which a form is imbued by its collocates'; semantic prosodies, Lowe says, are 'largely inaccessible to human' intuitions about language and they cannot be retrieved reliably through introspection'. Also, the semantic prosody is close to the boundary of the lexical item.

Like Sinclair (in the case of *brook*), Louw uses examples such as *utterly* and *symptomatic of* to show that semantic prosody can occur to the right of the core lexical item. For instance, in the manner of Louw, the word *utterly* also occurs in the Singapore ICE corpus, as Figure 3.6 shows:

```
1. …ure linguistic classes as he sees it as[[utterly]] useless to the child's understanding
2. … an aerogram from India, only to be    [[utterly]] disappointed it was actually my
3. … successfully allocated a flat. I am    [[utterly]] disappointed with the
4. …to his wife. Let's say he feels          [[utterly]] distraught and blames himself for this….
5. …, they said glibly. The man had lived   [[utterly]] alone for five years - no relative…
6. … She undid the gift eagerly and was     [[utterly]] dumbfounded at the sight of the …
7. …imagine it, could you? It would be      [[utterly]] inconceivable.
```

Figure 3.6 Concordance listing of *utterly*, from the Singapore ICE corpus, generated using *MonoConc for Windows* (see Appendix B)

There is a negative prosody associated with this word, as evidenced at N+1 position where such adjectives as *"useless, disappointed, inconceivable"* indicate a feeling of unfulfilled or lost expectations, appropriately modified by the adverb *utterly*. However, as in Section 3.1, a confirmation on the behaviour of *utterly* comes only when various sources of evidence are examined. *Utterly* does not have only a 'bad' prosody in all instances: *charmed* and *convinced* are some 'good' right-collocates that occur after *utterly*, as evidenced by various dictionaries. In spite of this, corpus evidence does suggest that *utterly* takes an 'overwhelmingly "bad" prosody' (as Louw says) in the English language. A corpus such as the million-word Singapore ICE corpus, while being a good source of initial lexicographic evidence, needs to expand in size for more adequate coverage (see the similar case of *fit into place* in Section 3.3).

In concluding this section, let us note Sinclair's (1995, 1996a) observation that 'so strong are the co-occurrence tendencies of words, word classes, meanings and attitudes that we must widen our horizons and expect the units of meaning to be much more extensive and varied than is seen in a single word.'

3.5 CONCLUSION

Two main issues surrounding the use of the corpus as a lexical resource have been considered in this chapter: representativeness and size. Also, in considering the transition from corpus to lexicon, it is important to know how lexical knowledge can be extracted from text and organised. By using the primary means of extracting lexical knowledge, the concordance, corpus data can be examined using a lexical framework offered by John Sinclair: this framework, suggested from data in the Bank of English, has been sketched and applied in a preliminary manner to two sublanguage corpora of business English. The framework is most promising for detailing the structuring of lexical information. However, the fields of information postulated by Sinclair – in particular, the fields of semantic preference and semantic prosody – are more easily learned by human than computer.

Therefore, in the next chapter, we will examine another issue in the transition from corpus to lexicon: whether it is possible to train the computer to learn to glean lexical information on its own. The chapter considers the selection of the most appropriate computational techniques of corpus processing in order to acquire the relevant kinds of linguistic information for the lexicon. Another not dissimilar lexical framework will be offered in order to complement the one outlined in this chapter.

3.6 STUDY QUESTIONS

1. In Chapter 1, Study question 6, we looked at the 'Wheel of Fortune' television programme, which is reflective of U.S. (American) English. The 'Wheel of Fortune Corpus' collected by Jackendoff (1992b, 1995) includes the following entries (N.B.: only samples from each classification are presented here; the full list is found in Jackendoff 1992b, 1995: 157–63):
   Compounds
   (a) Adj-N compounds: *Acoustic Guitar, Cellular Phones, Grizzly Bear, Overdue Library Book, Scholastic Aptitude Test*
   (b) N-N compounds: *Dolby Noise Reduction, Jerry Lewis Telethon, Meter Maid, Rhubarb Pie, Weenie Roast*
   (c) Participial compounds (V-ing-N, V-ed-N, N-V-er): *Chicken-Fried Steak, Poached Egg, Tongue Twister*
   (d) N's-N compounds: *Catcher's Mitt*
   (e) Verbal compounds: *Lip-Sync*
   (f) Num-N-N compounds: *Five-Story Building*

(g) [A-N]-N compounds: *Frequent Flyer Program, White Water Rapids*

(h) Odds and ends compounds: *Aloha Shirt, Honor Bound, Pop Quiz*

(i) Non-syntactic idioms: *Believe it or Not, Wait-and-See Attitude*

(j) Resultative idioms: *You Scared the Daylights Out of Me*

(k) Other VP idioms: *Eat Humble Pie, Not Playing with a Full Deck*

(l) NP idioms: *A Breath of Fresh Air, Stick in the Mud*

(m) PP idioms: *Off the Top of My Head*

(n) Names: *Dinah Shore, Rip van Winkle, Woodrow Wilson*

(o) Meaningful names: *Hostess Twinkies, Sergeant Joe Friday*

(p) Cliches: *A Toast to Your Health, Love Conquers All*

(q) Titles: *Little House on the Prairie, Watership Down*

(r) Quotes: *It's Miller Time, There's No Place Like Home*

(s) Pairs: *Mork and Mindy, Starsky and Hutch*

(t) Foreign phrases: *C'est La Vie, Tam-O'-Shanter*

(i) How many of these words are recognisable to you? What does it tell you about your own lexicon and the environment that you are in?

(ii) As mentioned in this chapter, the Bank of English is an extensive database of currently 323 million words of mainly British, and also American and Australian Englishes. Should this database contain as many other regional varieties as possible for the making of dictionaries? What would such a dictionary look like?

2. Consider the following (edited and shortened) concordance listing for the lexeme *veritable*, taken from the Bank of English.

```
making establishments, and so on. A veritable services sphere of their own, you
        rightly claim, as pepsico did, a veritable museum-without-walls in its
         see down to the Pritchetts # a veritable China Wall of wood. <p> In due
        a western sun, the desert air, a veritable army of counselors, and a
         <f> all mixed together here, a veritable painting! Look at the twelve
 and civilisation, as missionaries, veritable missionaries, for that is what we
influence of the environment become veritable wells of iniquity and crime, to
       to something, as if she was a veritable marquise - now, now, see here,
   act, that purposeless lunacy, that veritable treason - what a life! Now every
          an aggression, an outrage, a veritable crime! That shame, shame, shame,
     it was impossible to live in this veritable farm, where there wasn't one
     greatest cynicism; it was hell, a veritable hell, that kind of thing is
          by those illiterate fanatics, veritable primitive animals and enemies of
      sermon that was greeted as a veritable lesson in history, then declaimed
 and itching sensation, making it a veritable luxury to scratch. Any soldier
As a result they are driven into a veritable frenzy of wholesale helping,
parts of the political spectrum, a veritable hailstorm of criticism descended
facing Israel. He said there was 'a veritable flood" of Soviet military
   Evy in this book because she is a veritable scholar and sage of suffering -
     rural simplicity, lay the men, a veritable pile of them, their throats cut.
  dear! Aren't you? This place is a veritable <f> tomb, <f> what with Mary Ann
       here I am, a teacher, no less, a veritable pillar of a privileged community,
 it would be just one more item in a veritable cavalcade of personalised
   an abundance of fleshy warts - a veritable crop - scattered across his face
```

```
        with the second student he was a veritable Cicero. I thought I had never met
        military hospital she had been a veritable dictator; at home, bureaucratic
        and L. Cirino, 1973, Evans. This 'veritable <f> Guide Michelin" <f> to
He looked faintly amused. 'You're a veritable font of local color." <p> I did a
        him and hellip; Connie Bradshaw, a veritable museum of kitsch and hellip; that
     Pretty neat, huh?" The room was a veritable jungle of greenery and flowers -
           Her digestive system is a veritable cosmos in nature, the most
         from her master in Tibet. A veritable encyclopedia of occult wisdom,
        of a venture 'have created a veritable barrage of paperwork and
She's been there the whole time. A veritable beacon. I'm sure of it." <p> Oh,
      the roller disco's stage became a veritable electrical Fourth of July and the
       vitamin pill manufacturers spend veritable fortunes convincing us that a
   joke, the well-thrown wisecrack, a veritable pied piper of the boardroom. He
          here, a vice president there, a veritable raft of assistant vice
few years ago, and found them to be veritable methane factories. With a rapidly
them. Someone was saying, It was a veritable circus. I was embarrassed to be
     the pea soup fog. But Fran kept a veritable stream of information flowing
    a throw rug. We had met up with a veritable farewell party of harp seals and
```

Based on this listing, isolate the syntactic cooccurrence structure for the lexeme *veritable*, i.e. its semantic prosody, semantic preference, colligation, and collocational information.

3. Gather instances of the use of the phrase *bright future*. Although this term seems positive in tone, does corpus evidence suggest anything negative about the use of this term?

3.7 FURTHER READING

Read Clear (1992), Haan (1992), Leitner (1992), and Summers (1993, 1996) for studies on corpus design and sampling. For an introduction to other aspects of gleaning useful linguistic information from concordances, read Sinclair (1991). Stubbs (1993) details Firthian principles which have influenced Sinclair's thinking, as indeed they have of others such as the linguist Michael Halliday.

NOTES

1. In the ICAME Corpora Discussion List of June 1993, Jeremy Clear searched 120 million words of varied modern (mainly post-1990) British (75%) and US (25%) English texts forming part of the 'Bank of English' at COBUILD and obtained four instances, involving *has been being (followed), has been being (playing rich), has been being (in Las Vegas), and has been being (spent)*. Ken Church searched over nearly 1/2 billion words of text (e.g., Associated Press news, Hansards, Shakespeare, Bible, Wall Street Journal, Brown Corpus, etc) for *been being* and found only two examples from the Department of Energy abstracts, i.e. the following: *The thermal effects, accompanying the deformation process , have [[been being]] observed for a long time by the experimentalists and still remain the subject of a large number of publications; (2) In order to heighten the performance of turbocharger of the passenger car's engine, the development to have the turbocharger made of ceramics had [[been being]] made*. See also Francis and Kucera (1982) which details various long verb groups; however the longest passive one, e.g. *might have been being considered* does not occur at all.

2. A smaller text base, c. 50 million words, is available online for subscription. See Appendix B for the relevant Web site.

3. See Sinclair ((ed.) 1987) for a more detailed rationale for the text types and categories chosen for the COBUILD corpus.

Methods of lexical acquisition: 'Learning' a lexicon for real texts from real texts

4.0 INTRODUCTION

In Chapter 3, we saw how, through the concordancer, the corpus yields the most basic lexicon that represents the object of study which the corpus was gathered for in the first place. From such a concordanced lexicon, many linguistic generalisations can be made by an examination of the context which surrounds the word in question. Such generalisations are captured by the human through forming a frame of expectations, that is, from both an analysis of the concordance and a knowledge of how language works.

It would pose a challenge to train the machine to measure up to a similar degree of accuracy. In this chapter, I would like to examine emerging concerns regarding how the computer can be made to derive a lexicon from real texts, including the question of which computational techniques emerge as most suitable for deriving the relevant types of lexical information.

4.1 THE RELATION BETWEEN THE LEXICON AND THE CORPUS

In the enterprise of deriving a lexicon from real texts represented by a corpus, it would seem that there is a direct relation between the lexicon and the corpus. Strictly speaking, there is no such direct relationship, both entities being crafted for different purposes. However, the instances of words or phrases in a corpus, subjected to some means of processing to yield the various types of linguistic information, can be used to interface with a **lexical database**, a computerised lexicon which is structured to record morphological, syntactic, semantic, pragmatic, and sometimes phonological information about the word. Interfacing the corpus with such a database is done in order to update the database from time to time, since the corpus (in the sense of Sinclair's 'monitor corpus', as we have seen in Chapter 3) is updated with new texts to monitor the state of the language or sublanguage from time to time.

Formulated in this manner, the issue becomes one of seeing how a corpus can create or augment a lexical database (which stores the lexicon). In this connection, one notes Leech's (1987) cyclic conception of the relationship between a linguistic database and a corpus (see Figure 4.1), where **A** represents corpus data which is then processed in order to create/enhance **B**, the linguistic database, which in turn enhances the NLP system, **C**, itself seeking to improve the system's performance by processing new data in order to enhance the database.

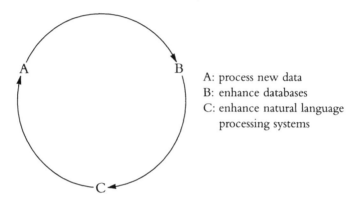

A: process new data
B: enhance databases
C: enhance natural language
   processing systems

Figure 4.1 The relationship between a linguistic database and a corpus (Leech 1987: 15)

The conceived database could contain information of the sort described by Beale (1987) where accessible frequency data in respect of grammatical tags, individual word forms and their collocations are provided. Although a linguistic database and a corpus can be regarded as independent in principle, in practice 'any system for processing of a large amount of NL text data must make use of a substantial linguistic database of one kind or other' (Leech, 1987: 14). For Leech, the close relationship between a linguistic database and a corpus is seen especially in probabilistic systems where 'the frequency data derived from corpora are virtually indispensable for system updating and enhancement' of the database (Leech, 1987: 15).

Leech and Fligelstone (1992: 123) assert that a lexical database of the sort postulated would be one 'adapted for both humans and machines as users: a lexicon [*sic*, presumably = a "system"] which is capable of parsing unrestricted natural language text is bound to need an extremely detailed lexicon, which itself has to draw upon corpus data as an authoritative warranty for its definitions, its sense distinctions, its ordering of senses by frequency, and other types of lexical information.' How such a lexical database can be adapted for both 'humans and machines' is not made quite clear: as it was seen in Chapter 2, under the rubric of CL2, printed dictionaries made for human consumption tend to be at the expense of machine-use. Indeed, the motivation for the creation of the data/knowledge base is perhaps one in which machine-use takes precedence over human consumption. However, there is perhaps some confusion over the use of the terms **linguistic database** and **lexical database**. Leech

(1987) uses 'linguistic database' for 1. a lexicon, 2. an idiomlist, 3. a tag-transition matrix, or 4. a probabilistic grammar: in this sense, a linguistic database is not a 'permanent lexical structure', and needs constant updating. The type of lexical database postulated by Leech and Fligelstone here is closer to my sense of **B** above, a permanent lexical structure, a theoretical linguist's dictionary stored in a computationally tractable form, as it were, which is reusable in the sense that it can be drawn upon for various purposes. For instance, the lexicographer can draw upon a (hypothetical) lexical database of business English in order to produce, say, a Dictionary of Business English for the advanced learner. The means to produce this permanent structure, in the second sense of Calzolari and Zampolli's (1991) and Heid and McNaught's (1991) use of the term 'reusability', is to use existing corpora/MRDs as reusable resources to produce and maintain this permanent structure. Given the linguistic position I have sketched in Chapter 1, the lexicon is the repository of linguistic knowledge, so it does not really matter whether one calls it a linguistic database or a lexical database. However, the term 'linguistic database' has been used in a non-lexicalist way: for instance, the Nijmegen Linguistic Database (see Halteren and Heuvel 1990) is one designed for the storage and search of large collections of parse-trees.

A lexical database should, as I have suggested in Chapter 1, be integrated in terms of grammar and lexicon: the lexicon is viewed as a richer structure of linguistic (and conceptual) knowledge which is stored in a computational format. Also, if one is committed fully to the notion of lexicalism, then the lexical database should be regarded more in the sense of a knowledge base where lexical entries are mutually integrated and the notion of lexical relations is immensely richer than those in a published dictionary (which restricts itself to such conventional relations as synonymy and antonymy): in this book, however, I do not want to make too strict a distinction between a lexical database and that of a knowledge base (see Chapter 5).

The linguistic information enhancing such a database should come from various sources, of which machine-readable dictionaries and textual corpora are probably the most significant. The extraction of lexical information using machine-readable dictionaries (MRDs) – instead of 'reinventing the wheel', since these MRD tapes are available and relatively inexpensive – into the database is a well-treated subject, especially for the LDOCE Dictionary (see the collection of papers edited by Boguraev and Briscoe 1989) and has been discussed in Chapter 2. On the other hand, the derivation/acquisition of lexical information automatically from machine-readable corpora is not an easy enterprise, given that it is raw text that is dealt with, unlike the semi-formal representation codes already existing in, say, LDOCE, which makes this MRD more amenable to exploitation. Such acquisition of unrestricted text is called **textual acquisition** (i.e. when texts are selected and put into a computational format). As in Chapter 3, corpus building or textual acquisition includes issues of representativeness and size, including the suggestion that there should perhaps be an emphasis on sublanguage texts.

The notion of a lexical data/knowledge base may be seen as one which involves the issue of the representation of linguistic/lexical knowledge. Formulated in this manner, the lexical database can then be viewed in terms of – to borrow a concept from knowledge-based systems – its **conceptual** and **computational** structures (Kim 1991: 129). A conceptual structure is a format suitable for humans to understand, whereas a computational or software structure is one more appropriate for computers. So, the nature of **B** (as indicated in Leech's figure) may be viewed in Figure 4.2:

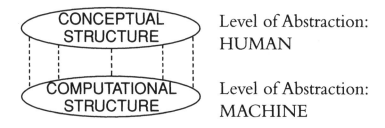

Figure 4.2 Representation phase of a lexical database, viewed from two abstractions: human and computer implementation

The computational structure is an explicit structure which directly reflects the conceptual structure, given the position (as in Chapter 1) that linguistic and conceptual structures are not dissimilar, unless proven otherwise. In turn, the conceptual structure of the lexical data/knowledge base assists in being a theoretical linguist's dictionary from which the lexicographer can utilise various knowledge structures in order to produce, say, a Dictionary of Advanced Learner's Business English (assuming of course that the lexical data/ knowledge base concerned is geared towards such a variety of English).

I interpret the phase **B → C** as one in which various **virtual lexicons** can be extracted, as and when necessary, for the data/knowledge base for the specific application purpose concerned (e.g. to enhance the lexical component of the NLP system). According to Ingria et al. (1992), it was Ken Church who introduced this notion, as distinct from that of a permanent lexicon. More generally, lexical entries can be generated on demand. More specifically, 'while the grammar used in a particular system may require that all the inflected forms of a lexical entry be available on demand, this does not mean that they actually need to be stored in the permanent lexicon (the lexicon that physically resides on disk or whatever storage medium is used). All that is required is that they be available when needed. A **virtual lexicon** [my emphasis] is a mechanism for doing just this; it stores the minimal amount of information required in the permanent lexicon and provides a mechanism, such as a morphological analysis program, for generating other entries when they are needed by the grammar' (Ingria et al., 1992: 347). Of course, this idea of having 'minimal' information in the lexicon does not mean that the conceived lexicon, as stored in the LDB/ LKB will be sparse; indeed, on the contrary, it is precisely because the permanent lexicon (i.e. the one stored in the LDB/LKB) is rich that various parameters of information can be extracted as (and when) it is needed – this latter meaning more approximates the notion of 'minimal' here. Again, the sense of 'minimal' here is different from the idea of minimality in the polytheoretical lexicon and the 'core reusable lexicon' (see Sections 2.7 and 2.8). Also, there is perhaps a difference of usage between a **permanent lexicon** ('permanent lexical structure', the LDB/LKB) and a **physical lexicon**. A physical lexicon approximates the notion of the extracted output. I have, admittedly somewhat imprecisely, conflated the notion of a physical lexicon with that of the virtual lexicon: it is, nevertheless, through the idea of selecting from the virtual lexicon that the physical output is obtained.

Let us now turn to the phase **A —> B**, which I interpret as one concerning the acquisition of lexical knowledge from a corpus. The basic idea in this phase is to derive lexical information from a corpus and integrate it in as automatic a manner as possible into the lexical database. In relation to CL2, the prospect of processing the corpus is not so much a matter of 'reinventing the wheel' (by not utilising the MRD as lexical resource) but as a complement to the utilisation of the MRD in order to identify important lexical information. This is necessary because existing MRDs, although largely reliable, lack comprehensive lexical coverage and accuracy: Boguraev and Briscoe (1989: 34) themselves point out that 'LDOCE is by no means the only example of a not fully reliable dictionary source'.

A published dictionary on printed paper, or indeed CD-ROM, should be regarded as the isomorph of a lexical database which, according to Boguraev et al. (1989), lends itself to flexible querying because both its data and structure are made fully explicit. Such a database has the potential 'to update and maintain dictionaries and check [coherence] within a dictionary or across related dictionaries, as well as enable the exchange and sharing of information among projects and even the automatic generation of several printed versions of a dictionary (e.g., a full version, a concise version and a pocket version)' (Ide and Veronis 1992: 145).

As part of the notion of reusability, the corpus offers itself as an existing lexical resource (i.e. **reuse_e**) from which 'accurate' and 'relevant' lexical information can be derived. This accuracy and relevance is interpreted in the following manner: firstly, evidence of the behaviour of 'real' language at a particular point in time (or synchronic measure) is obtained; secondly, an updating of the corpus in terms of the gathering of new data can lead to an updating of the LDB/LKB. Nevertheless the use of a corpus as an 'accurate and relevant' lexical resource is preceded by the assumption that it is 'representative' of the language under study.

As mentioned earlier, by itself, text is not directly related to lexicon. However, the present focus on using computational approaches to the lexicon for the analysis of language implies an agenda whereby lexicographically useful output is obtained and utilised by first manipulating available textual resources.

In summary, the steps in what is known as the 'cycle of reusability' may be a more complex picture than the one postulated by Leech (1987). I therefore see the situation as approximating more to the one schematically represented in Figure 4.3.

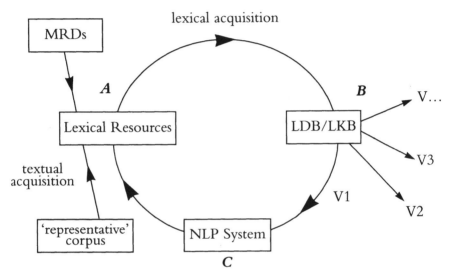

Figure 4.3 The cycle of reusability: aspects of the relationship between a linguistic database and the corpus as a lexical resource

Aspects of Figure 4.3 include the following. **A** is interpreted as representing (filtered) lexical resource data of which the two main existing sources are machine-readable dictionaries (MRDs) and machine-readable texts (MRTs). Where MRTs are concerned, **textual/corpus acquisition** takes place when a representative corpus (in contrast to an 'archive') is acquired from the process of corpus compilation and design: the objective of textual acquisition is to acquire representative texts, otherwise the corpus is unreliable as a resource for the acquisition of lexical knowledge. **Lexical acquisition** (the process of populating a lexicon) then takes place through the application of such techniques as the ones adopted in the Lexical Frame Analysis model. The created lexicon is stored in **B**, the lexical data/knowledge base (LDB/LKB), which is intended to be multifunctional in the sense that various virtual lexicons (V1, V2, V3 … etc) can be created from it as and when necessary. The construction of such a multifunctional resource will allow different NLP systems and human users such as lexicographers and linguists to extract – with appropriate interfaces – relevant lexical information. Enhancement of the lexical component of the NLP system, **C**, in turn means the system's improved ability to analyse new data (say, a more powerful parser) and the eventual enhancement of the database (by means of, say, an improvement in lexical acquisition methods which makes use of parsing) in this cycle of reusability.

Conceived in this manner, the term **lexical acquisition** may be regarded as a rubric for both 'lexical knowledge acquisition' and 'lexical data acquisition'. The two primary data for lexical acquisition include either MRDs (as mentioned in Chapter 2 and in the efforts of, say, Boguraev and Briscoe (eds) 1989) or corpora (which will be the main focus of this chapter), or a combination of both these main sources of lexical data.

As noted in the preceding section (as well as Chapter 3), the use of a corpus as an on-line textual resource for lexical acquisition is predicated, firstly, on the assumption that the corpus is (to an acceptable degree) representative of the variety of (sub)language it has been gathered for and, secondly, on the assumption that the tools used for such acquisition are sufficiently robust.

4.2 MANUAL LEXICAL ACQUISITION

Crafting a lexicon entirely by hand is certainly labour-intensive, but up to the present time it is probably the most frequently used method. This can be attributed to, at least, two main reasons, as noted by Ingria et al. (1992: 356). Firstly, the 'start-up' costs are low, since all that is required is a text editor: 'no corpora or existing dictionaries or lexicons need to be obtained and no automatic analysis programs need to be written.' Secondly, 'the lexicons of most natural language systems, excluding machine translation, are typically small, on the order of tens of words'; hence, consistency is not an issue since the size of the lexicon in NLP systems is small.

Consistency, however, becomes an issue with the increasing complexity of lexical information. As Section 2.1.1 has indicated, the central role played by the lexicon in a program such as Small's Word Expert Parser will mean that, in real-world applications, there is a need for acquisition programs to ensure that these complex lexical entries are well-formed. Also, the need to base the structuring of the lexical entry on corpus evidence (Section 2.3.1) will mean that, despite the start-up costs involved, the lexical entry will need to be informed not only by introspection.

Nevertheless, there are numerous efforts to construct a lexicon manually. An example of a large effort, showing sophisticated control of the manual acquisition process, is the approach first taken at the Centre for Machine Translation at Carnegie-Mellon University (henceforth CMT-CMU), represented by such projects as TRANSLATOR, ONTOS, and DIONYSUS to support multilingual applications by means of world-modelling, or ontology-building (see Nirenburg and Raskin 1987, Carlson and Nirenburg, 1992). The basic approach to lexicon building is that 'the work is done by humans assisted by an interactive aid which enhances productivity and ensures uniformity' (Nirenburg and Raskin, 1987: 277). For the CMT-CMU team, lexicon building in NLP involves the acquisition of three interrelated but distinct lexicons, which include the following:

> the world concept lexicon which structures our knowledge of the world, the analysis lexicon which is indexed by natural language words and phrases connected with concepts from the world concept lexicon, and the generation lexicon, which is indexed by concepts in the world concept lexicon connected with natural language words and phrases.
>
> (Nirenburg and Raskin 1987: 277)

The CMT-CMU approach has been to assign first priority to the building of the subworld concept lexicon. As such, the modules in the ONTOS system include a constraint language and an ontology (or set of general concepts). For Nirenburg and co-workers, a world model is a collection of **frames**. In turn, a frame is a named set of **slots**, 'interpreted as an ontological concept' (Carlson and Nirenburg 1992: 235). A slot represents an ontological property and consists of a named set of **facets**. A facet, in turn, is a named set of **fillers**. Finally, a filler can be a symbol, number, range etc. For instance, let us take the example of *coffee* (given in Carlson and Nirenburg).

> The concept frame COFFEE
> (COFFEE
>   (IS-A   (value *beverage))
>   (AGE   (sem(< 0))
>   (default (<> 0 4))
>   (measuring-unit *hour))

has a slot 'IS-A' which takes the facet 'value', which in turn is filled by the symbolic filler '*beverage', which names the ontological concept 'beverage'. In the 'AGE' slot, the 'sem' facet specifies an absolute constraint on the range of numerical values the slot can have; the 'default' facet expresses a typical range of values (which can be overridden, as long as the absolute constraint is not violated) for the age of COFFEE; and the 'measuring-unit' facet selects an appropriate measuring unit from the class TEMPORAL-UNIT, which in this case, is the symbolic filler 'hour'.

The concept COFFEE is linked to the word-sense *+coffee-n2* (i.e. the sense of *coffee*, 'the beverage') by means of the SEM zone in this entry. In general, such a lexeme in the analysis lexicon contains morphological and syntactic information, as well as word-to-concept ('lexical') mapping rules; in the case of a verb, there would be 'structural' mapping rules that 'link role structures of concepts with subcategorization patterns of their realisations in natural languages' (Nirenburg et al. 1989).

The CMT-CMU approach is predicated on the assumption that information needed for robust machine translation in particular and NLP systems building in general is not to be found in either dictionaries or corpora alone. Rather, the focus should be on the development of interactive systems for entering and updating lexical-semantic knowledge. Thus, the TRANSLATOR system (Nirenburg and Raskin 1987) uses a Lexicon Management System to facilitate the creation, modification, and testing of lexicons; the DIONYSUS system (Carlson and Nirenburg 1992) emphasises the interdependence of its modules – ontology, lexicon, and text representation – for the objective of world modelling as a component of knowledge support for NLP.

Ingria et al. (1992: 357) note that 'the lexicons associated with the CMT [-CMU] analysis and generation systems are among the largest and broadest available in NLP systems. This is due in part to the facility with which data is entered by the human knowledge engineer'.

Although the interactive tools available to the CMT-CMU projects might help to overcome the problem of inconsistency and incompleteness (and so the following assertion does not apply so strongly to the CMT-CMU lexicon), Velardi and Pazienza (1991: 157) make the point that 'a manual codification of the lexicon is a prohibitive task, regardless of the framework adopted for semantic knowledge representation; even when a large team of knowledge enterers is available, consistency and completeness are a major problem'.

Efforts are therefore ongoing to make use of automatic and semi-automatic methods for lexical acquisition. Even Nirenburg (1994: 342) postulates, for the future, it would be 'quite natural to introduce a measure of automatic lexicon acquisition into [a knowledge acquisition environment]' that is a mixture of automatic and manual methods.

4.3 AUTOMATIC AND SEMI-AUTOMATIC LEXICAL ACQUISITION

In the literature, two main sources of information concerning the emerging methods of (fully) automatic and semi-automatic lexical acquisition are Zernik ((ed.) 1991) and Boguraev and Pustejovsky ((eds) 1996). Some other discussions on lexical acquisition include Basili et al. (1992a, 1992b), Copestake (1992), and Brent (1994). However, the distinction between the efforts categorised either as 'automatic' or 'semi-automatic' (as also between 'manual' and 'semi-automatic') is not absolute: indeed, if one were to be severe in making this distinction, then all such current efforts would have to be considered semi-automatic, since mostly human intervention is involved in some phase of the lexical acquisition system. So, the question becomes instead one of how relative this human intervention is.

Efforts in the area of automatic and semi-automatic lexical acquisition may, broadly, be viewed on two dimensions: 1. the two different methodologies of either (a) extracting it from raw text or (b) processing the text first, and 2. the two different methodologies of using either (a) knowledge-based approaches or (b) statistical ones. Increasingly, however, there seems to be a tendency towards producing hybrid methodologies combining these methods, in various forms. In this section, I shall outline some of these different methodologies.

The extraction of word associations from corpora has been the subject of a number of studies, such as Anick and Pustejovsky (1990), Calzolari and Bindi (1990), Church et al. (1990, 1991), Zernik (1991), Jacobs (1992), and Smadja (1989, 1991). This focus on lexical co-occurrence knowledge has arisen, as Smadja (1989: 163) points out, because '[lexical relations] embody knowledge necessary for the proper usage of words ... and they represent the extent to which an item is specified by its collocational environment [independently of syntactic or semantic reasons]'. Besides being potentially useful to lexicographers and also to second language learners, the acquisition of lexical co-occurrence knowledge in 'computational dictionaries' becomes important in helping 'language generators correctly handle collocationally restricted sentences' (Smadja, 167). In other words, 'once [lexical collocations] have been supplied in a systematic way by a computational lexicon which is also annotated for frequency, [these collocations] can be helpful for lexical disambiguation in analysis and crucial for lexical selection in generation' (Calzolari and Bindi, 1990: 58). Or, to put it simply, the general motivation for the focus on co-occurrence knowledge, following Firth's (1957: 11) dictum, is that 'you shall know a word by the company it keeps'.

One of the earliest efforts which uses no linguistic pre-processing of the text is the system XTRACT (Smadja 1989, 1991). The system is used to acquire collocational relations from the statistical analysis of large textual corpora, i.e. a 300 thousand word corpus from the UNIX Usenet and a 2.5 million word corpus taken from the daily Israeli newspaper, *The Jerusalem Post*. The extraction algorithm 'takes as input a corpus, a span parameter (five) and a dictionary specifying closed-class words [i.e. articles, prepositions etc.]'.

Where the span is concerned, Smadja probably follows Martin et al. (1983: 65) who demonstrate that 'more than 95% of all relevant [lexical relations] is obtained by examining collocates within a span of -5 and +5 (disregarding punctuation)'. For Martin et al., the **span** is the 'co-text within which the collocates are said to occur', and the **span position** of a collocate is the number which specifies the distance of the collocate from the node. In turn, the **node** refers to 'the lexical item whose collocational pattern we are looking for' (Martin et al., 1983: 84), and a **collocate** may be defined as 'any lexical item which co-occurs with the node within the specified co-text' (Martin et al., 85). As an example, in the idiomatic expression *kick the bucket*, the collocate *bucket* appears at span position *+2* of the node *kick*. However, the way Martin et al. use the term 'span position' should not be confused with Sinclair's use of the term span as 'the number of lexical items on each side of a node that we consider relevant to that node' (Sinclair 1966: 415). Using the same example,

presumably Sinclair (1966) would consider the collocate *bucket* as appearing in
+1 span position, instead of *+2*. However, Sinclair (1991: 109–21) treats
collocation as 'the occurrence of two or more words within a short space of
each other in a text. The usual measure of proximity is a maximum of four
words intervening.'

Smadja's algorithm produces a list of tuples (w_1, w_2, f), where (w_1, w_2) is a
lexical relation between two open-class words (w_1 and w_2) identified in the
corpus, and *f* is the frequency of appearance observed' (Smadja 1989: 165). The
frequency of common appearance of the two items is derived from 11 numbers
representing the lexical relations in the corpus. Consider the following sample
output[1] produced by XTRACT

decision make	21.7657	2	3	1	61	1	21	2	5	3	1
decision court	5.321	1	2	3	5	64	1	1	19	2	2

The first figure is a factor which is empirically determined according to the
size and nature of the corpus, and the other ten are the values which range from
span position *-5* to *+5*, i.e. the attribute p_i (where $-5 \leq i \geq 5$ and $i \neq 0$). p_i
represents 'the proportion of common appearance of w_1 and w_2 in a position
where the relative distance of the two words is *i*' (Smadja 1991: 175). So, in the
case of *decision*, the most common frequency numbers are '61' at *-2* span
position (i.e. *make* occurs to the left of the node decision and is separated by
one word) and '64' at *-1* span position (i.e. *court* occurs immediately to the left
of the node *decision*), thus presumably making the most frequent expressions to
be *make (a/the) decision* and *court decision* (compound noun) respectively. This
extraction algorithm, as I have presented it, is a bit simplified: Smadja (1991:
174) details four necessary steps for the algorithm, which includes scanning,
compiling, lemmatising, and analysing/filtering. Applying these steps to a word
such as *protest*, Smadja's algorithm is said to retrieve the high-frequency
adjectival collocates *indignant, feeble, ineffective, earnest, passionate, respectful, strong*;
some high-frequency verbal collocates include *issue, anticipate, dismiss, deliver*,
and *maintain* (Smadja 1989: 166).

The approach used by Smadja is not dissimilar to that of Church and Hanks
(1990), and Church et al. (1991) who use the **mean** and **variance** of the
separation between a pair of words, *x* and *y*. For instance, in a fixed expression
such as *bread and butter*, presumably *butter* is at a *+2* span position from the node
bread (in the sense of Martin et al. 1983, see note 8). That is, the mean separation
is two, and the variance is zero (i.e. there is a very fixed word order). Church
and co-workers suggest the associations be filtered by using an **association
ratio**, which is used 'for measuring word association norms' (Church and
Hanks, 1991: 23). This association is based on the information theoretic
measure of **mutual information**.[2] That is, if *x* and *y* have probabilities $P(x)$
and $P(y)$, then their mutual information, $I(x,y)$, is defined as $I(x, y) = \log_2 (P(x,y)$

/ $P(x)$ $P(y)$). The joint probabilities, $P(x,y)$ are estimated by 'counting the number of time that x is followed by y in a window of w words[3], $f_w(x,y)$, and normalising by N, the size of the corpus' (Church and Hanks 1990: 23). The word probabilities $P(x)$ and $P(y)$ are estimated by obtaining the number of observations of x and y in the corpus, i.e. the frequencies $f(x)$ and $f(y)$, and normalising by N. Among other uses, the computing of such mutual inform-ation statistics for handling collocations can serve as an objective measure of what is significant (i.e. what to look for) in the concordance: a table of mutual information values could be used as an index to a concordance. This approach is also used by Jacobs (1992).

Unlike Smadja, though, the approach of Church and his co-workers also allows for the methodology of pre-processing or annotating the corpus, i.e. enriching the text in advance of information extraction. They show that a pre-processing of the corpus is necessary because the objective score alone 'cannot cluster words into appropriate syntactic classes without an explicit pre-process such as Church's parts program or Hindle's parser [Fidditch]' (Church and Hanks 1990: 29). The Fidditch parser (see Hindle 1994) is a deterministic phrasal parser. Although good results have been reported by Church et al. by first using Fidditch to yield SVO triples before applying the association ratio, Basili et al. (1992b: 114) point to two major disadvantages that the parser seems to have: Firstly, 'the Fidditch parser requires a lexicon including information about base word forms and, at least, syntactic constraints. Preliminary work is thus necessary in tuning the lexicon on the different domains and sublanguage ... A second problem with the Fidditch parser is poor performances [*sic*, ="performance"]: the recall and precision at detecting SVO triples are declared to be as low as 50%.' Briscoe (1992: 15) says that the output from this parser 'requires considerable manual editing', although at the moment, it is 'the only technology in practical use.' To balance this picture, Hindle (1994: 130) says that 'current parsers for unrestricted text are far from perfect, a situation likely to change only gradually. Despite these limitations, a parser like Fidditch can be quite useful in finding constructions in text. [Fidditch] ... always returns some analysis for any input ('grammatical' or not), though the analysis may consist of partial descriptions rather than complete tree structures, and it does this at a reasonable speed'.[4]

Church et al. (1991: 135–137) demonstrate that a part-of-speech tagger (such as Church's parts program) has at least three advantages. Firstly, the tagger and t-score[5] combination can be used to help the CL1 linguist design disambiguation rules (e.g. between *to* as an infinitive marker and *to* as a preposi-tion). Secondly, the same combination can be used to improve the coverage of complement structures. Thirdly, the combination can be used to spot likely sources of error in the tagged corpus. Following Zernik (1991: 20), perhaps the question to ask is: When is text processing effective and when is it not? For Church et al. (1991: 158), 'if one wants to study the distribution of predicates and their arguments, then it is extremely helpful to pre-process the corpus with a parser such as Fidditch. On the other hand, if one wants to look at the difference between the distribution of *Bank* and *bank* in A(ssociated) P(ress) stories, then such a transform would be ill-advised.' Moreover, since '[raw] text does not reveal the semantics of the things said' (Zernik 1991: 9), in highlighting relationships between subject, verb, object etc, the syntax might provide the means to 'bootstrap' the semantics.

In this respect, Basili et al. (1992a, 1992b, 1996) also offer a hybrid methodology which combines statistics with knowledge-based methods for lexical acquisition from corpora. This is demonstrated by both the CIAULA and the ARIOSTO_LEX system. The architecture and processing of the ARIOSTO_LEX system, a lexical learning system based on collocational analysis, consists of linearly going through the automated modules of morpho-logic[al] analysis, text segmentation, shallow syntactic analysis, semantic tagging (a phase which currently uses rapid human input), and clustered association. Of these various components, the clustered association data component forms the basis of their method 'to detect the important selectional restrictions that hold in a given sublanguage' (Basili et al. 1992a: 99). By clustered association data, they mean word associations augmented with syntactic markers and semantic tagging: 'clustered association data are syntactic pairs or triples (e.g. N_V (*John, go*),V_prep_N (*go to, Boston*), N_prep_N (*Boston, by, bus*)) in which one or both content words are replaced by their semantic tag (e.g. V_prep_N (PHYSICAL_ACT-to-PLACE), N_prep_N (PLACE-by MACHINE) etc.)' (Basili et al. 1992: 97). For Basili et al. (1992a: 98), a shallow syntactic parser is first used 'in order to cut texts into phrases (NP, PP, VP etc), and a phrase parser that is able to detect the following 15 links: N_V, V_N, N_ADJ, N_N, N_prep_N, V_prep_N, N_prep_V, V_prep_V, N_cong_N, ADJ_cong_ADJ, V_ADV, ADV_cong_ADV, V_cong_V, N_prep_ADJ, V_prep_ADJ.' (Note that Italian *congiunzione* ('cong') = English *conjunction* ('conj')). Such syntactic tags are then manually replaced by their respective semantic tags not only in order to increase the reliability of association data, but also for making explicit the semantic relations that hold between words. Clustered association tables are then built using the conditioned probability $f(C_1, synt\_rel, C_2) / f(synt\_rel)$, i.e the probability of co-occurrence of two classes C_1 and C_2 in the pattern C_1 *synt-rel* C_2, where *synt-rel* is one of the syntactic relations detected by the shallow syntactic parser.

The ARIOSTO system, together with the CIAULA system (Basili et al. 1996), has also been used to detect verb semantic restrictions more automatic-ally, i.e. the way(s) in which a particular verb functions in a given sentence (compare also Poznanski and Sanfilippo 1996). Since Basili et al. report good results with the hybrid (i.e. a mix of statistics and linguistics/knowledge-based) methodology adopted, such systems seem promising for the acquisition of lexical information from English corpora. The architecture for the lexical acquisition of English data would, however, have to be modified. For instance, the morphological component in ARIOSTO is highly developed, presumably because, typologically, Italian is more of an inflectional/synthetic language, whereas English is more of an analytic/isolating language (see Crystal 1987: 293). This supports Basili and his co-workers' (1992b: 115) claim that 'Italian morphology is much more complex than English and this allows a significant reduction in part-of-speech ambiguity during the subsequent syntactic processing'.

Another part of the success which Basili and co-workers claim is attributed to their ability to reduce the size of the input corpus needed to generate reliable statistics. The size of their training corpora is of the order of 500 thousand words, which is relatively small compared to the training corpus of 12 million words of Italian used by their Italian counterparts Calzolari and Bindi (1990: 55). So far as English is concerned, Jacobs (1992: 182) reports good results using a corpus of 3 million words while Church and Hanks (1990) complain that the size of the Associated Press (AP) corpus which they use has been 'small', even though the AP corpus contained 15 million words in 1987, which rose to 36 million words in 1988.[6] Generally, acquisition methods which rely on statistics cannot be applied *per se* to small corpora (of the order of, say, 60,000 words), since the statistics generated might not be reliable.

However, it suffices to note here that hybrid methodologies involving the right combination of statistics and rule-based approaches will not only be most practical but also most successful in the acquisition of lexical knowledge. No single strategy (statistics or knowledge-based, manual or automatic) is all-encompassing.

4.4 THE LEXICOGRAPHER/LINGUIST'S WORKBENCH FOR LEXICAL ACQUISITION

Semi-automatic lexical acquisition constitutes the immediate practical choice which balances the labour-intensive nature of manual acquisition against the developing nature of fully automatic lexical acquisition. However, each method of lexical acquisition has its own merits. For instance, Jacobs (1989), although in favour of automatic lexical acquisition methods, warns that the strategy of building lexical knowledge bases by hand should not be disregarded, especially 'where the lexicon must include information that simply cannot be obtained otherwise'. The inference to be drawn here is that lexicographic judgement has to be exercised, and this includes treating both human intervention and fully automated methods as taking place against the background of a convergence between 'i) lexical and textual projects, ii) computational and traditional lexicography, and iii) statistical and rule-based approaches' (Bindi et al. 1991: 172). In terms of the role of human intervention in lexical acquisition, it is useful to follow the approach taken by Church and co-workers, unlike a self-organising approach where the human role is limited to that of setting the parameters of automatic discovery procedures. Indeed, Church and his co-workers warn that where tools for natural language processing (including Hidden Markov Models[7] or neural networks) are concerned, 'it may be premature to attempt to use them in a self-organizing system' (Church et al. 1991: 161), until a time when a better understanding of when these tools are appropriate (and when they are not) is achieved. In the meanwhile, 'human judgement is required to select the appropriate tool and make sure that it doesn't run amuck' (Church et al., 161).

The relationship between human and computer is captured by the various kinds of computer processing or analyses that a corpus has to undergo in order to render it useful. Leech (1992b: 314) postulates four models concerning the role of corpus processing. Model A, the Linguistic Information Retrieval Model, is concerned with the processing of the corpus only to produce such lists as concordances in order to aid the human analyst in the study of language. Model B, the Induction Model, is concerned with the ability of the computer to induce generalisations (stated in probabilistic terms) from data. Model C, the Automatic Corpus Processing Model, is concerned with the ability of the system to annotate unrestricted texts with such linguistic information as grammatical relations in as automatic a manner as possible, since the system usually deals with thousands, even millions, of words of text. In the final model, the Self-Organizing Model or Model D (see Jelinek 1985), the computer learns to train itself by progressively fitting the analysis to the data concerned, by using iterative re-estimation algorithms such as the Forward–Backward algorithm (Sharman 1989a: 34).

For the present moment, we need the combination of human intervention and the appropriate (automated) tool to populate the lexicon. In this connection, the development of a CL1+CL2+CL3 workbench to assist in this process is to be welcomed, and does not seem far off (see below).

However, in the case of exploiting machine-readable corpora in an automatic manner, an important reason for the lack of success is that the tools for extracting higher-level linguistic information from them need to be developed and refined. Since Zernik (1991: 9) points out the home truth that 'unfortunately, text is given in raw form', the automatic linguistic enrichment of the text might constitute a first step towards lexical acquisition. Once the processed text is available, the task of lexical acquisition then consists of providing mappings between the lexical units and the elements of the processed text. Based on this assumption that learning can be achieved from processed text, a first step towards extracting lexical information from a corpus is ideally to annotate the text with such levels as the following, as characterised by Leech (1991a):

Linguistic level	*Annotations carried out so far*
phonetic/phonemic	widespread in speech technology corpora or databases
syllabic	none known
morphological	none known
prosodic	little (the LLC and SEC are notable exceptions)[8]
word class (i.e. grammatical tagging)	widespread
syntactic (i.e. parsing)	rapidly becoming more widespread
semantic	none known
pragmatic/discourse	little – but developing

(Leech 1991a: 24–25)

Since Leech (1991a), there have been several developments in the area of text processing and annotation (see Garside et al. 1997). Also, although my definition of CL3 (see Section 2.3) covers acoustic corpora, the processing tools listed below are, in the main, applicable to textual corpora only: this reflects the current technology which favours the handling of written texts first before dealing with spoken ones (although, of course, the assumption in linguistics is still that speech is primary). More advanced text-handling tools for the lexical analysis of texts, using an integrated CL1+CL2+CL3 workbench environment, which includes the ability for consistency-checking, will need to be developed to handle both textual and acoustic corpora. As a first step towards realising this ideal workbench, corpus lexical processing should take account of such processes and resources as the following for the semi-automatic acquisition of lexical information for a proposed lexical database. The following list suggested by Atkins et al. (1992: 3–4) is adapted here also for the reader to begin exploring the avenues relevant to text processing. Note that current information on software and projects can be obtained via a mix of e-mail, file transfer protocol (ftp), and accessing the World Wide Web. Since the World Wide Web is an evolving entity whose site addresses vary with time, the most useful option for the reader (in case the sites listed below should change) is to key in the relevant keywords when accessing the World Wide Web (using search engines such as WebCrawler, Magellan, Alta Vista, and Yahoo). See Section 5.9 and Appendix B:

Word frequency counts and Concordancing: This represents the basic tool of lexicographers. Keyword-in-context and word-frequency profiles can be generated using such software. Some software for achieving these types of information include Mike Scott's WordSmith Tools (one of the best currently available) and MicroConcord (whose number of concordance lines is limited co around 1,500), and Michael Barlow's MonoConc and ParaConc software. An early concordancer is the Oxford Concordance Program (Hockey 1988), whose forerunner was COCOA (word COunt and COncordance on Atlas): OCP permits the referencing of a text using this COCOA format to generate a listing where all instances of the word are grouped in the centre with columns to the left containing typological information previously referenced regarding the word.

WWW site for WordSmith:

http: //www.liv.ac.uk/~ms2928/wordsmit.htm

WWW site for MicroConcord:

http: //www1.oup.co.uk/oup/elt/software/mc?

WWW site for MonoConc and ParaConc:

http: //www.ruf.rice.edu/~barlow

Interactive searching: To search and display patterns, especially word strings. The UNIX tools *grep, sort, sed*, and *awk* represent powerful text-handling tools in this respect;

Lemmatisation: 'To relate a particular inflected form of a word to its base form or lemma, thereby enabling the production of frequency and distribution figures which are less sensitive to the incidence of surface strings' (Atkins et al. 1992 3). Beale's (1987, 1989) distributional lexicon project, for instance, incorporates automatic lemmatisation algorithms, based on a grammatically tagged corpus. There are a number of lemmatisation programs built into programs which carry out other linguistic tasks: this includes AUTASYS (see below: "Part-of-speech-labelling").

Word–Tag Extraction: This is a more sophisticated version of word count, frequency, and sorting tools whereby a wordlist can be extracted from a pre-processed text file (e.g. a CLAWS tagged file) in terms of the possible tags associated with the wordform and their various frequencies (Tony McEnery, personal communication).

Collocation: 'To compute the statistical association of word forms in the text' (Atkins et al., 1992 3). Smadja's distance-based algorithm (Smadja 1994) and Church's and his co-workers' association ratio have been mentioned. Another such measure is the Z-score, included in the TACT program (Bradley 1990). Although all such statistical measures become more reliable as the size of the text is increased, the computing of such a score on even a small corpus can help the lexicographer decide which collocate should be included in the lexicon.

WWW site for TACT: http: //www.chass.utoronto.ca: 8080/cch/tact.html

Part-of-speech-labelling ('grammatical tagging'): 'To assign a word class or part-of-speech label to every word. This allows simple syntactic searches to be carried out)' (Atkins et al. 1992 3). There is now an abundance of programs which make this type of annotation automatically possible. The CLAWS program (Garside et al. 1987) is one of the most comprehensive annotation programs for such an analysis of English texts and claims to have an accuracy of between 96% and 97% (depending on the type of text). In this connection, Atro Voutilainen and Mikko Silvonen's ENGCG tagger is also said to be 93-97% accurate. Other current part-of-speech taggers include Brill (1992), Cutting et al. (1992), and Paulussen and Martin (1992). Brill's tagger is mainly rule-based and seems to be widely used. Doug Cutting and Jan Pedersen's Xerox tagger can be used for the SUN Solaris and Windows platforms. There is also the AUTASYS annotation program, developed by the Survey of English Usage for the ICE project (cf Greenbaum and Nelson 1996). Because of the various tagging schemes that have become available, a comparison of these schemes forms a part of the AMALGAM project at Leeds.

WWW site for CLAWS:
    http://www.comp.lancs.ac.uk/computing/research/ucrel/annotation.html
WWW site for ENGCG:
http: //www.lingsoft.fi/doc/engcg/
Ftp site for the Xerox tagger:
    ftp: //ftp.parc.xerox.com/pub/tagger/
WWW site for the Brill tagger: http: //www.cs.jhu.edu/~brill
WWW site for the ICE range of software, including AUTASYS:
    http: //www.ucl.ac.uk/english-usage/software.htm
WWW site for the Amalgam project:
    http: //agora.leeds.ac.uk/ccalas/amalgam.html

Syntactic Parsing: 'To assign a fully labelled syntactic tree or bracketing of constituents to sentences of the corpus' (Atkins et al. 1992 3). No parser has yet been able to analyse unconstrained language or unrestricted text with, an accuracy of (say) 96% (which would be a dream come true!). Ide (1992: 66) says that current parsers can achieve an accuracy rate no 'more than about half of the time'. However, the shallow syntactic parser of the ENGCG project is claimed to achieve a 75-85% success rate. There also exists a limited form of parsing (through machine-accelerated manual input) known as 'skeleton parsing', which assigns partial phrase markers: see Leech and Garside (1991: 24). Other parsers worth evaluating include Satoshi Sekine's Apple Pie Parser (a chart probabilistic parser which is freely available), the PC-PATR generalised parser (which, though freely available, uses a toy English grammar), the Fidditch parser (Hindle 1994) and the ID/LP parser (Sharman 1989b; see Section 6.5).

WWW site for the Apple Pie Parser:
    http: //cs.nyu.edu/cs/projects/proteus/app
WWW site for the PATR parser:
    http: //www.sil.org/pcpatr
WWW site for the ENGCG (Constraint Grammar Parser):
    http: //www.lingsoft.fi/cgi-pub/engcg

Semantic tagging, parsing, and sense disambiguation: This type of annotation of unrestricted texts is an emerging enterprise and is similar to that for syntactic tagging and parsing, but is more ambitious in dealing with semantic categories, as we have seen in the discussion on the system developed by Basili et al. (1992a, 1992b, and 1996). A more modest system is the ACASD tagging system (Wilson and Rayson 1993) which uses text which has been pre-tagged with the CLAWS system. This tagged text is then fed into a semantic analysis program which assigns semantic tags representing the general sense field of words from a lexicon of single words and an idiom list of multi-word combinations (e.g. as a rule), which are updated as new texts are analysed. Some post-editing of the semantically annotated text is usually needed. Rayson and Wilson (1996) also discuss the ACAMRIT semantic tagging system.

Sense disambiguation or homograph separation is used in order 'to distinguish which of several possible senses of a given word is being employed at each occurrence. Early work in this area shows promising results by methods based on look-up in a machine-readable dictionary or on identifying collocational patterns' (Atkins et al. 1992 4). A recent development in this area includes Hearst (1991) who uses local context in large corpora to disambiguate noun homographs automatically. Using a million words of the Associated Press corpus, Sutton (1992) also builds a model which employs static (local context, -2 span, making use of n-grams) and dynamic (local and non-local context, using classification/decision trees) predictors for such word-sense disambiguation. Since the sublanguage approach is predicated on the assumption there should be less lexical ambiguity in specialised or domain-restricted texts, such sense disambiguation tools are probably more necessary for general language texts; however, this is not to say that they should not be applied to sublanguage texts as well. A related development is Sanfilippo and Poznanski (1992) where word senses across dictionaries are correlated, using semi-automatic techniques to recover syntactic and semantic information from MRDs. Also, Bindi et al. (1991: 181) show that many fields of word senses 'stake out fuzzy sets of meaning which appear to fade into each other, overlap, and collide along exceedingly finely grained borderlines': for this reason, such statistical tools as multi-dimensional scaling and factor analysis are necessary to uncover the underlying meaning dimensions when similar words are used.

Pragmatic tagging: Pragmatic tagging is probably the least developed in terms of being automatically possible. However, a first step in this direction is Fligelstone (1992), which details an anaphoric annotation scheme co-indexing pronouns and noun phrases within the broad framework of cohesion described by Halliday and Hasan (1976). The software used for this annotation (XANADU) is an X-windows interactive editor.

Link to lexical database: 'to integrate the instances of words or phrases in a corpus with a structured lexical database' (Atkins et al. 1992 4) which records morphological, syntactic, semantic, and pragmatic information about these words. This link between the corpus as a lexical resource and the data/ knowledge base is represented by the lexical acquisition process, as indicated in Figure 4.1. This lexical acquisition process, in turn, is such that the lexicon is specified at an adequately abstract level of analysis for representation in the lexical data/knowledge base. Many databases are now in existence, of which some will be discussed further in Chapter 5. An instance of an enterprise which tries to integrate the instances of words in a corpus into a structured lexical database is the Italian enterprise at the Istituto di Linguistica Computazionale. There is the DBT textual database system which has been used to manage very large text corpora; there are also monolingual and bilingual lexical data/ knowledge bases which integrate textual and lexical modules in the LWS or Lexicographical Workstation (see Calzolari 1991b; Calzolari and Picchi 1994).

WWW site for the Pisa enterprise: http://www.ilc.pi.cnr.it

4.5 A FRAMEWORK FOR LEXICAL ANALYSIS

As the preceding section has indicated, these corpus-based lexical resources for lexical acquisition should facilitate the integration of the instantiations of the word and the company it keeps in the corpus with a structured lexical data/ knowledge base system, which records the various levels of linguistic information about the word. These various levels of information in a corpus-informed lexicon can be obtained through the mediation of a bottom-up (corpus-processing) and a top-down (knowledge-based) approach. These levels are specified, at the conceptual level of representation, by what I call a **Lexical Frame Analysis** (or LFA), using attribute:value notation.

To recapitulate so far on the principles that have been looked at, some of the tenets of the LFA include the following:

1. The lexicon is the central repository of linguistic knowledge, and so any analysis of language should take the word/lexeme as the central unit within which grammatical and lexical information are integrated. This gives rise to various levels of linguistic information used to describe the word: (phonological – in the case of speech), morphological, collocational, syntactic, semantic, and pragmatic;

2. This linguistic information is described using categories that may be regarded as common (as far as possible) to varied linguistic theories. And even if the exact order of any of these categories remains controversial, the consensual point is that these facts have to be recorded in any lexicon of general application. Therefore, Quirk et al. (1985), by virtue of their (arguably) neutral metalanguage for linguistic description, might be useful as a starting point for the description of such categories;

3. Although linguistic and cognitive structures have their respective distinctiveness, they are not dissimilar, unless proven otherwise;

4. Linguistic knowledge may be viewed as declarative knowledge (as con-trasted with procedural knowledge);

5. A complementary view to language being structured as declarative knowledge is that the lexicogrammar may also be viewed as inherently probabilistic: statistical information such as frequency, mutual information and Z-scores for co-occurrence knowledge should therefore be recorded as facts in the lexicon;

6. Lexicographic information can be most comprehensively derived from the observation of language in use, i.e. from corpus data, as far as possible, and this can be supplemented by introspection and other sources (such as MRDs);

7. Lexical knowledge is derived from analysing how words are used. In order to derive this knowledge, the corpus (and the MRD) used should be representative of the phenomenon under study;

8. In many cases, it is helpful to process a corpus first by using the appropriate tool (ideally in a CL1+CL2+CL3 lexicographic workstation). In order to economise on human resources, the processing is to be done in as automatic a manner as possible. However, for a small corpus, existing automatic methods of lexical acquisition which rely on statistical methods cannot always be applied because the statistics are unreliable for small bodies of data. So, human intervention is inevitable: human intervention also serves, in initial exploratory stages, to ensure that the tools have been appropriately applied. A small corpus whose linguistic coverage might not be adequate may be complemented by a similar one which serves as a control and which helps to extend the linguistic coverage and accuracy of the first corpus;

9. A lexical frame (using attribute:value notation) is used as the basic data structure for the lexical entry. The frame is structured through a combination of 'letting' the processed data suggest what these types of frames should be and specifying a sufficiently abstract level of analysis;

10. In order to act as a general, multifunctional resource for NLP applications, a lexical entry (and the lexicon) should be translated and organised into a lexical data/knowledge base system which has a computationally tractable and expressive format.

4.6 CONCLUSION

In this chapter, we have considered the relation between the lexicon and the corpus, with a view towards lexical acquisition. Mention was made of two text resources for lexical acquisition: machine-readable dictionaries (MRDs) and text corpora. Each of these two resources has its strengths and weaknesses. As seen in Chapter 2, besides the criticism that they are inconsistent in their organisation of data, MRD sources tend to be incomplete in their coverage of the number of words and the properties of these words. However, this is not to say that text corpora are not without their disadvantages, especially in relation to the question of representativeness and the question of 'how to abstract the information acquired through "learning" from the learning mechanism itself' (Boguraev and Briscoe, 1996: 5).

Nevertheless, lexical acquisition is an exciting topic that will continue to assume importance. For this purpose, the chapter has introduced various methods of lexical acquisition: manual, semi-automatic and (fully) automatic. The chapter has also recapitulated the principles, gleaned in earlier chapters, for inducing linguistic information from corpus data in a semi-automatic manner: these principles are embodied in a framework loosely called the LFA (Lexical Frame Analysis).

4.7 STUDY QUESTIONS

1. Velardi et al. (1991: 158) somewhat humorously claim that 'corpora are more interesting than dictionaries as a source of linguistic knowledge, just as tribes are more interesting than "civilised" communities in anthropology'. Do you agree with this analogy?
2. Consider the following expressions: *bread and butter, drink and drive, computer scientist, United States, man and woman, man and women, refraining from, coming from, keeping from.* Can you categorise these expressions in terms of how 'fixed' these terms are? The following table, obtained from Church et al. (1991: 135) who processed the 1988 version of the Associated Press corpus, might help you:

Word x	Word y	mean	variance
bread	*butter*	2.00	0.00
drink	*drive*	2.00	0.00
computer	*scientist*	1.12	0.10
United	*States*	0.98	0.14
man	*woman*	1.46	8.07
man	*women*	-0.12	13.08
refraining	*from*	1.11	0.20
coming	*from*	0.83	2.89
keeping	*from*	2.14	5.53

3. If you have access to a browser such as Netscape, search for articles and sites containing
   (i)   the term 'lexical acquisition'. (N.B.: Of course, what you will find depends on the search engine used, e.g. 'Magellan', 'Yahoo', 'Lycos', or 'Infoseek'). In how many ways is the term 'lexical acquisition' used?
   (ii) the term 'corpus processing'. What further information can you gather?
4. The following example input and output of Name Identification is taken from Mani and MacMillan (1996: 42). Can you account for how such proper names and their semantic attributes might be derived automatically from such an input text?

Input:

Gen-Probe Inc., a biotechnology concern, said it signed a definitive agreement to be acquired by Chugai Pharmaceutical Co. of Tokyo for about $100 million, or almost double the market price of Gen-Probe's stock. ... Osamu Nagayama, deputy president of Chugai, which spends 15% of its sales on research and development, was unable to pinpoint how much more money Chugai would pump into Gen-Probe.

Output:

```
<org name="Gen-Probe Inc." type=company
business=biotechnology index=1>
<org name="Chugai Pharmaceutical Co." type=company
business=pharmaceuticals located-in=3 index=2>
<loc name="Tokyo" type=city located-in=Japan index=3>
<person name="Osamu Nagayama" occupation=corporate-officer
title=deputy-president org=1 index=4>
```

4.8 FURTHER READING

Read the various papers in Boguraev and Pustejovsky ((eds)1996) and Zernik ((ed.)1991) for a more detailed treatment than has been possible in this chapter. Pustejovsky et al. (1993) discuss knowledge acquisition techniques from corpora by means of first pre-processing the corpus (i.e. performing the resolution of unknown words in the corpus, corpus tagging, and partial parsing) and then extracting lexical information from the processed corpus of partially parsed sentences. Read also the proceedings of the various conferences on Computational Linguistics and the Computation and Language E-Print Archive material, found on the ACL World Wide Web site (see Appendix B).

NOTES

1. I have taken these figures from Smadja's paper in Zernik ((ed.) 1989), which reappeared in a paper of the same title in Zernik ((ed.) 1991), but these figures do not appear in the latter.
2. However, as Church and Hanks point out, 'technically the **association ratio** is different from **mutual information** in two respects. First, joint probabilities are supposed to be symmetric: P $(x, y) = P (y, x)$, and thus, mutual information is also symmetric: $I (x, y) = I (y, x)$. However, the association ratio is not symmetric, since $f (x, y)$ encodes linear precedence': see Church and Hanks (1990: 24) for a more detailed treatment.
3. The term 'window of w words' that Church et al. use may be taken as equivalent to 'span position'. Like Smadja, Church et al. set the span position to 5.
4. Since there is a continual improvement on the development of parsers, the reader should use a tool like Netscape (see Section 5.9) to update the information presented here.
5. See Church et al. (1991) and Woods (1986) for a detailed treatment of such statistical measures. Church et al. (1991), in particular, provide a tutorial on when to use **mutual information** (generally for cases where the measure of similarity between words is important) and **t-score** (generally for cases where the measure of dissimilarity between words is important).
6. Church et al. (1991: 145) give the figure for the 1988 Associate Press corpus as closer to 44 million words.
7. Hidden Markov models are stochastic (probability) processes that cannot be observed. See, for example, Black and Leech ((eds) 1993) and McEnery (1992).
8. This refers to the Spoken English Corpus (SEC) and the London-Lund Corpus (LLC): see Leech (1991a). For a more comprehensive account of the SEC, see Knowles, G. (1990). For an account of the LLC, see Svartvik (ed.) (1990).

Computational storage of the lexicon

5.0 INTRODUCTION

In Chapter 4, I indicated that the representation phase of a hypothetical LDB/ LKB, following Kim (1991), has two structures: conceptual and computational. In terms of conceptual structure, the last few chapters have indicated the possible form and content of the lexicon. In particular, a lexicon derived by what I call the LFA framework should record instances of corpus data and link them to the higher abstraction of a structured lexical frame.

In this chapter, I would like to discuss issues related to the computational organisation of this lexicon, as well as give an idea of various structures that have been used in the literature. Given the constant changes in computer hardware and software, note that computational mechanisms (reflecting the computational structure) will probably change at a faster rate than the conceptual structure of the lexicon. The survey in this chapter is not meant to be comprehensive; rather, it gives an indication of the notion of 'computerised lexicons', 'lexical databases', and 'lexical knowledge bases.'

5.1 THE QUESTION OF FORMALISM

Formalism refers to the encoding of linguistic or computational information in a manner that is as explicit as possible. It is useful then to see a distinction between two types of formalism. The first formalism (**formalism_1**) concerns linguistic theories such as GPSG (Gazdar et al. 1985) and LFG (Bresnan 1982) which are meant to embody particular linguistic claims (and are perhaps thus not 'theory-neutral'). Of course, by contrast, a grammar such as Quirk et al. (1985) does not have such in-built formalism, but might have an advantage of being theory-neutral as a general description of the language in keeping to categories which are perhaps maximally consensual. The second type of formalism includes such formalisms as Kay's FUG (Functional Unification Grammar), PATR-II (Shieber 1986), and DATR (Evans and Gazdar 1990) which are not intended to express linguistic generalisations as such, but serve as (general purpose) CL1 programming languages (**formalism_2**).[1] Note that formalism_2 can be evaluated in one of three ways: its 1. **linguistic felicity**: the degree to which descriptions can be directly (or indirectly) stated as linguists tend to state them, 2. **expressiveness**: which class of analyses can be stated at all in the formalism; 3. **computational effectiveness**: whether there exist computational devices for interpreting the grammars expressed in the formalism and, if such devices do exist, what computational limitations inhere in them. These criteria typically compete with each other (see Shieber 1992: 62).

In terms of the development of **formalism_2**, the tendency towards **unification** (constraint)-based (see Shieber 1986) and **typed-feature**-based (Heid and McNaught, 1991: 68) formalisms will undoubtedly influence the design of the multifunctional (**reuse_m**) LDB/LKB postulated in Chapter 2. **Unification** refers simply to a (linguistic) pattern-matching operation. It is 1. commutative (i.e. $f(x,y)=f(y,x)$) and associative, where the order in which unifications are applied to a series of terms does not matter (i.e. $f(f(x,y),z)=f(x,f(y,z))$); 2. monotonic, i.e. it merges information, but never removes any; and 3. bidirectional, i.e. variable binding may occur in both of the structures to be unified (see Knight 1992). **Typed-feature** formalisms allow types of (linguistic) features to be identified and grouped, each feature associating a slot (name) with one or more values.

Within the framework of the Text Encoding Initiative which has as its basic aim the widespread use of the Standard Generalized Markup Language (SGML) as a formal language for encoding and representing textual information, enabling the exchange of texts across systems, typed-feature and unification formalisms work well in encoding linguistic information in a maximally consensual manner.[2]

The typed-feature approach for the encoding of lexical entries is also known as the slot:value or attribute:value approach (as mentioned in Chapter 1). This notation may be viewed as similar to the notation of feature:value in unification grammar (Shieber 1986: 12), an f-structure (LFG), a feature matrix (GPSG), and a dag or directed acyclic graph (PATR-II).

An example of a such an entry is seen in Andry et al. (1992: 246–247) where, in conforming to Categorial Unification Grammar (see Pollard and Sag 1987, Zeevat et al. 1987), the lexical entry *arrives* constrains morphological, syntactic, and semantic information (see Figure 5.1).

In this entry, there are three main parameters in the lexical entry: **mor** ('morphological'), **syn** ('syntactic'), and **sem** ('semantic'). Also, 'the syntactic head features … help … determine the inflected form with an **args** list that constrains its environment within the phrase of which it is the head; the **sem** feature represents the semantic structure that will be assigned to that phrase'. The entry shows that the verb may optionally be followed by a prepositional phrase whose semantics 'will fill the semantic role **thetime**', and 'the argument preceding the verb is constrained to be third person singular nominative (i.e.

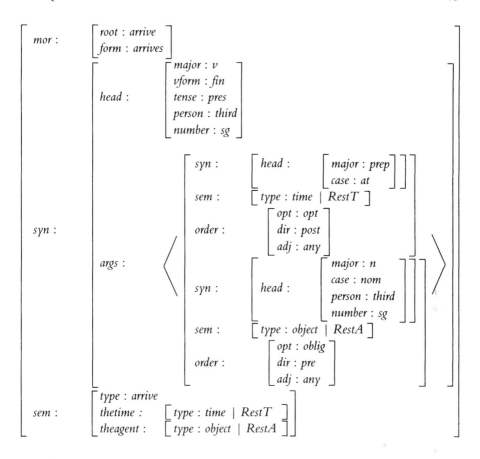

Figure 5.1 The lexical 'sign' for *arrives*: from Andry et al. (1992: 247)

not object-marked), and supplies the filler for the semantic role **theagent**'
(Andry et al. 1992: 247). The flow of information between these feature
structures is therefore constrained linguistically.

The structuring of a lexical entry in this manner may be viewed as an
instance of a lexical frame analysis, given that 'feature structures resemble other
data structures used in AI. Features are very similar to slots (Minsky 1975) and
whole feature structures can easily be viewed as frames' (Knight 1992: 1634).
The linguistic structure here forms part of the overall conceptual structure for
this lexical item. However, an important difference in methodology emerges as
to how this information is derived in order to encode this lexical entry. In the
present book, the emphasis on corpus lexicography means that corpus data
forms the primary basis for the description of a word's behaviour.

While the 'unification' and 'constraint' devices are noted for their simplicity
and elegance, a unification grammar is 'the result of having written some
higher level grammar [such as LFG and GPSG] and having that compiled out':[3]

it represents a **top-down** approach where theory plays a more important role than data in the description of language. On the other hand, a **bottom-up** approach takes data to be the basis of such description, and theory, if any, is relegated a second place. However, there is no reason why there cannot be an interplay of both approaches in order to provide a more adequate description of language.

The foregoing comments thus point to a trade-off in methodology, time, and resources available to incorporate all aspects of describing and representing the form and content of a lexical item.

5.2 LEXICAL DATABASE VS LEXICAL KNOWLEDGE BASE?

The formalisms discussed in the preceding section may be built into a lexical database or knowledge base.

Ingria et al. (1992: 360) assert that the term **lexical knowledge base** is not 'mere rhetoric' and has become a 'widely accepted one', referring to 'a large-scale depository of lexical information, which incorporates more than just static descriptions of words, e.g., by means of clusters of properties and associated values'. They postulate such an LKB as one which states '(1) constraints on word behavior, (2) dependence of word interpretation on context, and (3) distribution of linguistic generalizations'. They further add that this LKB is 'essentially a dynamic object, as it incorporates, in addition to its information types, the ability to perform inference over them and thus induce word meaning in context'. Amsler's conception is not dissimilar:

> A lexical knowledge base ... is a repository of computational information about concepts ... which contains information derived from machine-readable dictionaries, the full text of reference books, the results of statistical analysis of text usages, and data manually obtained from human world knowledge ... a lexical knowledge base is not intended to serve any one application, but to be a general repository of knowledge about lexical concepts and their relationships ... the task of constructing a lexical knowledge base is seen as a goal in itself, distinct from the task of building natural language processing programs that will use that knowledge base.
>
> (Amsler 1984: 458)

Such an LKB would subsume the notion of a **lexical database**, which F. Knowles (1990: 42) conceptualises as follows: 'A lexical database, as a concept, is a straightforward application to lexical data of the general database method used so widely, successfully, and routinely in areas such as commerce, finance, librarianship, etc., in fact, in simply any area of taxonomic analysis and logistic organization which requires highly structured data to be reliably stored, classified, manipulated, and retrieved in systematic ways dependent on various clustering and sorting methods – over a hundred different and sensible ways of selection exist for LDB's. Once that is done, developers must place their reliance on the facilities provided in the form of the database management system (DBMS).' I agree with Ide and Veronis (1992: 145), however, that 'lexical data, as is obvious in any dictionary entry, is much more complex than the kind of data (suppliers and parts, employees' records, etc.) that has provided the impetus for most database research'.[4] Nouns, verbs, adjectives, and adverbs vary in terms of the types of information needed to encode them. Thus the search for a lexical database system must take into account the variability of lexical structure.

While I view the LKB as a concept which is coming into its own, it might be better, at least for the present moment, to note also that

> the distinction between databases and knowledge bases is not a sharp one and has been the subject of some controversy ... To some, databases are 'simple' knowledge bases, where only propositions of a limited form are allowed, thus simplifying the task of generating inferences. To others, databases are mere data structures (relations, records) with no semantics ... Fortunately, it is becoming increasingly apparent that the distinction, whatever it is, is gradually disappearing as database research focuses on more powerful semantics including active objects (e.g., rules, object methods) and AI research focuses on knowledge bases that include rules, frames, facts, and data; on knowledge-base system performance and robustness; and on shared or cooperative knowledge-base systems.
>
> (Mylopoulos and Brodie 1989: 2)

Thus, I do not make such a severe distinction between these two notions in the present book. Instead, it is perhaps more helpful to view implementational efforts in this area as forming a linear continuum from a lexical database (one which is in a (relational) DBMS format) to a knowledge base (one which has the necessary computational and formal semantics), i.e.

LDB ⎯⎯⎯⎯⎯⎯⎯⎯⎯⎯⎯⎯⎯⎯⎯⎯⎯⎯⎯⎯⎯⎯⎯⎯→LKB
mere structured records   greater computational
with fields   and formal semantics

5.3 THE NOTION OF INHERITANCE

At the LKB end of the continuum, one of the central ways in which 'greater computational and formal semantics' can be achieved is structuring the lexical entry with **inheritance**. For this purpose, Russell et al. (1992: 311) note that 'the primary task of a computational lexicon is to associate character strings representing word forms with various types of information, able to account for their distribution within a sentence and for their contribution to the meaning of a text'; thus, 'in the interests of linguistic parsimony and sensible knowledge engineering, it is necessary for lexicalist approaches to factor away at the lexicon-encoding interface as many as possible of the commonalities between lexical items' (Andry et al. 1992: 247).

Inheritance relates, in the present context, to the organisation of a lexicon in such a way that a daughter node inherits some/all of the properties of a parent node. The main motivation for inheritance is in the interest of the economy principle, as indicated in the previous section, whereby information is stated in the most efficient manner.

What constitutes 'most efficient manner' is itself, in turn, controversial. In this respect, Daelemans et al. (1992) discuss the main types of inheritance networks listed in the literature. These include four possible scenarios: 1. monotonic single inheritance; 2. nonmonotonic single inheritance (default inheritance); 3. monotonic multiple inheritance; 4. nonmonotonic multiple inheritance (i.e. multiple default inheritance). Let us consider each in turn.

In monotonic single inheritance, a node inherits *all* (i.e. without exception) the properties associated with its parent node (hence '**monotonic**'). This is in such a way that that node has only a single parent, and hence has only one path through which properties may be inherited. For instance, a verb (taking the *-ed* past participle as one of its properties) might be structured as the root node of the network. This VERB node has two daughter nodes, i.e. TRANSITIVE_VERB and INTRANSITIVE_VERB, which inherit all the properties associated with the root. These nodes, in turn, consist of further daughters, such as *love* and *hate* (exemplifying transitive verbs), and *elapse* and *expire* (exemplifying intransitive verbs). Thus, while *love* has its own individual properties, such as being orthographically represented as /l o v e/, it inherits all the properties of transitivity from its immediate parent, as well as the properties of the root. However, this type of network presents problems for the description of natural languages. For instance, a transitive verb such as *beat* cannot be fitted into the transitive node because, unlike the other verbs, it takes the *-en* participle instead. If, then, a new node EN_TRANSITIVE is defined, this new node cannot be either a daughter of the TRANSITIVE_VERB node nor that of the VERB node simply because, in both instances, the past participle of *beat* conflicts with the *-ed* past participle property associated with these latter nodes. Another unsatisfactory solution would be to remove the -ed property from the VERB node in order to account for this irregularity, in which case, morphologically, the VERB node has the *-ing* participle as its only property. If this latter approach were followed, it would lead to the eventual stripping of all common properties traditionally associated with the VERB node (in order to satisfy other irregularities), which would render the 'VERB node' ineffective.

It seems clear that monotonic single inheritance has to be abandoned. A better solution would be to attach *beat*, in the case of the above example, to the TRANSITIVE_VERB node, but adopt the principle that the properties attached to a node take precedence over those inherited from the parent, i.e. **nonmonotonic** inheritance (better known as **default inheritance**) occurs.

This will mean that the contradiction encountered earlier disappears.

The third type of solution would be to use monotonic multiple inheritance. Using the same illustrative example, the network is reorganised in such a way that, under the VERB node (which is not given any other property), the TRANSITIVE_VERB and INTRANSITIVE_VERB encode only syntactic information, and two other equal nodes, EN_VERB and ED_VERB, are defined for morphological information. In this case then, while the transitive verb *love* takes its syntactic property from the TRANSITIVE_VERB node and its morphological property from the ED_VERB node, the transitive verb *beat* inherits its syntactic property from the TRANSITIVE_VERB node and its morphological property from the EN_VERB node.

The final type of structured inheritance would be to use nonmonotonic multiple inheritance, or more popularly known as **multiple default inheritance**.[5] Although Daelemans et al. (1992) do not extend the above example to illustrate this type of inheritance, presumably, *beat* would still inherit its syntactic property from the TRANSITIVE_VERB node and its morphological property from the EN_VERB node. In the case of the latter, it would seem that this would be a sufficient statement, but it is still necessary to make the nonmonotonic statement that the *-en* past participle property within *beat* takes precedence over any parent node, especially those which conflict. Associated with the idea of default inheritance comes the problem of preventing mutually contradictory information from two or more parent nodes. Daelemans et al. (1992: 209) mention two types of strategies to overcome this potential problem. The first is **orthogonal inheritance**, in which, say, morphological properties can be inherited from node **A** and syntactic properties from node **B**, but 'no single property can be inherited from more than one parent node'; the other is **prioritised inheritance**, in which ordering of the parent nodes takes place and 'the first parent in the ordering that is able to supply the property wins'.

5.4 THE DATR LEXICAL KNOWLEDGE REPRESENTATION LANGUAGE

One such mechanism which permits multiple default inheritance and prioritised inheritance, but enforces orthogonality, is the DATR lexical knowledge representation language (Evans and Gazdar 1989a, 1989b, 1990; Evans et al. 1993). DATR represents an object-oriented, declarative approach that allows the lexicon to be structured particularly by inheritance. As a lexical representation language, it might be suitable for use in a lexical database system, and can be considered a lexical database system in itself.

DATR is what I would call a **formalism_2** language. This language is one that '(i) has the necessary expressive power to encode the lexical entries presupposed by contemporary work in the unification grammar tradition, (ii) can express all the evident generalisations about the information implicit in those entries, (iii) has an explicit theory of inference, (iv) is computationally tractable, and (v) has an explicit declarative semantics' (Gazdar 1990: 1). DATR also does not commit the user to a particular computer language in the value expressions it returns, which consists of atoms or lists of atoms as values: 'a value list can be handed to over to the interpreter of other languages such as … LISP, [or] PROLOG, or whatever the application suggests is appropriate' (Gazdar 1990: 11). Let us interpret these statements in the light of the following.

In relation to the choice of a unification grammar, DATR is 'theory-neutral' in that it does not specify an adherence to, say, GPSG (see Gazdar et al. 1985), but it does presuppose a grammar formalism that depends, implicitly or explicitly, on paths of attributes and values. Existing DATR work also presupposes the primacy of the lexeme, which accords well with the LFA lexicon. In both these respects – feature structures and the ability to encode lexical entries – DATR is more suitable for representing lexical information than the PATR formalism (Shieber 1986).

An instance of the PATR formalism is the following for the lexeme *love* (with my comments enclosed in curly brackets), as detailed in Gazdar (1988):

Lexeme love: <syn cat> = v   {'syn cat' = 'syntactic category}
               <syn arg0 cat> = np
               <syn arg0 case> = nom
               <syn arg1 cat> = np
               <syn arg1 case> = acc
               <sem>= love2a.   {'sem' = 'semantics'; for instance, sense
                                        2a of the verb *love*}

The lexeme *love* (v) subcategorises for a nominative subject NP ('arg0') and an accusative object NP ('arg1').

PATR provides macros that can shorten the way a lexical entry is structured. For instance, using the same example, the entry for *love* could just be

               Lexeme love: syn_tV
                                   <sem> = love2a

where 'syn_tV' stands for the following transitive_verb macro:

               Macro syn_tV: syn_iV
                                   <syn arg1 cat> = np
                                   <syn arg1 case> = acc.

Apart from taking an accusative object, this transitive_verb macro is therefore similar to the one for intransitive verbs, i.e. syn_iV where

               Macro syn_iV   <syn cat> = v
                                   <syn arg0 cat> = np
                                   <syn arg0 case> = nom.

A more detailed treatment of the PATR formalism is given in Shieber (1986), Gazdar (1988) and Gazdar and Mellish (1989).

While PATR, as Kilbury et al. (1991: 137) note, has two ways of encoding lexical information (the first being the use of feature structures and the second the use of macros/templates), it has two disadvantages. Firstly, the encoded information in a PATR format is inherited monotonically, whereby only regularities can be expressed. Secondly, the use of macros in PATR will not be able to capture non-regular types of information (as in the case of the irregular *-en* past participle form that *beat* takes: see Section 5.3). A default inheritance network such as DATR, by contrast, is more appropriate for this purpose of capturing subregularities and exceptions. It should be noted, however, that DATR is not meant to compete with PATR: they are complementary to each other. Gazdar (1990: 11) makes the following comparison between DATR and PATR: 'The concrete syntax of DATR was deliberately made to look like PATR, but the semantics is quite different. PATR is designed for grammar definition, whereas DATR is designed for lexicon definition. Default inheritance is central to DATR, but unification plays no role. DATR is intended to be complementary to a language like PATR, not a substitute for it.' If DATR and PATR are structured for lexical and syntactic requirements respectively, on the theoretical level, the divide between lexicon and grammar (of course) still exists. However, it seems to me this gap is narrowing. For instance, Andry et al. (1992), in making abstractions over the lexicon, add the area of lexical-semantic relations to the already treated areas of morphosyntax and transitivity for DATR structuring.

While a more detailed treatment of the syntax, semantics and inferencing abilities of DATR is given variously by Evans and Gazdar, I will just list some basic features of DATR (without an exposition of the full notational system).

A verb, following Gazdar (1988), can be written as

    verb: <syn aux> == no
                 <syn cat> = v
                 <mor past> = root_ed
                 <mor present tense> == root_
                 <mor present participle> == root_ing
                 <mor present tense singular three> == root_s.

Similar attribute-path value assignments can be made for the past tense '<mor_past>'.

An auxiliary can take the following node:

    aux: <> === verb   {'<>' == 'just like'}
                 <syn aux> == yes
                 <syn arg> == vpcomp.

This says that 'aux' behaves similarly to items that fill the verb node, except that it is a primary auxiliary verb and its complement is a VP. A modal auxiliary verb is, therefore, a subclass of an 'aux' with the following

        modal1:   <> == aux
                           <syn form> == finite.

In the case of a verb with irregular morphology such as *be*, the following node applies:

        be_mor: <mor> == verb
                        <mor root> == be
                        <mor past participle> == been
                        <mor past tense singular one> == was
                        <mor past tense singular three> == was
                        <mor past tense> == were
                        <mor present tense singular one> == am
                        <mor present tense singular three> == is
                        <mor present tense> are.

Therefore, while *be* inherits all the properties of a verb, the specifications listed here take precedence over those of the verb node which conflict. The following individual lexical entries for *be* apply here:

be1:   <mor> == be_mor
       <syn arg> == npcomp
       <syn> == aux.   {as in a clause such as *Kim is an android*}
be2:   <> == modal1
       <mor> == be_mor.   {as in a clause such as *Kim is to leave*}
be3:   <> == aux
       <mor> == be_mor
       <syn arg syn form> == prp   {as in a clause such as *Kim is leaving*)

DATR is therefore a formalism_2 language that can handle lexical information without losing generalisations.

5.5 THE ACQUILEX LEXICAL KNOWLEDGE BASE

While DATR is designed specifically for lexical representation, the knowledge representation language (LRL) used for the ACQUILEX LKB is designed as a more general formalism 'because this [offers] the flexibility to represent both syntactic and semantic information in a way which could be easily integrated with much current work on unification grammar, parsing and generation' (Copestake 1992: 89). The LRL's main advantage is in facilitating the use of a parser in the LKB for testing lexical entries, as well as in experimenting with such notions as lexical rules and interlingual links between lexical entries. The LRL uses a typed unification formalism with minimum default inheritance, of which a specimen entry is the following (Figure 5.2).

    As in Section 1.2.1, this LKB builds in Pustejovsky's (1991; 1995) theory of semantic relations ('Qualia Structure') that hold between nouns (in the present instance): constitutive, formal, telic, and agentive.

$$
\begin{bmatrix}
\textbf{lex-uncount-noun} \\
\text{ORTH} = \textbf{whisky} \\
\text{QUALIA} =
\begin{bmatrix}
\textbf{comestible} \\
\text{AGENTIVE} = \textbf{nomagent} \\
\text{TELIC} = \boxed{\textbf{verb-sem}} \\
\text{FORM} = \begin{bmatrix}\textbf{nomform} \\ \text{RELATIVE} = \textbf{form}\end{bmatrix} \\
\text{CONSTITUENCY} = \boxed{\textbf{nomconst}} \\
\text{OBJECT-INDEX} = \boxed{1}\ \textbf{entity} \\
\text{PROPERTIES} = \begin{bmatrix}\textbf{phys-properties} \\ \text{STATE} = \textbf{liquid\_a}\end{bmatrix}
\end{bmatrix}
\end{bmatrix}
$$

whisky 1

$$
\begin{bmatrix}
\textbf{lex-count-noun} \\
\text{ORTH} = \textbf{whisky} \\
\text{QUALIA} =
\begin{bmatrix}
\textbf{comestible} \\
\text{AGENTIVE} = \textbf{nomagent} \\
\text{TELIC} = \boxed{\textbf{verb-sem}} \\
\text{FORM} = \begin{bmatrix}\textbf{nomform} \\ \text{RELATIVE} = \textbf{portion}\end{bmatrix} \\
\text{CONSTITUENCY} = \boxed{\textbf{nomconst}} \\
\text{OBJECT-INDEX} = \boxed{1}\ \textbf{entity} \\
\text{PROPERTIES} = \begin{bmatrix}\textbf{phys-properties} \\ \text{STATE} = \textbf{liquid\_a}\end{bmatrix}
\end{bmatrix}
\end{bmatrix}
$$

whisky 2

Figure 5.2 Lexical entries for *whisky* (from Vossen and Copestake 1993: 260)

While an LKB contains a lexicon which is structured as a multiple default inheritance hierarchy of typed-feature structures to which lexical and morphological rules (among others) can be applied, the ACQUILEX LDB is a system that just enables fast and flexible access to machine-readable dictionaries (MRDs) via index files (see Boguraev and Briscoe (eds.) 1989).

This LDB is central to the objective of the ACQUILEX project, which was conducted in two phases. Phase I emphasised semi-automatic lexical acquisition techniques for utilising monolingual machine-readable dictionaries (MRDs) in English, Italian and Dutch and bilingual MRDs for English-Italian and English-Dutch. The objectives of the project therefore included, firstly, the representation of multilingual syntactic and semantic information extracted from MRDs in a more reliable manner and, secondly, the construction of an LKB, the LRL formalism, and software tools which supported default inheritance, unification, and lexical rule application. In Phase II, the ACQUILEX project also considered the use of corpora and the development of such software tools for lexical acquisition.[6] The project ended in September 1995.

5.6 THE PROLEX PROLOG LEXICAL DATABASE

An experiment in the construction of lexical databases on a much smaller scale is Ooi (1987) which considers how PROLOG can be used to structure lexical entries for a corpus of business English using two well-known linguistic theories. As a programming language, PROLOG (Clocksin and Mellish 1981; 1994) is not only flexible enough to take into account the variability of lexical structure (as mentioned in Section 5.2) but facts and rules are also treated in a largely declarative manner, which accords well with the popular view that all linguistic knowledge can be regarded as declarative knowledge. In terms of linguistic principles, this database incorporates (and adapts) both the 'lexical functions' (i.e. relations providing lexical-semantic information) of the Russian linguists Mel'cuk, Apresyan, and Zholkovsky (see, for instance, Mel'cuk and Polguere 1987; Mel'cuk and Zholkovsky 1988; Mel'cuk 1996) and the 'metafunctional hypothesis' (i.e. the structural configurations that define the lexical unit at the level of the clause) of M. A. K. Halliday (see, for instance, Halliday 1985; 1994).

Halliday's Functional Grammar (see Section 1.1.2) has been developed specifically for the analysis of texts. The model uses a tristratal analysis of the clause: lexis is viewed as 'most delicate grammar', and the 'way' to the semantics is specified through the patterning of this tristratal analysis. For lexical-semantic analysis, Melcuk et al.'s lexical functions, expressing both paradigmatic and syntagmatic co-occurrence, can be used in order to represent both deep and surface lexical structure in an explicit manner. A combination of these two approaches provides rich linguistic information in terms of syntax and lexis.

Word and world knowledge is represented by the structuring of lexical frames, using a mix of top-down and bottom-up approaches. In terms of a top-down approach, four main lexical frames are structured. Using the noun lemma/lexeme *account* as an illustration, the first frame gives the part of speech, agreement information (singular/plural), and the ordering in the database for the entry. For instance, in *There are insufficient funds in your account,* the term *account* is represented as

>   *entrya(account,_, 10, noun, singular).*

This reads as 'The lexeme *account* is a count noun (singular) and occurs in con-figuration number 10 in the database'. The second frame defines the entry in terms of the lexical functions that we have mentioned. Thus for a sentence such as *There are insufficient funds in your account,* the entry

>   *entryb(account,_, 10, a1_minus_anti_ver_setp_pre,*
>   *['insufficient funds in']).*

reads as 'the lexeme *account*, of configuration 10 in the database, has before it a set phrase whose properties include being an adjectival element attributively modifying the headword, and having an attribute whose meaning is not "right" or proper.' Another example within this frame includes the following entry:

>   *entryb(account,_, 10, loc_pre, ['in'])*

which reads as 'the lexeme *account*, of configuration 10 in the database, has before it a preposition with the meaning of localisation in relation to the keyword.' The third frame relates to the **companions** (see Hudson 1984) that the word keeps, analysed in Hallidayan terms. There are three sub-frames, each corresponding to the ideational, interpersonal, and textual functions respectively. Thus an entry for *There are insufficient funds in your account* is represented in terms of the interpersonal function as

> *entryc(account,_, 10, interpersonal ([m (plus*
> *([s('there'), f(pres)]))])).*

This reads as 'the lexeme *account*, of configuration 10 in the database, occurs within a clause which includes, within the interpersonal function, a **mood** component (see Halliday 1985, 1994) consisting of the Subject and the Finite element in the present tense. The order s + f realises "declarative".' Another example of the interpersonal sub-frame is the following entry:

> *entryc(account,_, 10, interpersonal ([r (plus*
> *([c('insufficient funds in your account')]))])).*

This reads as 'the lexeme *account*, of configuration 10 in the database, occurs within a clause which includes, within the interpersonal function, a **residue** (see Halliday 1985, 1994) component which includes the Complement.' The textual sub-frame is illustrated in the following entry

> *entryc(account,_, 10, textual ([top_t('there'),*
> *rheme('are insufficient funds in your account')])).*

which reads as 'the lexeme *account*, of configuration 10 in the database, occurs within a clause which includes, within the textual function, the Complement as part of its **residue**.' For this third frame, the ideational sub-frame is illustrated by an entry such as

> *entryc(account,_, 10, ideational ([exisp('are'),*
> *existent('insuff 2icient funds'), circum_l('in your*
> *account')])).*

which reads as 'the lexeme *account*, of configuration 10 in the database, occurs within a clause which includes, within the ideational function an existential process verb, an existent, and a circumstance of location.' Finally, the fourth frame links or relates the entry to pragmatic, typological information. Thus the entry

> *entryd(account,_, 10,letter_number, 050).*

means that 'the lexeme *account*, of configuration 10 in the database, is part of text 50 in the corpus.'

In terms of a bottom-up approach, these lexical frames are manually structured not by introspection but primarily by using information gleaned from

concordanced listings obtained from textual processing of the PROLEX
corpus (see Webster 1984, and Chapter 6).

5.7 THE WORDNET LEXICAL DATABASE OF ENGLISH

Another example of a lexicon which is basically hand-crafted is the WordNet
lexical database (Miller (ed.) 1990; Beckwith et al. 1991), which is available
online in a variety of computer platforms.[7] This database is organised on
pyscholinguistic theories of human lexical organisation and memory. English
nouns ('n'), verbs ('v'), adjectives ('a') and adverbs ('r') are organised into
synonym sets (or 'synsets', corresponding roughly to Mel'cuk et al.'s notion of
'vocable' or 'family of lexemes'). Different kinds of lexical relations link these
synonym sets. The following search types are currently possible, as seen in
Figure 5.3:

-ants{n|v|a|r}	Antonyms
-hype{n|v}	Hypernyms
-hypo{n|v}, -tree{n|v}	Hyponyms & Hyponym Tree
-entav	Verb Entailment
-syns{n|v|a|r}	Synonyms (ordered by frequency)
-smemn	Member of Holonyms
-ssubn	Substance of Holonyms
-sprtn	Part of Holonyms
-membn	Has Member Meronyms
-subsn	Has Substance Meronyms
-partn	Has Part Meronyms
-meron	All Meronyms
-holon	All Holonyms
-causv	Verb Cause to
-pert{a|r}	Pertainyms
-attr{n|a}	Attributes
-faml{n|v|a|r}	Familiarity & Polysemy Count
-framv	Verb Frames
-coorn	Coordinate Sisters
-simsn	Synonyms (grouped by similarity of meaning)
-hmern	Hierarchical Meronyms
-hholn	Hierarchical Holonyms
-grep{n|v|a|r}	List of Compound Words

Figure 5.3 Searchtypes of lexical relations in the WordNet lexical database, Version 1.5
(UNIX)

The hierarchies of relations found in the WordNet system accord well with the
inheritance principle. Indeed, WordNet is claimed to be a lexical inheritance

system in which hyponyms (e.g. the organic sense of *tree*) are connected with their superordinates (i.e. *plant* as the hypernym of *tree*), as the following shows

> *woody plant, ligneous plant*
> > => *vascular plant, tracheophyte*
> > > => *plant, flora, plant life*
> > > > => *life form, organism, being, living thing*
> > > > > => *entity*

In the UNIX version of WordNet, a query syntax takes the following search form:

> wn word [-hgla] [-n#] -searchtype

-h	Display help text
-g	Display optional gloss
-l	Display license and copyright notice
-a	Display lexicographer file information
-n#	Search only sense number #

Therefore, a search of the various noun senses of the polysemous word *bank* is done by using

> wn bank -syns{n}

which yields the following, as shown in Figure 5.4:

Synonyms/Hypernyms (Ordered by Frequency) of noun bank
9 senses of bank
Sense 1
bank, side
> => slope, incline, side
Sense 2
depository financial institution, bank, banking concern, banking company
> => financial institution, financial organisation
Sense 3
bank
> => ridge
Sense 4
bank
> => array
Sense 5
bank
> => reserve, backlog, stockpile
Sense 6
bank
> => funds, finances, monetary resource, cash in hand, pecuniary resource
Sense 7

bank, cant, camber
    => slope, incline, side
Sense 8
savings bank, coin bank, money box, bank
    => container
Sense 9
bank, bank building
    => depository, deposit, repository

Figure 5.4 Results for the synonyms of *bank* (n) in the WordNet lexical database, Version 1.5

A noteworthy feature of the current database is that relations in this database are beginning to be ordered by frequency, especially in the case of synonyms. The frequency of a particular (sense of a) word in a representative corpus should determine the order in which a lexeme is structured (see Summers 1996). For instance, in the case of *bank*, it can therefore be claimed that the 'river bank' sense takes greater precedence in the mental lexicon than the 'financial institution' sense. However, it should be noted that such a generalisation might not be valid for all contexts: in Singapore, at least, with its dearth of rivers and the abundance of financial institutions, one can surmise that the 'financial institution' sense (which has been relegated to Sense 2 in the WordNet database) might take precedence over the 'river bank' sense.

5.8 THE CELEX LEXICAL DATABASE

Our final discussion concerning the notion of an LDB or LKB is the **CELEX** (**CE**ntre for **LEX**ical Information) database at Nijmegen (see Piepenbrock 1993 and Appendix B for their WWW web site),[8] whose objective is to provide an on-line lexical resource of present-day Dutch, English, and German.

There are a number of motivations for considering CELEX. Firstly, the CELEX database uses corpus frequency data, which is in line with the tenets of the LFA framework (as mentioned in Chapter 4), that such data should be recorded as facts in the lexicon. Secondly, the English component of CELEX is a 'distillation' or integration of three well-known general dictionaries, i.e. the LDOCE (Procter (ed.) 1978; Summers (ed.) 1987), OALD (Cowie (ed.) 1989), and COBUILD (Sinclair (ed.) 1987a) dictionaries: it represents an instance of an on-line resource of lexical information whose utilisation accords well with the principle that corpus data should be complemented by other sources of data such as MRDs. Thirdly, in showing how a lexical database may be structured, the CELEX database also provides a good illustration of a lexical database in action, corresponding to Martin Kay's idea of a dictionary server which would facilitate the creation of a 'virtual lexicon' targeted to one's specific needs, since the user interface design in the CELEX database contains the following phases: LEXICON DEFINITION $\rightarrow$ LEXICON DERIVATION (from the MASTER DATABASE) $\rightarrow$ VIRTUAL LEXICON $\rightarrow$ EVALUATION $\rightarrow$ PHYSICAL LEXICON (internal and external use) (see CELEX 1988a: 5). Also, by means of the user-querying language in CELEX, an on-line virtual lexicon can be created and exported back to the user: this is an instance of multifunctionality (Section 2.7) in action, whereby various lexicons can be created according to specifications from a single source. Fourthly, the use of such a database highlights the linguistic analysis that defines its 'theoretically-uncommitted' character.

In general, these multilingual databases are organised according to the following parameters of lexical information: orthography (variations in spelling, word hyphenation), phonology (phonetic transcriptions, variations in pronun-ciation, syllable structure, primary and secondary stress), morphology (derivational and compositional structure, inflectional paradigms), syntax (wordclass, word-class specific subcategorisations, argument structures, expressions and idioms), and frequency (summed word and lemma counts, based on recent and representative text corpora). The lexical information is stored in three separate databases using the ORACLE relational database management system format.

These databases contain dictionary information combined with frequency data taken from large text corpora. For instance, the Dutch database contains approximately 400,000 present-day Dutch wordforms. The first version of the German database was made available in August 1990 and contains 51,000 lemmas. The English database contains approximately 150,000 wordforms.

5.8.1 The CELEX English Lexical Database

The CELEX English Lexical Database is claimed to reflect present-day British English and contains a structure which provides identical orthographic, phonetic and syntactic representations with respect to both the LDOCE (the ASCOT version, see Akkerman et al. 1985, 1988) and the OALD (Roger Mitton's computer-readable version) dictionaries. This is a difficult task to achieve, considering that 'whereas [the] OALD provides only the most essential information (orthographic representations of headwords and inflections, pronunciation, wordclass and verbal subcategorisation)', the ASCOT/LDOCE contains 'detailed information on various grammatical properties as well as additional lexical characteristics with respect to word division, spelling variation (British English, American English etc.) morphological processes, synonymy and usage.' Apart from these two sources, the database takes its input from such sources as COBUILD for frequency information and Webster's for its syllabification (word-division) list. When all the morphological variants concerned are expanded, a total of 150 thousand wordforms is obtained.

In the most recent edition, the frequencies for these wordforms are available in their (as yet) undisambiguated form, based on the COBUILD Corpus. Thus, a wordform such as *cut* might be labelled as an adjective, noun and verb (base form, past tense, or past participle), but would only have one gross frequency figure in the database. In terms of word class tags, subcategory tags and argument structure information, the CELEX lexical database has main word-class features as well as subcategory features for every entry. For instance, a lexical entry for a verb may contain any of the following subcategory features: Monotransitive, Complex Transitive, Intransitive, Ditransitive, Copula, Phrasal verb, Prepositional verb and Phrasal Prepositional verb. This will be returned to later (see Section 6.4.1.3).

5.8.2 The structure of the CELEX English database

Individual lexicons can be created using the querying interface FLEX, which translates the user's queries into Structured Query Language statements. The contents of the lexicon can be defined and controlled by selecting and specifying restrictions on the selection of words from the various possibilities presented in the FLEX menus. The user is given the choice of retrieving either one of two 'lexicon types': a **lemma** or a **wordform** lexicon. However, CELEX follows the unusual practice of distinguishing between lemmas without a recourse to considerations of meaning. For instance, whereas the conventional dictionary would list the noun *bank* twice ('riverside', and 'financial institution'), there is only one lemma for the noun *bank*, which thus gets only one row in the database: a row corresponds to an entry or sub-paragraph in a dictionary. This may be considered a limitation (of the database) which arises partly as a result of not having the semantic parameter available yet, and partly from the constraints imposed by the conventional relational database method.

Let us examine further what this involves. In the CELEX database, five types of criteria are used for distinguishing lemmas:

1. Orthography of the wordforms. Thus, *peek* (n) and *peak* (n) are considered two different lemmas because they are spelt differently and have a different meaning.

2. Syntactic class. *Meet* (adj) *meet* (v) are different lemmas because they each belong to a different word class and have different meanings. Sometimes the difference in word class is itself the only way a difference in meaning is indicated, for instance, w*ater* (v) and *water* (n).

3. Inflectional paradigm. *Antenna* (n) ('radio aerial'), and *Antenna* (n) ('insect feature') are two different lemmas because the first has the plural *antennas*, while the second has the plural *antennae*.

4. Morphological structure. *Rubber* (n) ('someone or something that rubs – *rub + er*') and *rubber* (n) ('elastic substance') are two distinct lemmas because they differ in their derivational morphological structure.

5. Pronunciation of the wordforms. *Recount* (v) ('to count again') and *recount* (v) ('to tell a tale') are different lemmas because the first is pronounced with a stress on the first syllable, while the second has the stress on the second syllable.

These formal considerations are useful for perhaps most of the wordforms in the language, and any two homographs which differ from each other in just one of these five criteria can be considered as separate lemmas. However, these criteria would fail when applied to homonyms such as the two *banks* which get reduced (counter-intuitively) to just one lemma. The inference to be drawn here is that the use of formal criteria, while being a necessary condition, is not an all-sufficient one.

5.8.3 Accessing the database
The database is available both on-line (via ftp, telnet, and the World Wide Web) and on CD-ROM (from the Linguistic Data Consortium; see Appendix B).

The user-querying language FLEX allows one to inspect the lexicons available, manipulate a selected lexicon into a form suitable for one's purposes, and save it as a file. By means of the user interface, a lexicon can be defined by specifying the wordforms and the linguistic parameters required. Once this lexicon is defined, the user can then immediately access and query this virtual lexicon as if it were a separate database. The virtual lexicon can be made into a physical lexicon which can be exported to another computer by means of file transfer protocol and electronic mail.

5.8.4 Selected lexemes using the CELEX linguistic codes
In this section, selected linguistic parameters used in the CELEX database will be discussed for their rationale. Note that for each parameter, the first two columns (i.e. 'English lemma', and 'unique numeric id') are repeated, for ease of presentation.

A. Orthography
1. *English lemma*
2. *Unique numeric id*
3. *number of spellings*
4. *spelling number (1-n)*
5. *language code*

For ease of presentation, in a lexeme such as *account* (n), i.e.

1	2	3	4	5
account	*\190*	*\1*	*\1*	*\B*

I have numbered the columns accordingly: the number '1' just above the first column (let us call this 'A1') indicates the lemma, the number '2' for the unique numeric id, and so on. Column A1 indicates that *account* is a noun lemma (see D4 in this section) which is given an ordering number ('unique numeric identity') of 190 (Column A2). No two lemmas can have the same ordering number: *account* (v), for example, is given an ordering number of 191 in the database. With regard to the spelling (Column A3), *account* does not have any variants (Column A4) unlike, say, a wordform such as *generalize* (v) which has two spellings: *generalize* and *generalise*. These would be assigned a 'spelling number' of 1 and 2 respectively. For every (different) spelling, the language code records whether it is a British (B) or American (A) variant: by default, *account* has been assigned the British spelling (Column 5). Applying this criterion to the lemma *generalize*, presumably we get the forms *generalize* (A) and *generalise* (B).

B. Phonology
   1. *English lemma*
   2. *unique numeric id*
   3. *number of pronunciations*
   4. *pronunciation number (1-N)*
   5. *status of pronunciation*

Phonetic transcriptions
   6. number of phonemes – syllabified
   7. number of syllables – syllabified, with stress
   8. celex character set
   9. stress pattern

Phonetic patterns
10. CV pattern

For instance, in the row

1	2	3	4	5	6	7	8	9	10
account	\190	\1	\1\	P\	5\	2\	@-'kaUnt\	01	\V-CVVCC\

Column B3 indicates that the pronunciation for *account* is unambiguous, unlike, say, *dexterous*, which could be transcribed as [d.E.k.s.t.@.r.@.s]. and [d.E.k.s.t.r.@.s] (where @ stands for 'schwa'). As in column B8, the transcription uses the CELEX character set, which follows closely that of SAM-PA, a widely-agreed computer-readable phonetic character set.[9] In the case of *dexterous*, then, column B4 would assign the numbers 1 and 2 to the first and second pronunciations respectively. Column B5 concerns whether the pronunciation is 'primary' (P) or 'secondary' (S): these categories are assigned on the basis of the preferred pronunciation (see Jones 1977) in the case of alternative forms. Column B6 indicates that *account* consists of 5 phonemes. Column B7 states that the lemma has 2 syllables, while the primary stress is indicated in column B8. This primary stress is reflected in column B9, the stress pattern which shows how each syllable is stressed in speech. This takes one of three possibilities: primary (1), secondary (2), or 0 (neither). Finally, the 'phonetic pattern' (B10) is the syllable structure, or CV pattern in phonology.

C. Morphology
The presentation for this parameter is divided into two parts: the first (C1)

contains various types of derivational information for the word lemma; the second (C2) relates to information regarding the stem lemma and its affixes.

C1 – Status of morphological analyses
 1. *English lemma*
 2. *Unique numeric id*
 3. *Status*

Derivational/compositional information
 4. number of morphological analyses
 5. analysis number(0-N)
 6. status of morphological analysis
 7. noun-verb-affix compound
 8. derivation method
 9. compound method
 10. derivational compound method
 11. default analysis

Using the same example *account*, we have

1	2	3	4	5	6	7	8	9	10	11
account\	*190*\	*Z*\		*1*\	*1*\	*N*\	*N*\	*N*\	*N*\	*Y*\

Column 3 contains the value 'Z', which indicates 'zero derivation', i.e. *account* (n) has undergone the process of conversion from the monomorphemic *account* (v). The decision tree for establishing morphological status is the following: Is the lemma derived from another lemma identical in form but different in word class? If the answer is 'yes', then zero derivation ('Z') occurs. (However, CELEX seems to have the blanket principle that a noun sharing the same form as the verb is derived from the verb). If the answer is 'no', the next question becomes one of asking whether the lemma contains 'at least one modern, productive lemma or affix plus one other element' (CELEX 1991: 4–51). If the answer to this question is in the affirmative, then the next question reads as: 'Does the other element contain at least one productive lemma or affix?' If Yes, then a 'complex' ('C') status is assigned, otherwise it is considered 'obscure' ('O'). If the answer to the earlier question (i.e. productive lemma/affix + one other element) is 'no', then the next question reads as: 'Is the lemma a recent loanword?' If the answer to this question is 'yes', then the morphological status is 'undetermined' ('U'); if 'no', then the next question follows: 'Does the lemma contain at least one etymologically recognisable root?' If 'yes', then it is assigned the status 'root' ('R'), otherwise the lemma is 'monomorphemic' ('M').

The option 'number of morphological analysis' (Column 4) indicates how many analyses have been made for each stem, if applicable. In this case, it is left empty because there is just 1 stem which does not need to be analysed (whereas a wordform such as *flashbulb* containing 2 stems (i.e. *flash* + *bulb*) will be listed as having 2 analyses). Column 5 therefore identifies only one analysis of the stem *account*. In the lemma *flashbulb*, however, there would be two rows of which the first would be assigned the ID 'MorphNum 1', and the second 'MorphNum 2'. Thus, the status for *account* (N) is 1, indicating only one analysis. It seems to me that there is an overlap here between Columns 4 and 5 which would (arguably) mean some redundancy of information.

This lemma is unproblematic where the next few parameters are concerned, so it is assigned a default analysis status. In any case, a decision tree is formed, consisting of the following procedure: (a) Is the analysis SA (i.e. Stem–Affix) or AS or ASA acceptable? (b) If 'yes', then derivation takes place. (c) If the answer is 'no', then the next question becomes one of: Is the analysis SS or SAS acceptable? (d) If 'yes', then the word is a compound. (e) If the answer is 'no', then the next question becomes one of: Is the analysis SSA (or SASA) acceptable? (f) If 'yes', then the word is a 'derivational compound', otherwise it is monomorphemic. However, a word such as copy *editor* is problematic. The analysis for the word *copy editor* might take several possibilities, including being a compound (*copy + editor (edit+-or)*), ordinary derivation (*copy edit (copy+edit) + -or*), or derivational compound (*copy +edit + -or*).

C2 – Segmentations
  1. *English lemma*
  2. Unique numeric id

immediate segmentation
  3. stems & affixes
  4. class labels
  5. class & verb subcat labels
  6. stem/affix labels
  7. stem allomorphy
  8. affix substitution

complete segmentation (flat)
  9. stems & affixes
  10. class labels
  11. stem/affix labels

complete segmentation (hierarchical)
  12. stems & affixes
  13. stems & affixes, labelled
  14. empty brackets, labelled
  15. stem allomorphy
  16/ affix substitution
  17. opacity

other
  18. number of components
  19. number of morphemes
  20. number of levels

In

1	2	3	4	5	6	7	8	9	10
account\	190\	account\	V\	2\	S\	N\	N\	account	V\

11	12	13	14
S\	((account)	)\((account)[V])[N]\	(()[V])[N]\

15	16	17	18	19	20
N\	N\	N\	1\	1\	2\

Columns 3–8 concern the analysis of 'immediate segmentation' which is a simple, one-level breakdown of a stem into its next largest elements. At first sight, Column 4 – denoting the word class label – seems to be a mistake, since the number '190' is associated with a noun, whereas this column indicates it as a verb: however, in cases where the verb and noun forms are the same, CELEX treats the noun as being derived from the verb. In wordforms whose syntactic category takes the N (noun) label – for instance, *agreement, application, payment, shipment* – the morphological label 'Vx' indicates that these wordforms are made up of a verb and an affix (a derivation). However, a noun such as *business* is given the label 'Ax', which in this case indicates that it is derived from the adjective form 'busy' + the suffix. Other labels in C4 are largely self-explanatory, except that, in order to avoid the confusion between the adjective ('A') and adverb labels, the adverb label has been given a 'B' label (similarly, the Article category is indicated by 'D'). In Column 5, following the rationale that *account* (n) is derived from *account* (v), the syntactic categorisation of the verbal stem is given as '2' (i.e. indicating 'transitivity'). The database does not, however, seem to make a distinction between deverbal forms which are more clearly semantically related to the verb and those which are not. Taking the present example, the similarity of the meanings between the noun and verb forms of the word *account*, especially in business English such as *settling [one's] account* and *to account [for something]*, should be differentiated from those of the deverbal word *claim*, as in *settling [one's] claim* and *to claim [something]*. Yet, the CELEX database merely lists both a*ccount* (n) and *claim* (n) as derived from their respective verb stem. Returning to Column 6 of *account* (n), the value 'S' indicates a stem. 'A' would indicate an affix and F a flectional form of the stem. Thus, *emigration* is represented as SA, and *bagpipes* as SSF. The value 'N' in Column 7 indicates that *account* has a stem which does not involve any allomorphy. Otherwise, the possible values are 'B' (blending, as in *breathanalyse*), 'C' (clipping, as in *phone*), 'D' (derivational, as in *clarify*), 'F' (flectional, which is rare, as in *born* (adj) from *bear* (v)), and 'Z' (conversion, as in *belief*). Column 8, indicating affix substitution, identifies the process whereby an affix replaces part of a stem when that stem and the affix join to form another stem (e.g. a*ctive* is formed from *action* and the affix *-ive*, but the affix *-ion* disappears).

Columns 9–11 and 12–17 have been included for the purpose of illustrating that the morphological analysis in CELEX can be more detailed, if one chooses. Columns 9–11 contain information relating to the 'complete segmentation' of the morphemes that a stem has: the segmentation is considered 'flat' which means that the constituent morphemes are presented without containing details of the full morphological analysis carried out. Columns 12–14 contain a detailed, hierarchical analysis: this analysis is arrived at after immediate analysis has been carried out on every stem that can be identified within a larger stem. Columns 15–16 are a repetition of Columns 7–8 above. Column 17, which indicates opacity, is for words in which the meaning of the head element does not accord with the full meaning of the word. Words whose analyses are morphologically and semantically clear get the value 'N'. The value 'Y', however, in a word such as *accordion* stems from the head element *accord* having no direct semantic link with *accordion*.

Finally, the remaining three columns contain 'count' information of various sorts, which arguably are redundant types of information. Column 18 gives the number of components (i.e. stems and affixes) in the immediate analysis of each stem; Column 19 provides the number of morphemes a stem contains after complete segmentation; Column 20 indicates the number of levels involved in the complete hierarchical analysis of each stem.

D. Syntax
  1. *English lemma*
  2. *unique numeric id*

Word Class
  3. Numeric Codes
  4. Labels

Subclassification nouns
  5. Count
  6. Uncount
  7. Singular use
  8. Plural use
  9. group count
  10. group uncount

Subclassification verbs
  11. transitive
  12. transitive & complementation
  13. intransitive
  14. ditransitive
  15. linking verb
  16. phrasal

Subclassification adjectives
  17. ordinary
  18. attributive

19. predicative
20. postpositive
21. expression

Subclassification adverbs
22. ordinary
23. predicative
24. postpositive
25. combinatory
26. expression

Subclassification numerals
27. cardinal
28. ordinal
29. expression

The word class codes for identifying the syntactic class of each lemma in the database, D4, include the labels 'A' (adjective), 'ADV' (adverb), 'ART' (article), 'PRON' (pronoun), 'PREP' (preposition), and 'C' (conjunction). In examining the list, the database does appear to make adequate distinctions – especially in a wordform such as *like* for which the possibilities 'N', 'V', 'A', 'ADV', 'PREP', and 'C' are listed. However, the database has its limitations. A word such as *please* is listed only as a verb, without any provision for it being an adverb as well. Similarly, there appears to be a mistake in one of the entries for *better*, which is given as 'N', 'N', and 'V', instead of one of them being an 'A'.

Where Columns D5–8 are concerned, let us retain the same illustrative example, *account* (N),

1	2	3	4	5	6	7	8	9	10	11	12	13	14	15	16	17
account\	190\	1\	N\	Y\	Y\	N\	N\	N\	N\	N\	N\	N\	N\	N\	N\	N\

18	19	20	21	22	23	24	25	26	27	28	29
N\	N\	N\	N\	N\	N\	N\	N\	N\	N\	N\	N\

which is listed as a count noun in Column 5. The 'N' label in Column 7 indicates that this lemma does not only occur in the singular form – by the same token, Column 8 must take an 'N' label as well, since *account* can singular as well as plural. Finally, Columns 9 and 10 answer the questions 'Is this lemma a collective noun that has a singular *and* a plural form?' and 'Is this lemma a collective noun that has only a singular form, but *not* a plural form?' respectively.

For Columns D11–16, let us take *advise* (V) as an illustration.

1	2	3	4	5	6	7	8	9	10	11	12	13	14	15
advise\	437\	4\	V\	N\	N\	N\	N\	N\	N\	Y\	Y\	Y\	Y\	N\

16	17	18	19	20	21	22	23	24	25	26	27	28	29
N\	N\	18	N\	N\	N\	N\	N\	N\	N\	N\	N\	N\	N\

Here, *advise* (v) is said to be subcategorisable – variously taking a direct object, object complement, being intransitive, taking both the direct and indirect objects, but not ever being a linking or phrasal verb.

Where Columns D17–21 are concerned, let us take *full* (adj) as an example.

1	2	3	4	5	6	7	8	9	10	11	12	13	14	15
full	*11069*	2\	*A*	N\	N\	N\	N\	N\	N\	N\	N\	N\	N\	N\

18	19	20	21	22	23	24	25	26	27	28	29
Y\	Y\	N\	N\	N\	N\	N\	N\	N\	N\	N\	N\

In this instance, *full* is an adjective which is said to be 'ordinary', i.e. it can be used *both* attributively (e.g. *full details*) and predicatively (e.g. *details are full and complete*). The 'Y' (yes) in Columns 18 and 19 indicate that there are some contexts in which the adjective can be used either in attributive or predicative position. Column 20 indicates that *full* cannot be postpositive, unlike a phrase such as *life everlasting* in which the adjective can occur *after* the noun, whereas the normal position would be for the modifier to come *before* the noun. Column 21 asks the question: 'Is this adjective lemma only ever used in combination with certain other words to make up a particular phrase?' In this case, there does not seem to be any such idiomaticity involved. Nevertheless, it applies to other adjectives such as *bated* (which occurs only in *with bated breath*) and *put* (where the adjective form occurs only in the phrase *stay put*).

For columns D22–26, let us take the example of *kindly* (adv).

1	2	3	4	5	6	7	8	9	10	11	12	13
kindly	*15053*	7\	*ADV*	N\	N\	N\	N\	N\	N\	N\	N\	N\

14	15	16	17	18	19	20	21	22	23	24	25	26	27	28	29
N\	N\	N\	N\	N\	N\	N\	N\	Y\	N\	N\	N\	N\	N\	N\	N\

Here, out of the various columns, the only positive indication is given in Column 22, where the term 'ordinary' simply means that the adverb does not necessarily have any special subclassification features – it is taken just as an adverb which can modify a verb or an adjective. Like *kindly*, the other adverbial examples in the selected listing – *due, forward, however, like, the* – also behave in the same way. However, all these examples take the N label for Columns D23–26, so it would not be interesting to use them here to illustrate the meaning of the labels. Instead, for Column D23, an adverb such as *adrift* would get the code Y since it can be distinguished from ordinary adverbs on the basis of its predicative use with the verb *be*: thus, it is possible to say *the boat is adrift* but not *the boat is quickly*. Thus *adrift* is a predicative adverb, while *quickly* is not. In Column D24, as with the postpositive use of the adjective, an adverb such as *apart* will get the code Y, based on its occurrence in such a phrase as *several yards apart*. In Column D25, the question to ask is the following: 'Is this lemma an adverb which can be used in combination with a preposition or another adverb?' An adverb such as *clean* would get the Y code, as in *the sledgehammer broke clean through the door*, where the adverb combines with a preposition. In Column D26, the question to ask is the following: 'Is this adverb lemma only ever used in combination with certain other words to make up a particular phrase?' An example would be *amok*, as in the phrase *run amok*.

Finally, I shall not dwell on the 'subclassification numerals' since, suffice it to note, they do not apply to the selected listing, but are included here to indicate the full extent of the CELEX syntax codes.

E. Frequency
  1. *English lemma*
  2. *unique numeric id*

COBUILD all sources
  3. COBUILD frequency 17.9m
  4. COBUILD 95% confidence deviation 17.9m
  5. COBUILD frequency 1m
  6. COBUILD frequency, logarithmic

COBUILD written sources
  7. COBUILD written frequency 16.6m
  8. COBUILD written frequency 1m
  9. COBUILD written frequency, logarithmic

COBUILD spoken sources
10. COBUILD spoken frequency 1.3m
11. COBUILD spoken frequency 1m
12. COBUILD spoken frequency, logarithmic

Frequency information can be useful in a variety of ways, for instance, in being used by a probabilistic parser to select the most appropriate syntactic category for a word. The frequency information given here is taken from the 1991 version of the COBUILD Corpus, which contained 17.9 million words from mainly written sources. In terms of lexical ambiguity resolution, the disambiguation has been done by hand instead of using a procedure similar to Hearst (1991) or Sutton (1992).

For our illustration here, let us take the frequency figures for the verb *appreciate*.

1	2	3	4	5	6	7	8	9	10	11	12
appreciate	*1197*	*624*	*2*	*35*	*2*	*577*	*35*	*2*	*47*	*36*	*2*

The third column gives the plain COBUILD frequency count for the lemma, i.e. *appreciate* occurs 624 times (grouping its wordforms) in the 17.9 million word corpus. The fourth column indicates how accurate the frequencies in the previous column are by providing a deviation figure for each lemma.[10] Similarly, Column 5 gives the frequency figures as Column 3, except that they are scaled down to a normalised frequency of occurrences per 1 million: it is easier to say, for instance, that *appreciate* is 35 in a million than it does to say it is

624 words out of 17,900,000. Column 5 should compare well with such frequency figures for the LOB and Brown corpora, each of which has approximately a million words.

The logarithmic values for Column 6 (and by a similar token Columns 9 and 12) range from zero ($\log_{10}1$) to 6 ($\log_{10}1000000$). In the CELEX manual (p. 4–107), it is calculated that 'only words which occur 27 or more times in the COBUILD Corpus) have a logarithmic value greater than zero.'

The preceding discussion similarly applies to Columns E7–9 respectively, which are taken from the 16.6 million words of written texts in the corpus. Finally, Columns E10–12 represent figures taken from the remaining 1.3 million words that make up spoken texts in the COBUILD Corpus.

5.8.5 General comments on the CELEX database

Although I have raised the possibility that some of the syntactic information in the CELEX database does not make certain valuable distinctions, this is not so much a reservation aimed at CELEX as a reflection on the fact that such information cannot be culled from published dictionaries, which by themselves are not all-inclusive lexical resources. More positively, the focus on the linguistic codes in CELEX points to the 'theoretically' uncommitted representation, in terms of content, which enhances the multifunctional potentiality of the database. The CELEX database points to the awesome potentiality of automation which future users will have in accessing online multifunctional LDB/LKBs which might be physically located thousands of miles away and from which they can create their own customised lexicons, sending these lexicons back to themselves in no time at all.

5.9 USING THE WORLD WIDE WEB FOR LEXICAL RESEARCH

The foregoing comments point to the awesome and profound changes made by networked computing in the past few years. We now have the Internet which is the largest system of linked computer networks facilitating data communication services such as remote login, file transfer, electronic mail, and newsgroups. The Internet is currently the largest means of connecting and extending the reach of each computer network linked to it than would otherwise have been possible with a single network. It is made easier to use because of the World Wide Web, a hypertext system using the Internet as its transport mechanism: in such a system, the Internet is navigated by clicking hyperlinks displaying another documents containing also hyperlinks. These hyperlinks can contain text, sound, and video (graphics). What makes the World Wide Web such an exciting and useful medium is that the next document seen could be housed on a computer on a local site or an external one, thousands of miles away. Documents on the World Wide Web are accessed via browsers such as Netscape Communicator or Microsoft Internet Explorer.

What this means in practice for us is that the transfer, exchange, and study of lexicons (and of language) is greatly enhanced. Lexicons, as we have seen in the case of the CELEX system, can be created and e-mailed back to the end user. Lexical databases and knowledge bases can be accessed easily, since institutions which are concerned about the issue of copyright in releasing the source codes for their linguistic software can maintain a site where users can use the software there to process texts and access data or knowledge bases. Tagging and parsing can therefore be done on a site without any source codes being released at all. Greater sharing and portability of lexical and textual information is increasingly enhanced as we move into the 21st century.

Appendix B contains a few World Wide Web sites that I have found relevant to the discussions in this book. However, as the World Wide Web is an evolving entity, site addresses will tend to change over time. Of course, a central way of resolving this potential problem is to use the 'Net Search' option in any browser for the searching of the site by keying in the relevant word (such as the name of the site or the topic under study)

5.10 CONCLUSION

In this chapter, I have outlined issues related to the computational storage of the lexicon. In particular, I have sketched two notions of formalism: formalism_1 which is claimed to lead to a more linguistically motivated organisation of the lexicon, and formalism_2, which is claimed to lead to a more efficient computational organisation and representation of the lexicon. In terms of formalism_2, we have looked at the notions of inheritance, unification, typed-feature representation, and the formalisms used for PATR, DATR, and the ACQUILEX systems. We have also seen other databases in practice: the PROLEX PROLOG database, the WORDNET lexical database system, and the CELEX system. Although the examples used are primarily from English, it should be clear that similar principles can apply to the case of the computational storage of the lexicon for other languages.

5.11 STUDY QUESTIONS
1. Find out the meanings of *hyponym, meronym, pertainym* etc. which are listed in Figure 5.3.
2. Miller et al. assert that 'lexical inheritance systems ... seldom go more than ten levels deep, and the deepest examples usually contain technical levels that are not part of the everyday vocabulary'. A man-made artifact such as *roadster*, for instance, goes about six or seven levels deep, as the following output from the WordNet database shows:
    roadster, runabout, two-seater
       => *car, auto, automobile, machine, motorcar*
    (i) Can you think of a similar one where the hierarchy of persons runs to about four levels deep?

(ii) Why is it the case that lexical inheritance systems seldom go more than ten levels deep?

3. If *beak* and *wing* are meronyms of *bird*, and if *canary* is a hyponym of *bird*, what would the notion of lexical inheritance suggest?

4. A number of lexical databases are now available through the World Wide Web. In order to find out more about them, use a browser such as Netscape Navigator: perform a search for the terms "lexical database" and "lexical knowledge base." For example, my search yielded the following web site: *http://engdep1.philo.ulg.ac.be/decide/robcol.html* for the French-English Robert and Collins database at the University of Liège. This database allows the authorised user to query the database by means of the 'robcol' (Robert Collins) program. One of the central distinctive features of this database is its ability to return analyses of words using the lexical functions postulated by Igor Mel'cuk and his co-workers (see Mel'cuk and Zholkovsky 1988; Mel'cuk 1996; Wanner (ed.) 1996). This site contains a list of Mel'cuk et al.'s lexical functions, which represent one of the most incisive models for lexical analysis, containing over 50 primitives (most basic items) characterising language. Instances of lexical functions include the following: 'Mult' ('regular group/set) when applied to the lexeme *dog* will yield the corresponding word *pack* (i.e. 'a pack of dogs'), i.e. Mult (dog) = pack; the lexical function 'Son' ('typical sound') when applied to the lexeme *elephant* will yield the following: Son(elephant)=trumpet; the lexical function 'Anti' ('antonym') combined with the lexical function function 'Real' ('satisfy the requirements of') for the word *sail* will yield the following: AntiReal (sail)='stop sailing.'

The following (edited) examples indicate how the end user might query such a database:

> The main parameters for robcol (the program) are :
> "-h" for the headwords.
> "-i" for the italic words.
> "-pos" for the part of speech.
> "-lex" for the lexical functions.
> A wild card "*" can be used inside any query parameter.

"Let's go fishing"

> (1) Show the "parts" of a fish.
>   *robcol -i fish -lex part*
> (2) What do you call a "multitude" (group) of fishes.
>   *robcol -i fish -lex mult*

Magnification

> (3) How to say "big liar" ?
>   *robcol -i liar -lex magn*

"Let's go sailing"

> (4) How do you make a sail work?
> *robcol -i sail -lex real1*
> (5) How do you stop a sail working ?
> *robcol -i sail -lex antireal1*

"Sound"

> (6) The sound of a bell.
> *robcol -i bell -pos v* -lex *son*

In the last example, it would be nice if the sound of a bell could be heard at the same time for those who have multimedia machines! The integration of graphics, sound and text for the World Wide Web will mean that language analysis becomes increasingly more exciting.

5.12 FURTHER READING

The concept of a lexical data/knowledge base is dealt with in greater detail by Calzolari and her co-workers at the Istituto di Linguistica Computazionale. For aspects of the relationship between a corpus and a lexical database, read Souter (1993). The notion of semantic networks is dealt with in Sowa (1991, 1993). Read also Wilks et al. (1996) which gives a critical view of various projects, including a number of the ones mentioned in this chapter.

NOTES

1. Gazdar, in a discussion involving Fernando Pereira, Martin Kay, Aravind Joshi, Mitch Marcus, Steve Pulman and others, makes this point about there being two subcategories of unification grammar formalisms (see Wilks (ed.) 48–49). Shieber (1986: 38) also makes a similar point in separating formalisms serving as linguistic *tools* and those intended to be linguistic *theories*. For a discussion of Kay's FUG, see Kay (1984a), and Wilks (ed), pp. 44–46.
2. See the TEI Guidelines (http://etext.virginia.edu/TEI.html), especially the sections on Feature Structures and Feature Structure Declarations.
3. Steve Pulman's point, in the TINLAP discussion on unification formalisms. (see Wilks (ed.) 1989: 43).
4. Some of these relational database management systems for the PC include Oracle (used for the CELEX database), Database IV, Data-Ease, and more recently Microsoft Access (for its integration with the Windows environment).
5. For a discussion of the principles of default inheritance, see Gazdar (1987).
6. For an update on the ACQUILEX project, visit their WWW homepage: http://www.cl.cam.ac.uk/Research/NL/acquilex/
7. The current publicly available version is 1.5. Access their WWW homepage for the latest updates: http://www.cogsci.princeton.edu/~wn/.
8. The information contained this section, and the subsequent sub-sections, is taken from the CELEX User Guide – CELEX (1991) – as well as the following issues of the newsletter published by the Centre: see CELEX (1986, 1987, 1988a, 1988b, 1990). Besides these in-house publications, see also Piepenbrock (1993). I am grateful to Richard Piepenbrock and Marcel Bingley for setting up a trial account for me in 1992. Since then, with the expansion of the World Wide Web, the reader should refer to the CELEX homepage: http://www.kun.nl/celex/ for continual updates.
9. The acronym *SAM-PA* (Speech Assessment Methods – Phonetic Alphabet) arises from the SAM project, which is a European Community funded project. The development of the phonetic alphabet was co-ordinated by J C Wells with the intention of its becoming the standard European computer phonetic

alphabet. SAM-PA is designed specifically to handle Danish, Dutch, English, French, German, and Italian. See IPA (1987).

10. CELEX (1991, Section 4-104) gives the formula as

$$N \times 1.96 \times \sqrt{\frac{p(1-p)}{n}} \times \sqrt{\frac{N-n}{N-1}}$$

where N is the frequency of the string as a whole, n is the number of items which could be disambiguated in a random 100-item sample, and p is the ratio figure for the item when it belongs to one particular lemma.

6
A case study: Applying the LFA framework to two corpora of business English

6.0 INTRODUCTION

The principles that have been suggested in the preceding chapters for acquiring a lexicon using a corpus-based approach can be more clearly demonstrated through a case study. In this chapter, we will apply in particular the LFA framework to two sublanguage corpora for the acquisition of lexical information. Contextual information concerning how these corpora have come about is first detailed. The corpora are then processed so as to derive or acquire the respective lexicons from them. In so doing, we will also become acquainted with the workings of a (type of) lexicographic workstation in practice.

6.1 THE NOTION OF SUBLANGUAGE, GENRE, AND REGISTER

Two sublanguage corpora, the PROLEX corpus and the PROCOMPARE corpus, are chosen here. Besides using examples from these corpora for illustration and analysis, these corpora are chosen for their sublanguage properties, following both McNaught (1993: 233) and Frawley (1988), both of whom note that

1. Sublanguage is strongly lexically based;
2. Sublanguage texts focus on content;
3. Lexical selection is syntactified in sublanguages, thus
4. Surface collocation plays a major role in sublanguages;
5. Sublanguages demonstrate elaborate lexical cohesion.

For our present purposes, we may describe a sublanguage in terms of a sublanguage corpus A **sublanguage** is, following Harris (1991: 272), a part of natural language with a grammar of its own: 'certain proper subsets of the sentences of a language may be closed under some or all of the operations defined for the language.' In other words, a sublanguage is characterised by the notion of closure (see McEnery and Wilson 1996: Chapter 6), a language used by a 'particular community of speakers, say those concerned with a particular subject matter or those engaged in a specialized occupation' (Sager 1986: 2). Therefore, a sublanguage is similar to linguistic notions such as **register** and **genre**. **Register** (Halliday and Hasan 1985: 38, for instance), more popularly associated with the Hallidayan tradition, is a variety of language *according to use* which creates contextual meaning through its three elements: **field**, **tenor**, and **mode**. These three aspects of the social context always act upon the language as it is being used. In terms of a functional approach to language, register is a semantic concept whereby field, tenor, and mode are correlated with the **ideational**, **interpersonal**, and **textual** functions respectively (see Section 1.1.2). This methodology, whose framework is fully specified in Halliday (1985, 1994), can be – and has been – variously applied to the linguistic analysis of texts.

Working within the Hallidayan framework but using a methodology which focuses on the notion of **text structure**, Ruqaiya Hasan conceptualises a Contextual Configuration (CC) as a specific set of values that realises the field, mode, and tenor of discourse (Halliday and Hasan 1985: 56). The CC, through its specificity, is used to predict the obligatory and optional elements of text structure, that is, specifying the following:

> *What* elements *must* occur;
> *What* elements *can* occur;
> *Where must* they occur;
> *Where can* they occur;
> *How often* can they occur.

(Halliday and Hasan 1985: 56)

For Hasan, the specification of these elements constitutes a specification of the **generic structure potential** of a text: the agenda is to specify the total range of these elements in a way which exhausts the possibility of text structure (for every appropriate text). The specification of which discoursal elements are obligatory and which are optional is important because it is only the obligatory elements that define a **genre**: 'the obligatory elements define the genre to which a text belongs' (Halliday and Hasan, 61). Thus, for instance, when one walks into a McDonald's, an element which seems to be always obligatory is the part of discourse in which the salesperson asks whether the customer is going to eat in or take the food out: this element constitutes part of the language of such service encounters. In specifying a method which allows one to characterise a particular text as an instance of a particular genre, Hasan also maintains that the construction of such a text is a matter of social experience: one learns to make such a text.

On the other hand, for Biber (1988, 1993), a genre is determined on the 'external' basis of 'situational' use, and is to be distinguished from a text type which, as in Section 3.2, is determined in terms of specific 'internal' language features associated with it: '**genre** refers to classes of texts that are determined on the basis of external criteria relating to author's or speaker's purpose', whereas **text type** refers to 'classes of texts that are grouped on the basis of similarities in linguistic form, irrespective of their genre classifications' (Biber 1988: 206). The example cited by Biber here is that 'particular texts from press reportage, biographies, and academic prose might be very similar in having a narrative linguistic form, and they would thus be grouped together as a single text type, even though they represent three different genres.' So, text types and genres do not necessarily overlap; indeed, they should be distinguished. In this respect, Biber (1988, 1993) uses such quantificational methods as factor and cluster analyses to develop a typology of texts that describe the distinctive and common linguistic characteristics of spoken and written texts, in terms of 'multi-feature, multidimensional analysis'.

From a lexical perspective, these issues regarding a sublanguage are important for a resolution of what a sublanguage lexicon really is: further discussion is beyond the remit of this section. For our present purposes, a sublanguage will be taken, firstly, to refer to a sublanguage corpus, since 'the particular textual structures found in sublanguage corpora reflect very closely the structuring of the sublanguage's associated conceptual domain.' (McNaught 1993: 233) and secondly, a genre or a register.

6.2 THE PROLEX CORPUS

The first sublanguage corpus detailed here, the PRO(fessional) LEX(is) corpus of business English texts, was gathered between 1983 and 1984 (see Webster 1984, 1986). Samples of business English correspondence from both local and multinational firms in Singapore were collected with the result that the PROLEX corpus amounts to a text base of 566 samples which total approximately 65,000 words.

Details are included in Figure 6.1:

THE ***PROLEX*** (=THE ***PRO***(FESSIONAL) ***LEX***(IS) CORPUS)

Compiled by:	Jonathan Webster
Compiled at:	The National University of Singapore
Sampling period:	1983–1984
Language (variety):	Business English
Spoken/written:	Written
Size:	c. 65000 words

Details of material: Material is drawn from local and multinational organisations in Singapore. The names of these organisations, upon their request, may not be disclosed. As a rule, every occurrence of each organisation's name has been blanked out to protect the confidentiality of business transactions.

Classification: A text base of 566 samples which are classified as 12 Questionnaires, 165 Telexes, 303 Letters and Memorandums, 17 Order Forms, 33 Lists of Terms and Conditions, 36 Statements of Account.

How transcribed: Original version in upper-case. However, the UNIX **tr** command can translate this version into just lower-case letters.

Use: Some of the objectives of the PROLEX project, as outlined by Webster (1984, 1986), include the following which I will elaborate in this section: 1. to provide a syntactically sophisticated computer-processed frequency-count of professional lexis with systematic indications given of the social and geo-graphical source of the form; 2. to classify text samples according to those typological categories deemed to be sociolinguistically significant; 3. to discover the collocational range of those lexemes constituting the professional lexis under review, and 4. to develop PROLEX into an expert system for word knowledge, not just another on-line dictionary.

Storage details: Stored on DEC Digital UNIX at the National University of Singapore.

Availability: Currently unavailable.

Figure 6.1 The PROLEX corpus: a summary

In gathering and analysing a sublanguage corpus, especially one which is as small as the PROLEX corpus, the following principles (modified from Webster 1984, 1986) might be useful:

Firstly, a description of the usage rules governing the appropriate use of a given profession's technical vocabulary and style of expression (i.e. in this context, business English) is needed. This means a discovery of the system of rules underlying the sociolinguistic competence of members of this socially-defined group. While such 'sociolinguistic competence' issues are beyond the remit of this book, the notion of the lexical frame (as detailed in Section 1.3) is a useful one, in this context, of indicating the business profession's default usage of the term.

Secondly, there is a need to do justice to what there is in human sociopsychological reality by organising the representation of professional lexis by frequency, collocational range, and semantic nesting. As Makkai's Associative Lexicon (see Section 1.1) shows, there is the concern that alphabetical dictionaries do not mirror the natural clustering, or 'nesting', of lexemes. Roget's Thesaurus is a good example of a 'semantic nesting' in practice. A similar idea in AI which has been developed in recent years is the notion of 'semantic network' (see Sowa (ed.) 1991). Where frequency is concerned, some reliable indications can be given even in such a small corpus. Where collocational range is concerned, a corpus such as this is at present too small for an extended study using existing statistical methods which require vast amounts of data (see Section 4.3): nevertheless, a preliminary step towards measuring collocational strength (in a statistical sense) is the use of the Z-score (see Section 6.7).

Thirdly, there is a need to provide a syntactically sophisticated, computer-processed frequency-count of professional lexis with systematic indications given of the social and geographical source of the form': this is partially fulfilled by pragmatic tagging (as outlined in the next principle). The annotation of a corpus (by means of tagging, parsing, etc) is needed in order to prepare it to be useful for further linguistic purposes.

Fourthly, there is a need 'to classify text samples according to those typological categories determined to be sociolinguistically significant': this relates to the first and third principles and presupposes some prior classification of texts by whatever criteria can be shown to be sociolinguistically significant. This principle is also related to the wider issue of resolving the traditional divide regarding linguistic and encyclopedic knowledge. Pragmatic knowledge is an essential part of the lexicon's task of relating the word to its use in context: for this reason, texts gathered should detail the correspondence between two parties, rather than mere forms (for instance, bank application forms for the purchase of bank drafts, pay-in slips for cash/cheque deposits, etc).

Fifthly, the corpus should be processed for its lexical content and then 'transformed' into a lexicon that can eventually be made available to various professionals and learners by virtue of its reusability. A first step towards this objective is to store the corpus in a computational format;

Sixthly, using the corpus as a lexical resource means a need to store and organise such a corpus-derived lexicon into a lexical data/knowledge base: such issues were detailed in Chapter 5.

In the case of the PROLEX corpus, an adherence to these principles means that there was a need to ensure that this corpus was collected during a given period; that the texts collected reflected the form of letters written to certain local and multi-national organisations which had been chosen carefully on a prior assessment of their prominence and reputation in Singapore's business circle; that, in the context of a second-language English situation such as Singapore (with its developing variety of Singapore English), it was necessary to make sure that the corpus reflected, say, letters written by educated speakers, not learners: hence, the title of this project (PROLEX) emphasises the Business profession. Further, it is not unusual to find a few minor typographical errors in the corpus, but they should be tagged as such.

In order to give a flavour of the form of the texts in PROLEX, Figure 6.2 contains a number of sample texts extracted from the corpus. For this purpose, I have chosen to use a version of the PROLEX corpus which has been pragmatically-tagged (see Section 6.9 for an explanation of the pragmatic codes contained within angled brackets):[1]

<n 013><s 7><x 1><a 2><p 1>dear sirs
<p 4>re : overdue account
<p 2/1/3>according to our records, the following bills are over-due for payment :{list}
<p 2/2/3><a 3>if payment for the above-mentioned bills have somehow been overlooked, we would be most grateful if you would now forward your cheque in settlement of the total outstanding. if you have any reason for non-payment of, or any query regarding the above account, please do not hesitate to contact us.
<p 2/f/3>kindly ignore this letter if you have already mailed your cheque to us.
<p 3>yours faithfully

<n 019><c 2><a 2><x 1><s 7><p1>dear sirs
<p 2/1/3>referring to your account which is now slightly past due, <a 3>we hope that you will consider this just a routine courtesy reminder and that we may hear from you soon.
<p 2/2/3>if <e +> you <e -> cheque is on the way, please ignore this reminder.
<p 2/f/3><a 3>thanking you in advance for your prompt attention.
<p 3>yours sincerely

<n 020><a 1><p 1>dear sir
<p 2/1/3>you may have overlooked our statements and earlier reminder requesting for settlement of your account which is now considerably past due.
<p 2/2/3><a 2> please note that our credit policy requires all statements be paid in full within 30 days on presentation. <a 3> may we hear from you by return mail within the next ten days.
<p 2/f/3>thanking you in advance for your prompt attention.
<p 3>yours sincerely

<n 021><a 1><p 1>dear sir
<p 2/1/2>we refer to our previous reminders regarding your outstanding account and <a 2>regret that you still have not responded to our request for payment.
<p 2/f/2><a 3>please arrange to remit us your cheque in full settlement within seven days upon receipt of this letter or we will have no alternative, but to cancel your credit privileges with our hotel.
<p 3>yours sincerely

<n 022><a 1><p 1>dear sir
<p 2/1/2>we refer to our previous reminders regarding your above long outstanding account and <a 2>regret that you still have not responded to our request for payment.
<p 2/f/2><a 3> please note that unless your account is settled within seven days upon receipt of this letter, we will have no alternative, but to refer this matter to our lawyer for legal action to be taken against you. take notice that you will also be liable to pay for the legal costs of such proceedings.
<p 3>yours sincerely

Figure 6.2 Sample texts from the PROLEX corpus

6.2.1 The PROLEX Lexicon

Even without concordancing the PROLEX corpus for the lexeme *account*, one can note the progression of a harsher, more insistent demand for settlement of the account concerned in the sample text (Fig 6.2) above. The series of letters first begins with reference to the 'overdue' account, and moving progressively to 'slightly past due' account, 'considerably past due' account, 'outstanding' account, and finally 'long outstanding' account.

However, a concordance listing is necessary in order to show systematically the use of the lexical item: the following (edited and shortened) concordance listing obtains for the lexeme *account* (see Figure 6.3):

```
1.  ...fully, n013. dear sirs, re : overdue   [[account]] according to our records, the
2.  ...nt of, or any query regarding the above [[account]], please do not hesitate to contact us....
3.  ...y, n019. dear sirs, referring to your   [[account]] which is now slightly past due, we hop...
4.  ...nder requesting for settlement of your  [[account]] which is now considerably past due. p...
5.  ...s reminders regarding your outstanding   [[account]] and regret that you still have not res...
6.  ... regarding your above long outstanding    [[account]] and regret that you still have not res...
7.  ... payment. please note that unless your    [[account]] is settled within seven days upon rece...
8.  ...nge to remit us a cheque to clear this   [[account]] at your earliest convenience. we apolo...
9.  ...faithfully, n047. dear sir / madam,      [[account]] number {number}. your account has beco...
10. ... madam, account number {number}. your    [[account]] has become overdrawn to the extent of
11. . cheque number {number} for $ {amount};   [[account]] no: {number} . please note that we have
12. ...s there are insufficient funds in your   [[account]] to meet it. in addition, your account ...
13. ... account to meet it. in addition, your   [[account]] has been debited with ${amount} being ...
14. ...ingapore. the present balance of your    [[account]] is ${amount} and we shall be pleased if...
15. ... are insufficient cleared funds in your  [[account]] to meet them to be most unsatisfactor...
16. ...ternative but to ask you to close your   [[account]]. yours faithfully, n051. dear sir / ...
17. ..madam, cheque number for ${amount};      [[account]] number {number} please note that we
18. ...s there are insufficient funds in your   [[account]] to meet it. in addition, your account ...
19. ... account to meet it. in addition, your   [[account]] has been debited with ${amount} being ...
20. ...singapore. the present balance of your   [[account]] is $ {amount} and we trust you will pa...
21. ...legraphic transfer through {cname}, for  [[account]] of {cname} branch singapore, for cred...
22. ...ranch singapore, for credit of {name}    [[account]] number {cname} to advise {cname} vide
23. ...tal invoice amount in us${amount}. the   [[account]] receivable represented by this invoice ...
24. ...graphic transfer to {blank}, new york    [[account]] number {number}. regards, n113. {bla...
25. ...tal invoice amount in us${amount}. the   [[account]] receivable represented by this invoice ...
26. ... comma {blank}, new york, new york       [[account]] number {number} . please confirm recei...
27. ...ame day funds to {blank}, new york for   [[account]] of {blank}, international division (a...
28. ...t of {blank}, international division      [[account]] number {number}). the above is for par...
29. ...l invoice amount in us$: {amount}. the   [[account]] receivable represented by this invoice ...
30. ...he letter of credit are to be for the    [[account]] of openers and the letter of credit is ...
31. ...] [tanjong] pagar will be for {blank}    [[account]]. please advise documentation instructi...
32. ...of {number} barrels gasoil in {cname}'s  [[account]] to {blank} on {blank},{blank}, thereby...
33. ...as well as in new york are for buyers    [[account]]; payment in {blank} days from bill of ...
34. ... receipt figure at will be for {blank}   [[account]]. kindly acknowledge regards n153. yo...
35. ...documents have been prepared as {blank}  [[account]] instead of {blank} account {blank}. ...
36. ...as {blank} account instead of {blank}    [[account]] {blank}. in view of above, {blank} has...
37. ...{blank},{blank}, new york for credit of  [[account]] {number}. the letter of credit shall ...
38. ...the letter of credit are to be for the   [[account]] of openers and the letter of credit is ...
39. ...ter of credit shall not be for seller's  [[account]]. quality / quantity: shall be based on...
40. ... branch where you usually maintain your  [[account]], at your earliest convenience. we ar...
41. ...t to the branch where you maintain your  [[account]]. following our first {cname_obj} servi...
42. ...k; request a statement for your current  [[account]]; change your secret personal number an...
```

```
43. …leeps, through your savings or current  [[account]] [which] can be operated 24 hours a day,…
44. …eived since its inception. all personal  [[account]] holders of {cname} group are welcome t…
45. …umber} drawn on {cname}; debit current   [[account]]; debit {cname} branch account; debit …
46. … current account; debit {cname} branch   [[account]]; debit issuing bank account. yours fa…
47. …me} branch account; debit issuing bank    [[account]]. yours faithfully, n217. dear sirs, …
48. …with, please honour to the debit of our   [[account]] under advice to us. upon receipt of r…
49. …ith, please honour to the debit of our    [[account]] under advice to us. yours faithfully, …
50. …lloted by you) in favour of {blank} for    [[account]] of {blank} to the extent of candf (us…
51. …nking charges outside singapore are for    [[account]] of beneficiary. 10 per cent more or 1…
52. … open irrevocable credit favour {blank}    [[account]] {number}. amount covering motorcycle …
53. …e credit {blank} favour {cname} osaka      [[account]] covering yen {amount}. free on board j…
54. …ursement requests to the debit of our      [[account]] with you. your reimbursement charges a…
55. … your reimbursement charges are for our    [[account]]. yours faithfully, n225. dear sir, …
56. …ity to pay, avoiding duplication; your      [[account]] credited on {blank}. see attached ad…
57. …umber if any; the beneficiary's name /      [[account]] number is not on our file. please ins…
58. …are required; beneficiary(ies) paid /       [[account]] credited on {date}. see attached advice…
59. …stated discrepancies will be for your       [[account]]. kindly indicate your approval / disa…
60. …ttlement, we authorise you to debit our     [[account]] with the sum of ${amount} which inclu…
```

Figure 6.3 Concordance listing of *account*, from the PROLEX corpus, generated using *MonoConc for Windows* (see Appendix B)

A cursory glance at this concordanced listing shows a number of codes used in the corpus. These codes have come about because of the following: as a condition for obtaining their sensitive material, certain organisations requested that they should not be identified. For this reason, in the PROLEX corpus, the abbreviation {cname}, enclosed in curly brackets, is used as a substitute for names of companies/institutions whose names may not be disclosed for reasons of confidentiality. In turn, {cname_obj} is used to denote the name of the company product concerned. {Blank} is used to delete sensitive person's names or account numbers. {Lname} is a composite term for a person's last name in order to maintain authorial anonymity. Similarly, ${amt} is used as a substitute for the actual sum of money transacted. There are also (self-explanatory) terms such as {date} and {city} in the corpus.

In examining this listing, there are at least two main senses of the lexeme *account* in the PROLEX corpus: the settlement of an account with either an organisation or more specifically, a bank. In both cases, there does seem to be a syntactic co-occurrence structure governing the lexeme. Using Sinclair's theory (see Chapter 3), we may say that there is a semantic prosody of equilibrium, one which the account is supposed to be in. The prosody thus gives rise to a semantic preference expressed as verbs such as *debit, regarding, maintain, credit* and noun phrases such as *settlement of* and *insufficient funds in* sometimes before (pre-) and at other times after (post-) the core lexical item. There is also a colligation favouring such determiner pronouns as *your, our, the, these* and a collocation of *current, outstanding, personal* etc. The choice of an item does not come by chance but reflects the state of equilibrium that the account is perceived to be in. More will be said about this lexeme, and others, in Section 6.11.

6.3 THE PROCOMPARE CORPUS

Since the PROLEX corpus is manifestly small, a way to check any inadequacy that might arise in its linguistic coverage of the domain of Business English would be to compare it with another similar corpus. In this section, I also detail the PROCOMPARE corpus which was used as a control, providing a comparison with the PROLEX corpus.

The process of gathering and compiling a corpus is a time-consuming task. I therefore began to search for another existing corpus of business English texts, ideally, one of a comparable size. The only one that bore a remote resemblance to such a corpus, as far as I could gather was the following, found in a supplement to *PC-Shareware Magazine*:

> Over 600 sample business letters and legal forms are included for your boilerplating. All are in plain ASCII text for inclusion and customisation in your word processor. Most are quite short. Includes Accounting, Business, Legal, Employee, Product order, Sales letters, and some common forms. A complete index is also provided.
>
> (PC-Shareware 1992: 28)

At first sight, these 'boilerplates' purport to show how the various subparts of Business communication take place: presumably these are frames which purport to provide a range of stereotypes or scenarios of how Business English works. Since each text has been specifically referred to as a 'boilerplate', the templates, as it were, suggest (perhaps in a simplistic way) that all that is required for being a successful Business English writer is to choose, from the index, a text that best describes the situation and then customise the text by just filling in the blank spaces provided.

The various files have been merged into a large file, totalling approximately 60 thousand words, which is similar to that of the PROLEX corpus. These texts might also constitute a 'corpus', that is, the more this data is analysed and found to characterise Business English, the more it can claim to be a sublanguage corpus. Since the question of representativeness depends partly on the aims for which the data has been gathered, very little (unfortunately) is known of the source, apart from the publisher's blurb that has been noted.

As in Section 6.2 where I give a flavour of the form of the texts in the PROLEX corpus, Figure 6.4 contains a number of sample texts extracted for *account* from the PROCOMPARE corpus.

Text 1
Dear
We feel that there must be a reason why you haven't answered
any of our inquiries about your overdue account in the amount
of $
If there is a problem regarding the enclosed bill, won't you
please telephone me at the above number, so that we can

discuss the situation. Whatever the source of the problem is,
we are in the dark until we hear from you.
If this has been an oversight, please use the enclosed envelope
to mail us a check for the full amount today.
Thank you for your anticipated cooperation in the prompt
handling of this matter.

Text 2
Dear

Would you believe that we simply detest writing letters
such as this one? We know that you certainly can't enjoy
hearing from us under these circumstances.
I am, of course, referring to the fact that your account
has fallen very far behind.
We want you to remain a customer of ours, to continue to
buy our merchandise, and to know when we are planning an
outstanding sale.
What do you say? Can we hear from you today?
We are so anxious that we even placed a stamp on the
envelope for your remittance.
If you are unable to send us the payment, please give me
a call at the above telephone number. Thank you.

Text 3
Dear

It is because we do not want you to experience unnecessary
embarrassment, that we are writing this letter to you.
As we have reminded you, your account is past due and I am
sorry to inform you that if you were to present your charge
card at our store today, our sales personnel could not
accept the charge without an okay from the credit
department. This would necessitate your going to the credit
department to discuss the status of your bill before the
charge would be approved.
You have been too good of a customer in the past to have to
go through this procedure, but unless we receive your payment
we have no other alternative, due to our company policy.
We have enclosed a self-addressed envelope for your
convenience and are requesting that you please mail us your
payment today. Thank you for your anticipated cooperation.

Figure 6.4 Sample texts from the PROCOMPARE corpus

Since the source of the PROCOMPARE corpus is not known, one way to understand it better is to compare it with the PROLEX corpus in the manner of Halliday and Hassan (1985). This involves an examination of the register, which, as preceding sections in this chapter have noted, can be defined as a diatypic variety, 'a variety [of a language] according to use' (Halliday and Hasan 1985: 41). The register is characterised by the field, mode, and tenor of discourse. Where the field of discourse of this variety is concerned, we may say that both the PROCOMPARE and the PROLEX corpora concern the exchange of written business communication between two parties in order to effect a business transaction or for the parties to communicate regarding some business matter. Where the tenor of discourse is concerned, it would also certainly seem that the PROCOMPARE texts achieve the feeling of relative informality through (for instance) the use of contractions (e.g. Text 1, *haven't* and *won't*) and simpler lexical items (e.g. Text 3, *okay* instead of *approval*), as well as a more frequent use of the second person pronoun. However, in adopting the strategy of sounding more personal – perhaps hoping to win the addressee's cooperation as well as take less reading time – the PROCOMPARE texts do also seem more formulaic (e.g. *you*, the second person pronoun, is blankly used, without referring specifically to any addressee). By so doing, they arguably have the advantage of being more generally applicable. On the other hand, the PROLEX texts are more specific in intent, since both addresser and addressee are known. Also, the PROLEX texts are more specific in content, and so perhaps give a clearer indication of what the business profession do actually write about. Perhaps because they are less formulaic, the strategy adopted is such that the cooperation of the addressee is obtained by not adopting a patronising tone of voice. Where the mode of discourse is concerned, both types of texts are generally written to be read.

The register or genre of business correspondence tends towards a standard dialect (in the sense of a variety of language, as used by Halliday and Hasan 1985). The PROLEX texts are more indicative of the British variety (since Singapore adopts Standard British English as the model), whereas the PROCOMPARE ones are more American (e.g. in Text 1, 'check' is used for 'cheque'). Also, in some of the other PROCOMPARE texts, the dates used suggest that these texts were written/collected in the early eighties, which is similar to that for the PROLEX corpus.

A related notion to dialect and diatype is that of **contextual configuration** (Section 6.1; Halliday and Hasan 1985: 55–56). We may view the PROLEX and PROCOMPARE texts as part of the genre or register of Business English because they conform to the business letter format, i.e. Salutation, Body, Complimentary Close, etc. However, what precisely characterises the contextual configurational structure of business English – the dynamics between its obligatory and optional elements – falls outside the remit of this book, although it constitutes an inviting field of research (see Ghadessy (ed.)

1993). The computer might assist in such a field of research, since, for instance, at a later stage when semantic and pragmatic tagging methods are more refined, a content analysis (in the sense of Wilson and Rayson 1993; Rayson and Wilson 1996) of these two corpora might assist in the yielding of such obligatory and optional elements more automatically.

6.3.1 The PROCOMPARE lexicon

A cursory reading of the sample texts in Figure 6.4 shows similar progression in the need to achieve equilibrium for the lexeme *account*. The series of letters notes that the lexeme is *overdue, fallen very far behind,* and *past due.* The 'threats', as it were, to enforce this equilibrium are dispersed throughout the letter, as in the case of the PROLEX corpus, but remain part of the semantic prosody for equilibrium. Figure 6.5 provides an edited and shortened concordance for the lexeme *account.*

```
1. ...merchandise and issue a credit to your    [[account]] in the amount of $ .
2. PROFILE AND PRESENCE IN                       [[ACCOUNT]] INVENTORY:____
4. ...current balance in the above referenced    [[account]] is $ Since this amount does not agree ...
5. .... Dear Thank you for opening an            [[account]] with our company. As one of the leade...
6. ...and conditions for maintaining an open     [[account]] with our firm. Invoices are payable wi...
7. ... you may have regarding your new           [[account]]. I can be reached at the above number....
8. ... We wish to thank you for your valued      [[account]] and know that you will understand the ...
9. ... will be credited to the customer's        [[account]]. At the time of our service call we w...
20. ... the undersigned warrants that said       [[account]][s] are just and due and the undersigne...
27. Re: Loan #_____or Savings            [[Account]] #_____, I hereby authorize re
2_____ Savings                   [[Account]]: Date Opened_____ Present
29. ...ure. Dear A review of your loan            [[account]] indicates that you have had three chec...
30. .pleasure to notify you that a charge        [[account]] has been approved in your name. We we...
31. ..enjoy the convenience of your charge       [[account]]. We have established a credit limit ...
32. ...have established a credit limit on your   [[account]] in the amount of $ At such tim...
33. ...to shop with us. Dear My charge            [[account]]with your company is currently held in ...
34. ... change the name and address on my         [[account]] to the following: A...
35. ...t to the following:                         [[Account]] Number: Name: ...
36. ...ou that we are unable to open a charge     [[account]]for you at present due to information o...
37. ... that we will be able to open a charge     [[account]] for you some time in the future. Th...
38. ...reviewed your application for open         [[account]] terms, and at this time are unable to ...
39. ... and at this time are unable to open an    [[account]] for your company. Should circumstance...
40. ... After careful review of your charge       [[account]], it pleases us to inform you that we h...
41. ...IT: $ Furthermore, this change in          [[account]] status qualifies you for use of our in...
42. ...alifies you for use of our installment     [[account]]. Should you require additional inform...
43. ... additional information about this new      [[account]], please see one of our credit represen...
44. ... is our pleasure to inform you that an      [[account]] has been opened for your company. P...
45. ...ompany. Please feel free to use your        [[account]] as often as you wish. A descriptive br...
46. ...e terms and conditions upon which this      [[account]] has been opened. Should your credit ...
47. ... have any questions regarding your new      [[account]], call this office and ask to speak to ...
48. ... office and ask to speak to one of our      [[account]] representatives. When you call, please...
49. ...tives. When you call, please have your      [[account]] number available, in order that we mig...
50. ...nsibility for prompt payment in full of     [[account]]. If materials are ordered to be deli...
51. ... Date: _                                    [[Account]] Name _ Street _ City _ ...
52. ..._ State _                                   [[Account]] Status: Current $_ 30 Days ...
53. ... Comment or agreement for payment from      [[account]]: _ Recommended action: _ ...
```

```
54. … have your latest instructions on this   [[account]]? We ask this because collection has be…
55. … Debtor judgment-proof; 5. Claims          [[account]] is paid recovery doubtful B….
56. … 17. Claims returned merchandise E.        [[ACCOUNT]] CLOSED: on _____  …
57. …f our reminders advising you that your     [[account]] has fallen seriously behind. We are …
58. …ending the date for our payment of the     [[account]] until [date] This will enable us t…
59. …the seller of any claim for damages on     [[account]] of the condition, quality, or grade of …
60. …ify seller of any claim for damages on     [[account]] of the condition, grade or quality of t…
```

Figure 6.5 Concordance listing of account, from the PROCOMPARE corpus, generated using *Monoconc for Windows* (see Appendix B)

Although this concordance, like the others in this chapter, has been pruned for reasons of space, a more general frame of expectations, as it were, obtains for the use of the lexeme *account*. The lexeme has to be customised in order to suit one's needs: for instance, there is a general reference to a 'said' account, which does not occur in the PROLEX corpus; there are also more blank spaces to be filled in by the addresser of the template text. However, as in the use of the term in the PROLEX lexicon, one can still see Sinclair's framework being applicable to the 'semi-packaged' way of using this term: 'payment' can be made to ('credit') and from it ('debit') in order to maintain the semantic prosody of equilibrium.

Further discussion of both the PROCOMPARE and PROLEX lexemes will be made in Section 6.11. In the following sub-sections, I shall outline the pre-processing undertaken with respect to these corpora.

6.4 CORPUS TAGGING

As indicated in Section 4.4, part-of-speech tagging has been the most successful corpus annotation scheme to date: a number of taggers are available for researchers to annotate their texts. In this connection, I have chosen to use the CLAWS[2] program (Garside et al. 1987; Black and Leech (eds) 1993) for tagging the PROLEX and PROCOMPARE corpora. This annotation involves 'assigning to each word in a text an unambiguous indication of the grammatical class to which this word belongs in this context' (Garside 1987: 30). Of course, while manual tagging is possible in principle, in practice the tagging of a sizeable corpus is feasible only if done automatically: this ensures not only speed but consistency of tagging practice.

Using the same texts as in Figure 6.2 for illustration, Figure 6.6 contains an edited version of the output and indicates the success with which CLAWS was able to perform the analysis: while there is a high degree of accuracy in the system, some mistakes are made and so human post-editing is needed, following a set of guidelines.

<n 013>
dear_JJ sirs_NNS2

re_II :_: overdue_JJ account_NN1

according_II21 to_II22 our_APP$ records_NN2 ,_, the_AT following_JJ
bills_NN2 are_VBR overdue_JJ for_IF payment_NN1 :_: list_NN1

if_CS payment_NN1 for_IF the_AT above-mentioned_JJ bills_NN2 have_VH0
somehow_RR been_VBN overlooked_VVN ,_, we_PPIS2 would_VM be_VBI most_RGT
grateful_JJ if_CS you_PPY would_VM now_RT forward_RL your_APP$ cheque_NN1
in_II settlement_NN1 of_IO the_AT total_JJ outstanding._NNU if_CS you_PPY
have_VH0 any_DD reason_NN1 for_IF non-payment_NN1 of_IO ,_, or_CC any_DD
query_NN1 regarding_II the_AT above_JB account_NN1 ,_, please_RR do_VD0 not_XX
hesitate_VVI to_TO contact_VVI us._NNU

kindly_RR ignore_VV0 this_DD1 letter_NN1 if_CS you_PPY have_VH0 already_RR
mailed_VVD your_APP$ cheque_NN1 to_II us._NNU

yours_PP$ faithfully_RR

<n 019>
dear_JJ sirs_NNS2

referring_VVG to_II your_APP$ account_NN1 which_DDQ is_VBZ now_RT
slightly_RR past_II due_JJ ,_, we_PPIS2 hope_VV0 that_CST you_PPY will_VM
consider_VVI this_DD1 just_RR a_AT1 routine_JJ courtesy_JJ reminder_NN1 and_CC
that_CST we_PPIS2 may_VM hear_VVI from_II you_PPY soon._NNU

if_CS you_PPY cheque_NN1 is_VBZ on_II the_AT way_NN1 ,_, please_RR
ignore_VV0 this_DD1 reminder._NNU thanking_VVG you_PPY in_II advance_NN1
for_IF your_APP$ prompt_JJ attention._NNU

yours_PP$ sincerely_RR

<n 020>
dear_JJ sir_NNS1

you_PPY may_VM have_VHI overlooked_VVD our_APP$ statements_NN2 and_CC
earlier_RRR reminder_VV0 requesting_VVG for_IF settlement_NN1 of_IO your_APP$
account_NN1 which_DDQ is_VBZ now_RT considerably_RR past_II due._NNU

please_RR note_VV0 that_CST our_APP$ credit_NN1 policy_NN1 requires_VVZ
all_DB statements_NN2 be_VBI paid_VVN in_RR21 full_RR22 within_II 30_MC
days_NNT2 on_II presentation._NNU may_VM we_PPIS2 hear_VV0 from_II you_PPY
by_II return_JB mail_NN1 within_II the_AT next_MD ten_MC days._NNU

thanking_VVG you_PPY in_II advance_NN1 for_IF your_APP$
prompt_JJ attention._NNU

yours_PP$ sincerely_RR

<n 021>
dear_JJ sir_NNS1

we_PPIS2 refer_VV0 to_II our_APP$ previous_JJ reminders_NN2 regarding_II your_APP$ outstanding_JJ account_NN1 and_CC regret_VV0 that_CST you_PPY still_RR have_VH0 not_XX responded_VVN to_II our_APP$ request_NN1 for_IF payment._NNU

please_RR arrange_VV0 to_TO remit_VVI us_PPIO2 your_APP$ cheque_NN1 in_RR21 full_RR22 settlement_NN1 within_II seven_MC days_NNT2 upon_II receipt_NN1 of_IO this_DD1 letter_NN1 or_CC we_PPIS2 will_VM have_VHI no_AT alternative_NN1 ,_,but_CCB to_TO cancel_VVI your_APP$ credit_NN1 privileges_VVZ with_IW our_APP$ hotel._NNU

yours_PP$ sincerely_RR

<n 022>
dear_JJ sir_NNS1

we_PPIS2 refer_VV0 to_II our_APP$ previous_JJ reminders_NN2 regarding_II your_APP$ above_JB long_JJ outstanding_JJ account_NN1 and_CC regret_VV0 that_CST you_PPY still_RR have_VH0 not_XX responded_VVN to_II our_APP$ request_NN1 for_IF payment._NNU

please_RR note_VV0 that_CST unless_CS your_APP$ account_NN1 is_VBZ settled_VVN within_II seven_MC days_NNT2 upon_II receipt_NN1 of_IO this_DD1 letter_NN1 ,_, we_PPIS2 will_VM have_VHI no_AT alternative_NN1 ,_, but_CCB to_TO refer_VVI this_DD1 matter_NN1 to_II our_APP$ lawyer_NN1 for_IF legal_JJ action_NN1 to_TO be_VBI taken_VVN against_II you._NNU take_VV0 notice_NN1 that_CST you_PPY will_VM also_RR be_VBI liable_JJ to_TO pay_VVI for_IF the_AT legal_JJ costs_NN2 of_IO such_DA proceedings._NNU

yours_PP$ sincerely_RR

Figure 6.6 Sample CLAWS output (uncorrected) for PROLEX texts on the lexeme *account*

Some of the more common tags used in this scheme include the following: APP$ = possessive pronoun, pre-nominal; AT=article; CC=coordinating conjunction; CSA=*as* as conjunction; JJ=general adjective; MC=cardinal number; NN=common noun; NN1=singular common noun; NN2=plural common noun; NNJ=organization noun; NNT2=plural temporal noun; NNU=unit of measurement; PPIS2=*we*; RR=general adverb;VB0=base form 'be'; VBDZ=*was;* VBN=*been*; VBR=are; VVD=past tense of lexical verb; VVG=-ing participle of lexical verb;VVN=past participle of lexical verb.

6.5 CORPUS (SYNTACTIC) PARSING

It is important to note that grammatical tagging is only part of a larger enterprise. Another method of processing the corpora involves the syntactic analysis (or parsing) of a corpus: from a parsed corpus, it is possible to retrieve information about more abstract grammatical categories which cannot be specified in terms of words or word-classes, for example, types of phrases or clauses. With parsing, one could automatically extract, for instance, valency information which would not be possible with just tagging.

Following this rationale, an attempt has been made to parse the texts using Sharman's experimental ID/LP[3] parser, which does the tagging and parsing at the same time (Sharman 1989b). Sharman's parser, using a probabilistic ID/LP grammar, 'has the capability to parse any sentence of English, although it would not expect to do well on genres which are dissimilar to the Associated Press (corpus)' (Sharman, 9). Furthermore, Sharman reports that while 'initial reports indicate that tagging accuracy is quite good ... parsing accuracy is less good' (Sharman, 10).

Using the same texts as in Figure 6.2, Figure 6.7 gives the output from the parser. It also contains the form of the texts required by the parser: sentence numbers are inserted before each sentence, the texts converted to mixed upper-lower case, and unwanted lines removed.

N001
{N Dear_NP1 Sirs_NN1 N}
N002
{? ?}
N003
{S {P According_II {Tg to_II Tg} P} {N our_APP$ records_NN2 N} ,_, {N the_AT {X following_JJ X} bills_NN2 N} {V are_VBR {N overdue_JJ {P for_IF {N payment_NN1 N} P} N} :_: V} S}
N004
{Fn If_CS {N payment_NN1 {P for_IF {N the_AT above-mentioned_NN1 bills_NN2 N} P} {X have_VH0 somehow_RR X} N} {V been_VBN overlooked_VVN V} ,_, {S we_PPIS2 {V would_VM be_VB0 {N most_DA grateful_JJ N} {Fa if_CS {N you_PPY N} {V would_VM now_RT {N forward_NN1 N} V} Fa} {N your_APP$ cheque_NN1 {P in_II {N settlement_NN1 {P of_IO {N the_AT total_NN1 outstanding_JJ N} P} N} P} N} V} ._. S} Fn}
N005
{? ?}
N006
{S {N Kindly_NN1 N} ignore_VV0 {N this_DD letter_NN1 {Fr if_CS {N you_PPY N} Fr} N} {V have_VH0 {X already_RR mailed_VVN {Ti {N your_APP$ cheque_NN1 N} to_TO Ti} X} {N us_PPIO2 N} V} ._. S}
N007
{N yours_PP faithfully_NN1 N}
N008
{N Dear_NP1 Sirs_NN1 N}
N008
{S {N Referring_NN1 {P to_II P} N} {N your_APP$ account_NN1 which_DD N} {V

is_VBZ now_RT {X slightly_RR past_JB due_JJ X} V} ,_, we_PPIS2 {V hope_VV0 {Fn that_CS {N you_PPY N} {V will_VM consider_VV0 {N this_DD N} V} just_RR {N a_AT routine_JJ courtesy_NN1 reminder_NN1 N} and_CC that_CS {N we_PPIS2 {V may_VM hear_VV0 {P from_II {N you_PPY N} P} V} N} soon_RR Fn} V} ._. S}
N009
{S {Fa If_CS {N your_APP$ cheque_NN1 N} {V is_VBZ {P on_II {N the_AT way_NN1 N} P} V} Fa} ,_, {X please_RR ignore_VV0 {N this_DD reminder_NN1 N} X} ._. S}
N009
{S {V {N Thanking_NN1 you_PPY N} {P in_II {N advance_NN1 {P for_IF {N your_APP$ prompt_JJ attemtion_NN1 N} P} N} P} V} ._. S}
N010
{N yours_PP sincerely_NN1 N}
N011
{N Dear_NP1 Sir_NNS N}
N011
{S {N You_PPY N} {V may_VM have_VH0 overlooked_VVN {N our_APP$ statements_NN2 {X and_CC earlier_RRR X} reminder_NN1 N} requesting_VVG {P for_IF {N settlement_NN1 {P of_IO {N your_APP$ account_NN1 which_DD N} P} N} P} is_VBZ now_RT {X considerably_RR past_JB due_JJ X} V} ._. S}
N011
{S {N Please_NN1 note_NN1 {Fn that_CS {N our_APP$ credit_NN1 policy_NN1 N} {V requires_VVZ {N all_DB statements_NN2 N} be_VB0 V} Fn} N} {V paid_VVD {P in_II {N full_JJ {P within_II {N 30_MC days_NNT {P on_II {N presentation_NN1 N} P} N} P} N} P} V} ._. S}
N011
{S {V May_NPD1 {N we_PPIS2 N} hear_VV0 {P from_II {N you_PPY N} P} {P by_II {N return_NN1 mail_NN1 {P within_II {N the_AT next_MD ten_MC days_NNT N} P} N} P} V} ._. S}
N012
{S {V {N Thanking_NN1 you_PPY N} {P in_II {N advance_NN1 {P for_IF {N your_APP$ prompt_JJ attention_NN1 N} P} N} P} V} ._. S}
N013
{N yours_PP sincerely_NN1 N}
N014
{N Dear_NP1 Sir_NNS N}
N015
{S We_PPIS2 {V {Ti refer_VV0 to_TO {N our_APP$ previous_JJ reminders_NN1 {P regarding_II {N your_APP$ outstanding_JJ account_NN1 N} P} N} Ti} and_CC regret_VV0 {Fn that_CS {N you_PPY N} still_RR {V have_VH0 not_XX responded_VVD {Ti to_TO {N our_APP$ request_NN1 {P for_IF {N payment_NN1 N} P} N} Ti} V} Fn} V} ._. S}
N016
{Fn {N Please_NN1 {Ti arrange_VV0 to_TO Ti} {P remit_II {N us_PPIO2 N} P} N} {N your_APP$ cheque_NN1 {P in_II {N full_JJ settlement_NN1 {P within_II {N seven_MC days_NNT {P upon_II {N receipt_NN1 {P of_IO {N this_DD letter_NN1 N} P} N} P} N} P} N} P} N} P} N} or_CC {S we_PPIS2 {V will_VM have_VH0 {N no_AT

alternative_NN1 N} V} ,_, {V but_CC {Ti to_TO cancel_VV0 {N your_APP$ credit_NN1 priveleges_NN1 {P with_IW {N our_APP$ hotel_NN1 N} P} N} Ti} V} ._. S} Fn}

N017

{N yours_PP sincerely_NN1 N}

N018

{N Dear_NP1 Sir_NNS N}

N019

{S We_PPIS2 {V refer_VV0 {Ti to_TO {N our_APP$ previous_JJ reminders_NN1 {P regarding_II {N your_APP$ {X above_II long_RR outstanding_JJ account_NN1 and_CC regret_VV0 {Fn that_CS {N you_PPY N} still_RR {V have_VH0 not_XX responded_VVD V} Fn} X} N} P} N} to_TO {N our_APP$ request_NN1 {P for_IF {N payment_NN1 N} P} N} Ti} V} ._. S}

N020

{Ti {N Please_NN1 note_NN1 {Fn that_CS unless_CS {N your_APP$ account_NN1 N} {V is_VBZ settled_VVN {P within_II {N seven_MC days_NNT {P upon_II {N receipt_NN1 {P of_IO {N this_DD letter_NN1 N} P} N} P} N} P} V} ,_, {N we_PPIS2 N} {V will_VM have_VH0 {N no_AT alternative_NN1 N} V} ,_, but_CC Fn} N} to_TO refer_VV0 {N this_DD matter_NN1 N} to_TO {N our_APP$ lawyer_NN1 {P for_IF {N legal_JJ action_NN1 N} P} N} to_TO Ti}

N021

{S {V Take_VV0 notice_VV0 {Fn that_CS {N {X you_PPY will_VM also_RR be_VB0 liable_JJ {Ti to_TO pay_VV0 {P for_IF {N the_AT legal_JJ costs_NN2 {P of_IO {N such_DA N} P} N} P} Ti} X} proceedings_NN2 N} Fn} V} ._. S}

N022

{N yours_PP sincerely_NN1 N}

Figure 6.7 Sample parser output for PROLEX texts on the lexeme *account*

The ID/LP Parser uses the following non-terminal categories treebank (see Leech and Garside 1991; Black and Leech 1993): *Fa* (adverbial clause), *Fc* (comparative clause), *Fn* (noun clause), *Fr* (relative clause), *G* (genitive), *J* (adjective phrase), *N* (noun phrase), *Nr* (temporal adverbial noun phrase), *Nv* (non-temporal adverbial noun phrase), *P* (prepositional phrase), *S* (sentence), *Tg* (-ing clause), *Ti* (to-infinitive clause), *Tn* (past participle clause , *V* (verb phrase), *?null* (unlabelled constituent). In addition, the symbols *&* and *+* respectively represent initial and non-initial conjuncts of a coordinate construction.

If human post-editing of these texts is done using these treebank conventions, the following corrected version is obtained. Figure 6.8 shows the corrections in bold:

N001
{S {N Dear_JJ Sirs_NNS2 N} S}
N002
{? ?}
N003
{S {P According_II to_II {N our_APP$ records_NN2 N} P} ,_, {N the_AT following_JJ bills_NN2 N} {V are_VBR {J overdue_JJ {P for_IF {N payment_NN1 N} P} J} :_:V} S}
N004
{S {Fa If_CS {N payment_NN1 {P for_IF {N the_AT above-mentioned_JJ bills_NN2 N} P} N} {V have_VH0 somehow_RR been_VBN overlooked_VVN V} Fa} ,_, {N we_PPIS2 N} {V would_VM be_VB0 {J most_RR grateful_JJ J} {Fa if_CS {N you_PPY N} {V would_VM now_RT forward_VV0 {N your_APP$ cheque_NN1 N} {P in_II {N settlement_NN1 {P of_IO {N the_AT total_NN1 outstanding_JJ N} P} N} P} V} Fa} ._. S}
N005
{? ?}
N006
{S Kindly_RR {V ignore_VV0 {N this_DD letter_NN1 N} {Fa if_CS {N you_PPY N} {V have_VH0 already_RR mailed_VVN {N your_APP$ cheque_NN1 N} {P to_II {N us_PPIO2 N} P} V} Fa} V} ._. S}
N007
{S {N yours_PP N} faithfully_RR N} S}
N008
{S {N Dear_JJ Sirs_NNS2 N} S}
N008
{S {Tg Referring_NN1 {P to_II {N your_APP$ account_NN1 {Fr {N which_WP N} {V is_VBZ now_RT {J slightly_RR past_II due_JJ J} V} Fr} Tg} ,_, {N we_PPIS2 N} {V hope_VV0 {Fn {Fn& that_CS {N you_PPY N} {V will_VM consider_VV0 {N this_DD N} V} {N just_RR a_AT routine_JJ courtesy_NN1 reminder_NN1 N} Fn} and_CC {Fn+ that_CS {N we_PPIS2 N} {V may_VM hear_VV0 {P from_II {N you_PPY N} P} V} soon_RR Fn+} Fn} V} ._. S}
N009
{S {Fa If_CS {N your_APP$ cheque_NN1 N} {V is_VBZ {P on_II {N the_AT way_NN1 N} P} V} Fa} ,_, {V please_RR ignore_VV0 {N this_DD reminder_NN1 N} V} ._. S}
N009
{S {Tg Thanking_VVG {N you_PPY N} {P in_II {N advance_NN1 N} P} {P for_IF {N your_APP$ prompt_JJ attention_NN1 P} Tg} ._. S}
N010
{S {N yours_PP N} sincerely_RR S}
N011
{S {N Dear_JJ Sir_NNS N} S}
N011
{S {N You_PPY N} {V may_VM have_VH0 overlooked_VVN {N {N& our_APP$ statements_NN2 N&} and_CC {N+ earlier_JJR reminder_NN1 N+} {Tg requesting_VVG {P for_IF {N settlement_NN1 {P of_IO {N your_APP$ account_NN1

{Fr {N which_DD N} {V is_VBZ now_RT {J considerably_RR past_JB due_JJ J} V} N}
P} N} Fr} Tg} N} ._. S}
N011

{S {V Please_RR note_VV0 {Fn that_CS {N our_APP$ credit_NN1 policy_NN1 N} {V
requires_VVZ {N all_DB statements_NN2 N} be_VB0 V} Fn} N} {V paid_VVD {P
in_II {N full_JJ {P within_II {N 30_MC days_NNT {P on_II {N presentation_NN1 N}
P} N} P} N} P} V} ._. S}
N011

{S May_VM {N we_PPIS2 N} {V hear_VV0 {P from_II {N you_PPY N} P} {P by_II {N
return_NN1 mail_NN1 N} P} {P within_II {N the_AT next_MD ten_MC days_NNT
N} P} V} ._. S}
N012

{S {Tg Thanking_VVG {N you_PPY N} {P in_II {N advance_NN1 N} P} {P for_IF {N
your_APP$ prompt_JJ attention_NN1 N} P} V} ._. S}
N013

{S {N yours_PP N} sincerely_RR S}
N014

{S {N Dear_NP1 Sir_NNS N} S}
N015

{S We_PPIS2 {V {V& refer_VV0 {P to_TO {N our_APP$ previous_JJ reminders_NN1 {P
regarding_II {N your_APP$ outstanding_JJ account_NN1 N} P} N} P} V&} and_CC {V+
regret_VV0 {Fn that_CS {N you_PPY N} still_RR {V have_VH0 not_XX
responded_VVD {P to_IN {N our_APP$ request_NN1 {P for_IF {N payment_NN1 N}
P} N} P} V} V+} V} Fn} ._. S}
N016

{S {S& {V Please_RR arrange_VV0 {Ti to_TO remit_VV0 {N us_PPIO2 N} {N
your_APP$ cheque_NN1 N} {P in_II {N full_JJ settlement_NN1 {P within_II {N
seven_MC days_NNT N} P} {P upon_II {N receipt_NN1 {P of_IO {N this_DD
letter_NN1 N} P} N} P} N} P} S&} or_CC {S+ we_PPIS2 {V will_VM have_VH0 {N no_AT
alternative_NN1 N} V} ,_, {P but_II {Ti to_TO cancel_VV0 {N your_APP$ credit_NN1
priveleges_NN1 {P with_IW {N our_APP$ hotel_NN1 N} P} N} Ti} P} S+} ._. S}
N017

{S {N yours_PP N} sincerely_RR S}
N018

{S {N Dear_NP1 Sir_NNS N} S}
N019

{S We_PPIS2 {V {V& refer_VV0 {Ti to_TO {N our_APP$ previous_JJ reminders_NN1
{P regarding_II {N your_APP$ above_JJ long_RR outstanding_JJ account_NN1 N} P} V&}
and_CC {V+ regret_VV0 {Fn that_CS {N you_PPY N} still_RR {V have_VH0 not_XX
responded_VVD {P to_II {N our_APP$ request_NN1 {P for_IF {N payment_NN1 N} P}
N} P} V+} V} ._. S}
N020

{S {V Please_RR note_VV0 {Fn that_CS {Fa unless_CS {N your_APP$ account_NN1
N} {V is_VBZ settled_VVN {P within_II {N seven_MC days_NNT N} P} {P upon_II
{N receipt_NN1 {P of_IO {N this_DD letter_NN1 N} P} N} P} V} Fa} ,_, {N we_PPIS2
N} {V will_VM have_VH0 {N no_AT alternative_NN1 N} V} ,_, {P but_II to_TO
refer_VV0 {N this_DD matter_NN1 N} {P to_II {N our_APP$ lawyer_NN1 N} P} {P

for_IF {*N legal_JJ action_NN1 N*} *P*} *N*} {*Ti to_TO **be taken against you** ._. S*}
N021
{*S* {*V Take_VV0* {*N notice_NN1 N*} {*Fn that_CS* {*N you_PPY N*} {*V will_VM also_RR*
be_VB0 {*J liable_JJ* {*Ti to_TO pay_VV0* {*P for_IF* {*N the_AT legal_JJ costs_NN2* {*P*
of_IO {*N such_DA proceedings_NN2 N*} *P*} *N*} *P*} *Ti*} *J*} *V*} *Fn*} *V*} ._. S*}
N022
{*S* {*N yours_PP N*} *sincerely_RR S*}

Figure 6.8 Corrected parser output for PROLEX texts on the lexeme *account*

As it can be seen from a manual parse of the texts (Fig 6.8), the Sharman parser needs to be improved substantially in order to achieve a higher degree of accuracy. However, it must also be mentioned that the Sharman parser is a step in the right direction for the analysis of texts: it is applicable to unrestricted text, employs a probabilistic grammar adapted to corpus analysis, and uses a parsing scheme which is as theoretically 'neutral' as possible, and is hence suited for a wider variety of uses.

6.6 CORPUS WORD-EXTRACTION

In order to sort the output from the CLAWS word-tagging (Section 6.4), I have used Tony McEnery's Extraction Program (personal communication) which is designed to extract the frequency count of the possible tag(s) associated with each wordform in the tagged file. Thus, a combination of the CLAWS program and this extraction program acts as a kind of lemmatiser, in the sense that the morphological variants of the word are indicated. This facilitates the structuring of the morphological parameter in the lexical entry (see Section 6.10.1). Of course, a lemmatiser (in the sense most commonly understood) would, by means of inbuilt morphological rules, relate a wordform to its lemma so that the frequency figures for these tags would not only be based on surface strings.

6.7 CORPUS COLLOCATION

Where collocational information is concerned, I now turn to the TACT program developed at the University of Toronto (see Bradley 1990, and Appendix B). TACT assists in textual analysis by retrieving parts of text according to the wordform specified: it allows such facilities as concordancing, frequencies, indexing and displaying the results in graphs, lists, and tables.

An advantage of using TACT is that it includes a Z-score facility for the collation of word types related to the headwork. In statistics, the Z-score is a measure based on the standard deviation, involving the process of standardising so as to facilitate the comparison of scores (see Woods et al. 1986: 43). More immediately, for readers of linguistics (see Barnbrook 1996; Oakes 1998), the Z-score is a standard statistical measure which can be used to indicate the **significance** of the frequency of co-occurrence of the collocates with the selected wordform in question. In this connection, note that the term **significance** means different things in different communities. This is seen in some attempts at automatically generating 'collocational significance.' In statistics, the t-score and the Z-score are obviously related, the first being a measure of part of the dataset (i.e. sample) whereas the latter measures the whole dataset. Both the t-score and the Z-score are thus measures of confidence intervals. Mutual information (as used by Church and his co-workers) measure 'significance' in a statistical sense in that it is a statement about **expectations** rather than **confidence intervals**. In the statistical sense, expectations are (roughly speaking) statements about first moments, whereas confidence intervals (or variances) are statements about second moments. The sense in which I use the term 'significance' for the Z-score is thus one which is concerned more with confidence intervals than expectations. The term **collocational significance** in a lexicographic sense refers to linguistically interesting pairs, which may or may not refer to either confidence intervals or expectations.

For example, in looking at an unfamiliar text (indexed in TACT), substantive words that occur with a high frequency can be called up, and the Z-score calculated on each of the words. This will bring up a list of words occurring within a span of (say) 5 words (as indicated in Section 4.3) on each side of the target word and ordered by the Z-score, i.e. showing the degree of significance of each word as a collocate. TACT facilitates the transition from the Z-score list to the text itself in order for the user to follow up a given collocation.

Let us elaborate on this non-trivial statistical measure, the Z-score, which is applied to measure collocational strength. Bradley (1990: 12–13) states that 'it takes the observed frequency of a word in the 'mini-text' (the sequence of words near the selected positions)[4] and compares this with a theoretical frequency (assuming the word was distributed randomly within the full text) of occurence [sic,="occurrence"] within the same mini-text'. Given that Woods et al. (1986: 44) define the Z-score as the standardised X-score described by the single formula

$$Z = X1 - X2 \, / \, s \text{ where } s = \text{standard deviation}$$

TACT uses the following formula, as suggested by Barron Brainerd (Bradley, 1990: 13):

$Z =$ (Observed frequency of collocate $- E$) $/ s$
where $P =$ frequency of collocate in full text $/$ length of text
$E = P$ x length of the mini-text
$s = \sqrt{\text{(length of the mini-text x P x (1-P))}}$.

The statement that 'a higher Z-score means more significance of the co-occurrence in a statistical sense' (Bradley 1990: 12) becomes clearer in the light of the following. From the statistical tables of the Standardized Normal

Distribution (White et al. 1979: 15), an absolute value of the Z-score greater than 1.96000 will mean that there is a 95% certainty factor that what is observed is different from what would happen if the words came up at random near each other: this would mean that the words would be occurring significantly more times (i.e. observed frequency of collocate > E), or significantly less times than expected (i.e. observed frequency of collocate < E). Similarly, an absolute value of the Z-score being greater than 1.64485 will mean a 90% certainty factor of significance.

I have dwelt at length on the Z-score (and for that matter, measures of statistical significance such as mutual information) because such information should also be recorded in the lexicon: an illustration is indicated in the specimen lexical entries in Appendix A.

6.8 CORPUS SEMANTIC TAGGING AND PARSING

The processing of a corpus need not be restricted to grammatical analysis. For example, automatic tagging of semantic classes or of discourse features has been undertaken by the ACASD project (Wilson and Rayson 1993) and the ACAMRIT project (Rayson and Wilson 1996) for content analysis, as well as the 'anaphoric treebank' project (Fligelstone 1992) for the marking of anaphor-antecedent relationships.

Semantic tagging (of a corpus) is a technique still in its infancy. Nevertheless, semantic analysis is clearly an important level to apply to the extraction of lexicographic information from corpora, and major advances are being made to strengthen this aspect.

6.9 CORPUS PRAGMATICS

In business English, it is clear that questionnaires and statements of account represent mere formulaic texts where communication or correspondence cannot be said to occur between two parties. This, if we are interested in pragmatic information (i.e. 'meaning in interaction'), the first step is to exclude such formulaic texts before we process the corpus in this manner. The second step is to detail pragmatic information by referencing, either manually by hand or using an automatic computer program, the remaining texts for such information. By first processing the corpus for pragmatic information, we can later derive a lexicon that will 'mirror' speaker and hearer's knowledge, thus working towards the achievement of an all-inclusive lexicon (as mentioned in Chapter 1). Indeed, in an expanded view of the (business English) lexicon, each lexical entry 'should be informed as to the 'type' of text within which use of the term has been included ... typological information tells us *who* uses the term ('A term used by merchants'), to *whom* they address the term ('An enquiry, usually to a bank'), *where* they use the term ('on bills of exchange or drafts', 'in invoices and accounts'), *when* they use the term ('when quoting the price', 'in making contracts') and in *what* area of business and management activity the user participates ('in overseas trade', 'in bookkeeping', 'in commerce')' (Webster 1986).

In keeping with this approach, the referencing of each sample text in the corpus has specified the type of correspondence (letter, memo, telex, report, etc.) the business organisation from which the sample has been obtained, the function or purpose of the text (enquiry, complaint, etc.), the speech acts and discourse moves involved, and the specification of which part of the text in which a lemma is found. These parameters, seven in all, are each discussed in turn for the PROLEX corpus only. Because the PROCOMPARE corpus contains a variety of texts that cannot be regarded as correspondence between two parties – indeed, this latter corpus being a series of templates – there was no attempt to reference the material for the PROCOMPARE corpus in the manner I have just indicated.

The first label, the **S** (Subject) label, might perhaps be better called the F (Functions) label since it contains the following functional categories:

  0. miscellaneous, for correspondence which does not fit into the other categories
  1. *advertising* (own company's image and products)
  2. *personnel*
  3. *goodwill, public relations*
  4. *quotes, estimates, tenders, offers*
  5. *orders*
  6. *complaints, adjustments, and claims*
  7. *settlement of account* (billing, credit, invoice)
  8. *credit* (in the sense of lending)
  9. *authorisation* to act on behalf of
  10. *shipping* (in the sense of transportation)
  11. *samples* (of products)
  12. *travel arrangement*
  13. *trade enquiry*
  14. *transfer of funds*
  15. matters relating to *sealing of contract*

Under the second label, the **C** (Company) label, are listed the names of the business organisations from which the sample texts are obtained. These business organisations include the following:

  0. miscellaneous (smaller texts from various organisations)
  1. a major multi-national organisation in Singapore and Malaysia
  2. a major hotel in Singapore
  3. a leading foreign bank in Singapore
  4. an internationally-renowned hotel
  5. a major Singaporean broadsheet
  6. an institution of higher learning in Singapore

7. a leading local bank in Singapore
8. a major shipping company
9. a large U.S. multinational company
10. a major petroleum company
11. a leading insurance company
12. one of the world's largest computer companies

The third label, the **X** (eXchange) label,[5] refers to the discoursal moves of either

1. *initiate* or
2. *respond*

For this, I follow a suggestion by Ghadessy and Webster (1988: 114–115) who point out that

> written business communication starts either with a would-be client, customer, buyer, etc. or a company, bank, store, etc. For example if a person writes to his bank manager for a loan, he has *initiated* the communication to which the manager in almost all cases should *respond*. On the other hand, if a bank sends to its customers a new savings plan, the bank has initiated the communication to which clients may or may not respond.

Ghadessy and Webster also make the suggestion that 'whether one is initiating a letter or responding to a letter the function of the business communication is one of Informing, Requesting or Directing. The three letter types (for all business communication) then are: *Informative, Request(ive), Directive.*' However, in examining the texts, I find it difficult to draw the boundary between where a request ends and where a directive begins. Furthermore, there are paragraphs in the letters whose function do not seem to fit neatly into either of the three categories proposed: rather, such paragraphs more definitely have the function of acknowledging another person's prior communication, or recalling one's own previous communication to the addressee. I therefore include the following speech acts under the fourth label, the **A** (Acts) label:

1. *acknowledge* (other persons' communications) / *recall* (one's own previous communication)
2. *inform* (providing new information)
3. *enquire/request/direct* (eliciting from the addressee information and/or a course of action

The fifth label, the **T** (Type of Text) label, is used to specify whether the word-form occurs as part of a

1. *letter*
2. *telex*
3. *memorandum*

The next parameter, the **P** (Part of Document) label, divides the text into different sections, so that it is possible to know where the word-form occurs within the text. The numerals assigned to these sections include the following (those in quotes are the wordforms, the occurrence of which indicates natural segments in the text):

1. *greetings*
2. <P 2/*n1*/*n2*> where *n1*=the paragraph number in which the word is found, and *n2*=the total number of paragraphs. If *n1* is the final paragraph, it is signalled by *F*.
3. *closing* (including the complimentary close, 'Sincerely', etc.)
4. '*re:*'/*subheading*/*subtitle*
5. '*enclosure*'
6. '*attention*'
7. '*post script/n.b.*'
8. *receiver's reply*
9. '*terms and conditions*'
10. *checklist*

The seventh label, the **N** (Number) label, is used to mark the position in linear order in which the sample text occurs in the corpus. It is a text location identification marker.

The final label, the **E** (Error) label, is used for typographical and linguistic errors found in the original texts. Two values are assigned to **E**: + and -. The plus sign indicates that the word-form is an error found in the sample text concerned; the minus sign, on the other hand, indicates that there does not seem to be any such error.

6.9.1 The COCOA format for referencing the PROLEX corpus

The typological categories as proposed in the preceding section are used to reference the corpus, with each number corresponding to the respective category. Using the COCOA (word COunt and COncordance on Atlas) format adaptable for programs such as the Oxford Concordance Program (Hockey 1988) and TACT (Bradley 1990), the texts are referenced by placing the typological labels between angled brackets. For instance, in the label <S 1>, S (i.e. Subject) indicates the category label, and the number 1 indicates the value (i.e. Advertising). Such formulae are inserted into the text where appropriate.

6.9.2 Extraction of typological frequency from the PROLEX corpus

Thus, the OCP program has the capability of generating a keyword-in-context output, whereby a listing of the typological tags associated with the word are placed on the left of the keyword concerned. In this connection, a utility similar to the one detailed in Section 6.6 has been written in order to sort this listing. This is done in order to elicit the frequency of occurrence of the various pragmatic parameters (*C*, *S*, *T*....etc) associated with the word. This UNIX shell script makes use of the utilities *awk*, *sort*, and *uniq*.

6.10 STRUCTURING LEXICAL ENTRIES FROM THE PROLEX AND PROCOMPARE CORPORA

Once a corpus is processed for the various types of linguistic information, it becomes much easier to structure a lexical entry from it. For processed corpora such as the PROLEX and PROCOMPARE corpora, not only can collocational, syntactic, semantic, and pragmatic information be derived but frequency information detailing which of several related wordforms (e.g. *advise, advising, advised, advises*) is most basic can also be obtained. However, as pointed out by Hudson (1988) and also in Section 1.1, the process of structuring a lexical entry should not obscure the relationship between the entry and other words. Such a relationship obviously includes that between similar wordforms. For this reason, the notion of a vocable becomes useful: according to Mel'cuk and Zholkovsky (1988: 47), a **vocable** is 'a family of dictionary entries for lexemes which are sufficiently close in meaning and which share the same signans [i.e. identical stem]'.

The algorithm in a lemmatiser should be able first to group on the basis of similar stems into one vocable and then to distinguish the respective lemmas in this vocable through morphological rules. However, whether or not these forms are 'sufficiently close in meaning' is difficult to determine by any existing program, because even the human finds it difficult to agree on what constitutes 'sufficient' closeness in meaning.

In retaining the notion of a lexical entry – albeit an expanded one – I have not assumed that lexical entries are unrelated to one another: indeed the contrary holds true. Nevertheless, conceptually, the word is a universe (as it were) in itself: a word may be regarded as 'a text in microcosm, a "universe of discourse" of its own in which the semiotic properties of a text reappear on a miniature scale'.[6] Parallel to the idea that, in practice, the information properties of a text are viewed in context, word knowledge is not regarded as totally isolated from world knowledge: the dividing line between these two types of knowledge seems quite thin.

I have therefore structured four basic parameters of information for the selected PROLEX and PROCOMPARE lexemes: morphology, syntax, semantics, and pragmatics – of which the first three may be regarded as word knowledge and the fourth, world knowledge. This compares well with, say, Gazdar and Mellish (1989) and Evans and Gazdar (1990) who use the first three parameters for their lexical entry. However, as I have argued throughout this book, the richer the analysis of a word is, the richer its potentiality is for NLP applications.

Appendix A gives the sample lexical entries, structured using the following notation:

1. The frame ('attribute:value') notion is used. Let us call the 'attribute' side the left hand side (LHS) and the 'value' side the right hand side (RHS). Let the = sign be 'isa'. Thus given XXX="YYY", it is usually the case that XXX=attribute/slot, and "YYY"=value (the instantiation). However, sometimes it is XXX= <A B C D> where A B C D might be permanent slots, in turn containing values. Within "YYY", frequency data is mainly included, so "YYY (***)" is such that *** stands for some frequency value.

2. As indicated in (1), the angle brackets < > are used to enclose some particular combination of parameters in that slot. Sometimes, however, because the item in question (on the RHS) is the form which realises a particular value, I have left it unenclosed in such brackets, e.g.

   <syn post LEX noun_colloc real>= "number (17), receivable (4), holders (1)"

   <syn post LEX noun_colloc form>= Ncompound (LEX+N)

   where 'LEX+N' stands for 'the lemma concerned + a noun' to form a noun compound, e.g. *account receivable, account number.*

   The parameters of information enclosed within the angle brackets are generally mnemonic. Thus, using the same example, this reads as: 'in terms of syntactic information, *account* is a lexeme which collocates with a noun which occurs after it.' Thus, the terms 'pre' and 'post' indicate items to the left and to the right of the lexeme in question respectively.

3. On the LHS, the abbreviation 'real' stands for 'realisation', which is reflected on the RHS by " " which encloses actual occurrences. In general, on the RHS, these values are ordered by their frequency of occurrence, i.e. the most frequent items come first. Notice that, in the previous example, 'real' occurs before 'form', which is the complement of 'real'.

4. The numbers in round brackets '( )' stand for the number of occurrences (raw frequency count) of the item in question.

5. The empty square brackets [] are used in a number of ways. Generally, they stand for the empty set /non-occurrence of the item in question (Sometimes, (0) is used instead, for zero frequency). Sometimes, [] represents an object which is implicit: an instance of this is the implied second person pronoun in the imperative clause *Please advise me.* Also, in the CLAWS output (Morphology section), for ease of reading, I have used these square brackets to distinguish them from the round ones.

6. The curly brackets {} enclose those types of information, mainly for the PROLEX corpus, which maintain the confidentiality of business transactions. Thus, for the most part, I have abbreviated names of organisations as {*cname*}, together with such (self-explanatory) terms as {*date*} and {*city*}.

7. On the LHS, morphological information is enclosed as <mor ...>, syntactic information as <syn ...>, semantic information as <sem ....>, and pragmatic information as <prag ...>.

6.10.1 Morphology

Taking *account* (N) as the same illustrative example,

Prolexnoun_LEX account (103):

reads as '*Account* is a PROLEX noun lemma which consists of 103 occurrences of inflectional variants, i.e. of *account* (singular noun) and *account* (plural noun)'. In terms of morphology, the Morphology Frame for nouns thus specifies two basic slots:

<mor LEX F> = "account (91) [NN1 91]"
<mor LEX -S>= "accounts (12) [NN2 12]"

which indicates that the singular root/stem (**F**) form occurs 91 times, and its plural form (-s affix) 12 times. These frequency figures, with the respective CLAWS tag(s), are derived from McEnery's Word-Extraction Program (see Section 6.6) which takes its input from a CLAWS output file.

For verbs, the various inflectional variants are specified through the following slots

<mor LEX F> = "advise (87) [VV0 64 VVI 23]
<mor LEX -S> = "advises (0)"
<mor LEX -ED>= "advised (19) [VVN 15 VVD 4]"
<mor LEX -ING>= "advising (3) [VVG 3]"

where the <-ed> slot takes into account stemforms with this suffix. For verbs, this can occur either as a past participle (VVN) or simply as the regular past tense form (VVD).

For adjectives, the comparative and superlative slots are specified in inflectional morphology, thus in the case of *full* (Adj)

<mor LEX F> = "full (40) [JJ 40]"
<mor LEX -ER>= []
<mor LEX -EST>= "fullest (1) [JJT 1]"

there is a single instance of a superlative form, but the comparative slot remains unfilled.

Finally, for adverbial inflectional morphology,

<mor LEX F> = "please (275) [RR 275]"

the subjunct *please* just specifies the stem slot.

Where derivational morphology is concerned, the values in the slot

<mor LEX related_wordforms>= "accountant (1) [NN1 1], accountee (2) [NN1 2], accounting (2) [JB 1 VVG 1]"

indicate the other related lemmas in this family of lexemes. The form *accounting*, for instance, which occurs twice, is either an attributive adjective (JB) or the non-finite verb (VVG). Thus, the CLAWS program may be regarded as a kind of lemmatise in its own right. Also, it is significant that *account* (v) does not occur at all in the PROLEX corpus; as we shall see later, evidence from the PROCOMPARE corpus also suggests that, where the stem *account* is concerned, it is overwhelmingly the noun form which populates the sublanguage lexicon of Business English.

For the verb *advise*,

<mor LEX related_wordforms>:= "advice (29) [NN1 29]; advisable (1) [JJ 1]; advising (2) [JJ 2]; advisor (1) [NN1 1]"

a confusion might arise in comparing the orthographic form *advising* here with the same under the inflectional morphology section. Here, under derivational morphology, *advising* has the adjectival function, as in *the advising bank*, whereas in the inflectional morphology section, *advising* is the non-finite *-ing* form of the verb lemma *advise*.

In concluding this section, both the derivational and inflectional morphological parameters of information can be taken to specify variant wordforms and related lexemes, which form a vocable.

6.10.2 Syntax
In terms of syntactic information, general information for the noun lemma *account* includes the following:

<syn LEX cat>= N [X]; Ndeverbal []
<syn LEX N class>= Count [X]; Mass []

This reads as: *account* is a lexeme whose category is a noun (but not a deverbal noun – unlike *claim*) and whose class label is a count noun.

Moreover, if the noun *account* functions as the 'Head' of a noun phrase, then, the following slots are obtained for a Noun Phrase Subframe.

SYN_NP_SUBFRAME:
LEX= H
<syn pre H det real>= "your (26), our (10), the (6), {cname's} (5), this (5), the beneficiary's (2), opener's (2), all (1), these (1), a (1), buyer's (1), seller's (1)"
<syn pre H premod real>= "current (8), (long) outstanding (5), (considerably) overdue (4), above (2), personal (2), following (2), new (1); posb (2), savings (1), bank (1); head office (1), singapore dollar (1),{cname} branch (1), {cname} osaka (1); issuing bank (1)"
<syn pre H premod form>= Adj+LEX (24); N+LEX (4); Ncompound (N+N) +LEX (4); Adj+N+LEX (1)
<syn post H postmod real>= "of {cname}(6), of openers (2), of beneficiary (1); with you (2), with the post office savings bank (1), with the sum of ${amt.} (1); which should have been settled a long time ago (1), which is now slightly past due (1), which is now considerably past due (1); represented by this invoice

(2), rendered by our office in {place} and {city} (1); under advice to us (2); covering ${amt.} (1)"

<syn post H postmod form>= PP (of) (9) / PP (with) (4) / wh rel clause (3) / -ed clause (3) / pp (under) (2) / -ing clause (1)

Thus, a noun phrase can be taken as consisting of an H element which is preceded by a determiner + a premodifier, and postmodified by elements such as a prepositional phrase and a nonfinite clause. Notice that the premodifier itself can be regarded as a slot containing collocational information.

Outside the noun phrase, the following subframe obtains for collocational information in the PROLEX noun lexeme *account*.

SYN_LEX_COLLOCATE_SUBFRAME:
<syn pre LEX noun_colloc real>= "debit of (3),settlement of (2), balance of (2), funds in (2), credit of (2), statement of (1)"
<syn pre LEX noun_colloc form>= N+prep+LEX
<syn post LEX noun_colloc real>= "number (17), receivable (4), holders (1)"
<syn post LEX noun_colloc form>= Ncompound (LEX + N) (22)
<syn pre LEX verb_colloc real>= "debit (6), regarding (3), maintain (2),favouring (2), to credit (1), will be for (1), to debit (1), to settle (1), referring to (1), to clear (1), to close (1)"
<syn pre LEX verb_colloc form>= V(transitive)+LEX (20)
<syn post LEX verb_colloc real>= "has been debited (2), has been transferred (2), has become overdrawn (1); was credited (2); is (not) settled (2); can be operated (1); is (1)"
<syn post LEX verb_colloc form>= LEX+V(perfective) (5) / LEX+V(passive) (4) / LEX +V(modal) (1) / LEX + copula (1)
<syn post LEX adj_colloc real>= "((long) overdue) (1)"
<syn LEX zscore real>="debit (17.170), receivable (12.373), represented (10.357), debited (9.831), current (9.678)"

Thus, for example, one can '*debit an account*' or have an account which '*has been debited*', or have a *long overdue account*.

For the Z-score – which is an indication of the statistical significance of the collocates that occur with *account* – I have selected just the five most significant collocates to fill this slot. Since the Z-score (as used by the TACT program) is more a measure of confidence intervals than one of expectations (as indicated in Section 6.7), some of these collocates might seem to be counter-intuitive.

Turning now to verbs, the types of general information in the verb *advise* include the following syntactic subframe,

<syn LEX cat> = V
<syn LEX modals>= "will (10), could (2), would (2), shall (1), can (1)"
<syn LEX perfective>= " have **V**ed" (2),"have been **V**ed" (2)
<syn LEX progressive>= **V**ing (3)

<syn LEX passive>= "as **V**ed" (3), "[] (2) / shall (2) / can (1) / will (1) + be
+**V**ed", "keep...**V**ed" (1), "would be kept **V**ed (1)"

Slots are therefore reserved for the forms of the verb, which can take either
progressive or perfective aspect (or both), with an indication of any passive
form that occurs, as well as the modals that do occur with the verb. As a
predicate, the verb takes the following subframe, where the first parameter of
information in the verb *advise* concerns its subcategorisation possibilities:

<syn pred0 Copular= []
<syn pred0 Monotransitive>= []
<syn pred0 Ditransitive>= <arg1 arg2 arg3 arg4>
<syn pred0 Complex_Transitive>= []

Advise is a ditransitive predicate verb which takes 4 arguments. The structure
is something like the following, as indicated under the pragmatic level of
information: Concerning Z (arg2), X (arg1) advises (pred) Y (arg3), under
circumstance C (arg4)'. X and Y are variously realised, as the values in the
following slots show:

<syn pred0 arg1 real>= "[] (45), we (31), you (6), i (2), {cname} (3)"
<syn pred0 arg1 form> = NP
<syn pred0 arg1 function>= S
<syn pred0 arg1 status> = implicit (45), explicit (42)
<syn pred0 arg3 real>= "[] (55), you (14), us (9), {cname} (2), beneficiary
(1); your malaysian / singapore offices (1)"
<syn pred0 arg3 form> = NP
<syn pred0 arg3 function>= IO
<syn pred0 arg3 status> = implicit (55), explicit (14)

Notice that the values in Arguments 1 and 3 are frequently the same
orthographically (i.e. [], {cname}, and you); in terms of deixis, though, the
interpretations are different, i.e. it depends on who is being referred to. The
implied value [] is derived from utterances such as *Please advise us*, where the
subject is implied. Argument 1 is used, in this case, to refer to the person/
organisation which does the 'advising', e.g. *we* or {cname1} in *We advise you*,
whereas Argument 3 is the 'advised' (i.e. notationally marked {cname2}, in order
– as in the case of {cname1} – to maintain the confidentiality of the organisation
involved).

Argument 2, in the case of *advise*, refers to the matter in hand, i.e. *what* is
advised. In terms of grammatical function, this is a direct object (DO), as in

<syn pred0 arg2 form> = NP (22) / that-clause (21) / wh-clause (13) / []
(9) / PP (of) (5) / PP(on) (3) / if-clause (2) / ing-clause (1)
<syn pred0 arg2 function>= DO

Provision is also made for any special features that might go with the argument. For instance, in

<syn pred0 arg2 feats>= IF <T2>, prep ("on") optional, determiner optional; IF <T2> PP(on) substituted by NP

the term *advise* is a regular feature in Telexes which occurs 61 times (i.e. T2, see Section 6.9), so ellipsis (in this case the omission of 'on' and/or 'the') is expected to occur, as in *Please advise date of payment,* and *Please advise any interest.*

For *advise,* Argument 4 refers to Circumstantial elements such as *accordingly* in *Please advise accordingly.* I have grouped these elements broadly into 5 categories: Temporal, Cause-Reason-Purpose, Condition-Contrast, Manner-Means-Instrument, and Location, as in

<syn pred0 arg4 feats> = Temporal (12); Cause-Reason-Purpose (8); Condition-Contrast (6); Manner-Means-Instrument (6); Location (1)
<syn pred0 arg4 status> = optional

The 'status' feature here is 'optional' because the adverbial/adjunct element is by tradition considered non-essential – unlike the verbal element – to the structure of the clause.

Let us now turn to adjectival information. The adjective *full* can function as the Head element of an NP, for example in the phrase *pay in full.*

LEX= H
<syn pre H prep real>= "in (2)"

More often than not, the adjective functions as a premodifier in another noun phrase, as in the following slots

LEX= premod
<syn pre H det real>= "a (6), the (2), its (1)"
<syn LEX attr H premod real>= "LEX & final (2)"
<syn LEX attr H real>= "set (8), details (4), settlement (3), interest (2), invoice (2), address (1), capacity (1), page (1), understanding (1), payment (1), recovery (1), time position (1), extent (1), range (1), discharge (1), force (1), use (1); telephone number (1), commitment rate (1)"
<syn LEX attr H form>= LEX+N (31); LEX+Ncompound (2)

where the adjective occurs in attributive position. Here, *full* occurs attributively in the phrases *the full set* and *a full settlement* or co-occurs with another pre-modifying element to the head, as in *a full and final settlement.*

Predicatively, another adjective such as *complete* can collocate with *full,*

<syn LEX pred adj_colloc real>= "LEX & complete (1)"
as in the phrase *full and complete.*

Finally, we turn to *please* as an example of an adverb. Where adverbial information is concerned, the following classes specify the main types:

<syn LEX adv class>= adjunct []; subjunct [X]; disjunct; conjunct []

The adverb *please* in the PROLEX corpus may therefore be regarded as a subjunct or, more precisely, a **courtesy subjunct**, which is a formulaic expression 'of politeness or propriety' (Quirk et al. 1985: 569).

Although an adverbial/adjunct element is often highly mobile, the 'POSN' subframe determines the possible positions that any A element (in general English) can occur in:

<syn LEX pre S V>= []
<syn LEX post S Faux>= [][7]
<syn LEX post S copula>= []
<syn LEX pre Vfinite>= Adv + V (269); Aux+S+Adv+Vfinite (6) (interrogative)
<syn LEX pre Vfinite feats>= Aux in Aux+S+Adv+Vfinite realised by "would (5)" and "could (1)"; S ellipted in Adv+V pattern, thus Adv initial
<syn LEX post S V>= []

Therefore, out of the 5 possible positions, *please* (adv) in the PROLEX corpus occurs in only one of them. Most of the time, it occurs immediately in initial position before the finite verb, as in the imperative clause *Please advise*, with the Subject ellipted. The flexibility of the LFA approach is seen in allowing for the marking of important types of information by creating a 'feats' (features) slot whenever necessary. In this case, Quirk et al. (1985: 570)'s assertion that 'with *please*, I [initial position] is usual but *eM* [end medial] is possible for some speakers; *iE* [initial end] is by no means unusual, and *E* [end] is quite common' can be made more definitive by the use of such frequency figures that indicate the precise behaviour of this subjunct. In the PROLEX corpus, the adverb occurs 269 times just before the finite verb.

In an interrogative form such as *Would you please advise?* the auxiliaries used are either *could* or *would*, and while the data is too small (just 6 occurrences) to enable a greater generalisation, it is these hypothetical auxiliaries which enhance the impression of politeness, without being too tentative (as would be the use – otherwise – of 'might').

In terms of collocation, while the slot

<syn pre LEX adv_colloc real>= "herewith (1), kindly (1), also (1), so (1)"

indicates some of the other adverbial elements that can collocate with *please*, the following slot shows the range of verbs that collocate with the adverb *please*:

<syn post LEX verb_colloc real>= "advise (36), note (25), confirm (16), contact (12), find (8), arrange (7), remit (7), accept (5), complete (4), send (4), convey (3), honour (3), refer (3), acknowledge (2), debit (2), ensure (2), include

(2), instruct (2), place (2), present (2), proceed (2), relay (2), send (2), telex (2), write (2), airmail (1), attend (1), bring (1), cancel (1), carry (1), clarify (1), close (1), congratulate (1), coordinate (1), direct (1), endorse (1), expedite (1), follow (1), furnish (1), give (1), ignore (1), indicate (1), issue (1), investigate (1), liaise (1), lodge (1), nominate (1), notify (1), prepare (1), provide (1), read (1), recall (1), re-direct (1), release (1), reply (1), return (1),revert (1), revise (1), sand (1), return (1), signify (1), sign (1), submit (1), supply (1), transfer (1); let ... have (15), let ... know (8), pass on (3), attend to (3), take note (1), have ... done (1), have ... completed (1), rest [assured] (1), keep ... informed (1), keep ... appraised (1), look ... up (1), look out for (1), draw on (1), give ... ring (1), deal..with (1); [do not] hesitate to contact (8), [do] call (4), [do not] hesitate to call (2), [do not] add (1), [do not] forget (1);be informed (6), be advised (6), be guided (2), be assured (2), be reminded (1); investigate and arrange (1), check and advise (1), arrange and advise (1), assist and advise (1), complete and return (1); feel [free] to contact (2), continue to insure (1)"

<syn post LEX verb_colloc form>=V(finite) (196) / V(phrasal (prep)) (40) / Aux(do)+(not)+V(finite) (16) / Aux(be)+V(-ed)/Adj(-ed) (17) / V+&+V (5) / V+to+V (3)

Notice that the general principle of ordering the instances here – as elsewhere – is to group them into the respective formal categories and then, within the formal category, sort these instances in terms of descending highest frequency. For *please*, the frequency information shows that it collocates very strongly, for instance, with *advise*: this is also borne out by the Z-score ranking. The point here is that such types of information can be very useful for the lexicographer to extract for the creation of, say, a Dictionary of Business English Collocations for the advanced learner.

6.10.3 Semantics

Admittedly, the boundary between this parameter and the others is not as clear-cut as these various categorisations (morphology, syntax, semantics, pragmatics) suggest. For instance, corresponding to the Adverbial element (as discussed in the preceding section), the Circumstantial elements – Temporal, Cause-Reason-Purpose, Condition-Contrast, Manner-Means-Instrument – are both grammatical and semantic in their orientation. This link between the semantic and syntactic (grammatical) parameters is therefore reflected, in the case of *advise* (v), in the following:

<sem pred0 arg4 case> = Circumstance

where *advise* is a predicate which takes four arguments, of which the Circumstance is classified as the fourth argument. The other three arguments, whose respective case roles correspond to their syntactic form and functions, are

<sem pred0 arg1 case> = Actor
<sem pred0 arg2 case> = Content
<sem pred0 arg3 case> = Recipient

These cases characterise the 'superordinate' predicate (pred0) *advise*, from which these cases are inherited into the two senses of the verb in the PROLEX corpus, i.e.

<sem LEX> = ADVISE1 (pred01), ADVISE2 (pred02)

While Fillmore's case roles are developed more particularly for the verb – which thus has a richer semantic description – only this slot <sem LEX> is used for the other categories of noun, adjective, and adverb at the present moment: it should, however, be possible to incorporate a richer semantic description for these latter categories with, say, Pustejovsky's Theory of Qualia Structure (Pustejovsky 1991). In the case of a deverbal noun such as *claim*, however, aspects of verbal behaviour have to be recorded, even though the noun form is the one treated.

Returning to the slot <sem LEX> for *advise*, ADVISE1 has the sense of 'informing', while ADVISE2 takes the sense of 'directing /requesting' the addressee to a particular course of action.

6.10.4 Pragmatics

The contextual situation associated with the verb *advise* in the preceding section is more widely reflected in a 'macro frame' / script, which takes a structure such as the following:

<prag pred01 structure>= Concerning Z (arg2), X (arg1) ADVISE/inform (pred01) Y (arg3), under C (arg4), where X=SUPPLIER / BANKER / EMPLOYER / CNAME1, Y= CUSTOMER/ EMPLOYEE / CNAME2, Z=CONTENT, C=CIRCUMSTANCE; Y (Initiator)—>X(respondent) permissible

<prag pred02 structure>= X (arg1) ADVISE/directs/requests (pred02) a course of action Z (arg2) to Y (arg3), under C (arg4), where X= SUPPLIER / BANKER / EMPLOYER / CNAME1, Y=CUSTOMER / EMPLOYEE / CNAME2, Z= CONTENT, C= CIRCUMSTANCE; Y (Initiator)—>X(respondent) permissible

In other words, the stereotype presented in the PROLEX corpus for this verb is that it tends to be the institution/person initiating the discourse (be it the supplier, banker, employer, or more generally 'cname1') which/who does one of two things: either informing or directing the addressee (be it the customer, employee, or more generally 'cname2') regarding a particular state of affairs or course of action. For *advise*, it is also permissible for the second party in the discourse, {*cname2*}, to initiate the piece of discourse as well. However, in the case of *claim*, which takes two related senses from the field of insurance, the second sense in which the insured party makes a demand on the insurer for payment under an insurance policy is the more usual situation, whereas the insurer (as 'ower') is unlikely to initiate the piece of discourse to pay out a claim without any request for them to do so.

<prag arg02 structure>= X (arg1) files Z (arg2=arg02) against Y (arg3) under C (arg4), where X=CLAIMANT, Y=OWER, Z = CLAIMED, C= CIRCUMSTANCE, Y (Initiator)—>X (Respondent) impermissible

The foregoing discussion in this section – indeed, throughout the preceding sections – is generally applicable to the PROCOMPARE corpus as well. However, for the rest of this section, I now turn to the typological categories in the PROLEX corpus (see Section 4.4.6 for a detailed listing of the codes used).

Recall that there are 8 postulated categories. This includes the following labels:

<prag pred0 typological_information>= <S C X A T P N E>

where S = Subject/Functions, C=Company, X= Exchange, A=Acts, T=Type of Text, P=Part of Document, N=Number (Location Identification Marker), and the E=Error label (i.e. typographical and/or linguistic error occurring in the clause where the word occurs).

For each of these categories, let us take our illustration from the noun lemma *account*. From the following listing

<prag arg0 S>= S0 (5) S1 (5) S2 (5) S3 (0) S4 (2) S5 (0) S6 (1) S7 (47) S8 (18) S9 (1) S10 (3) S11 (0) S12 (0) S13 (0) S14 (6) S15 (10)

it can be noted that most instances of *account* come from those texts which relate to the 'settlement of account' (i.e. S7, 47 times), followed by those relating to 'credit' (i.e. S8, 18 times), rather than, say, those relating to promoting goodwill / public relations (i.e. S3, no occurrences).

Where the next label is concerned, the listing

<prag arg0 C>= C0 (4) C1 (2) C2 (6) C3 (12) C4 (0) C5 (0) C6 (2) C7 (24) C8 (9) C9 (14) C10 (13) C11 (10) C12 (9)

indicates that there are a fair number of texts (24) drawn from a local bank (i.e. C7 – a major bank in Singapore), but on the whole, *account* is quite well distributed across the range of institutions from which the texts containing *account* have been obtained.

Next, the eXchange label

<prag arg0 X>= X1 (74) X2 (29)

indicates that there are more discoursal moves of 'initiation' (i.e. X1, 74 times) than 'response'. This accords well with the expectation that those who manage the account – the bank manager, supplier etc – are the ones (because of their institutional role) who are more likely to initiate a piece of discourse to the customer regarding the *account*, than vice-versa.

This institutional role tends to be mostly one of *informing* the account-holder regarding the state of affairs, as the following indicates (i.e. A2, 62 times):

<prag arg0 A>= A1 (13) A2 (62) A3 (28)

In turn, it is not unexpected that A3 (requesting the addressee to a particular course of action) occurs more than A1 (acknowledging the addressee's letter), since it is the initiator, the one who manages the account, who does more of initiating the discourse, as the previous label listing suggests.

Where the mode of discourse in written business communication is concerned, this tends, for *account*, to take the form of a letter, as the following indicates:

<prag arg0 T>= T1 (80) T2 (23) T3 (0)

Memoranda mentioning *account(s)* do not occur, presumably because communication regarding the customer's account tends to take on a more formal tenor of discourse. This label 'Type of Text', incidentally, is not to be confused with Biber's 'text-type' (see Sections 4.4 and 4.5).

The next label

<prag arg0 P>= P1 (0) P3 (0) P4 (13) P5 (0) P6 (1) P7 (0) P8 (0) P9 (5) P10 (8) P11 (0) P12 (0) P2/1/2 (11) P2/1/3 (7) P2/1/4 (5) P 2/1/14 (1) P2/2/3 (8) P2/2/4 (9) P2/2/5 (2) P2/2/6 (1) P2/3/4 (5) P2/3/5 (2) P2/3/6 (1) P2/4/5 (3) P2/4/6 (1) P2/5/6 (2) P 2/6/14 (1) P2/f/1 (3) P2/f/2 (7) P2/f/3 (6) P2/f/4 (1)

gives a sense of how long the text is or, more specifically, where the word *account* tends to occur in the text. For instance, it is obvious that *account* would never occur in the 'greetings' (as in *Dear Sir*) or the 'closing' (as in *Yours sincerely*) but is likely to occur in the subject title of the letter (P4), and even in the 'checklist' (P10), in which the addresser has included some preworded piece of text (e.g. *(★★★) original letter of credit; (★★★) debit issuing bank account*). Moreover, in the main body of the text (<P2/n1/n2>), *account* is a word which tends to occur towards the beginning rather than the end. For instance, while the code <P2/1/2> (11) informs us that 11 instances of *account* are found in the first paragraph of a two-paragraph text, <P2/2/4> (9) indicates that 9 instances of *account* are found in the second paragraph of a four-paragraph text.

The next label, N,

<prag arg0 N>= N013 (2) N019 (1) N020 (1) N021 (1) N022 (2) N035 (1) N047 (2) N050 (6) N051 (4) N073 (2) N112 (2) N122 (2) N133 (1) N137 (1) N140 (1) N142 (1) N149 (1) N152 (1) N182 (3) N200 (1) N201 (1) N202 (2) N203 (1) N208 (3) N217 (2) N218 (1) N219 (1) N221 (1) N222 (1) N223 (2) N230 (3) N240 (1) N246 (1) N249 (1) N251 (2) N285 (3) N287 (1) N301 (3) N302 (2) N316 (1) N332 (1) N333(2) N361 (1) N364 (1) N365 (2) N369 (1) N372 (2) N373 (2) N382 (1) N453 (1) N455 (2) N456 (3) N502 (2) N516 (1) N517 (1) N524 (1) N527 (1) N540 (1) N541 (2) N542 (2) N543 (1) N548 (1) N564 (2) functions not only as the location identification marker but also gives a sense of how *account* is distributed in the PROLEX corpus, in order to allow for any 'skewing' or 'bias' that might affect the interpretation of these frequency figures. There does not seem to be any evidence of skewing here.

Finally, the category

\<prag arg0 E\>= E- (103) E+ (0)

indicates that *account* does not appear to be part of any clause that has linguistic and/or typographical errors.

6.11 A DISCUSSION OF THE PROLEX AND PROCOMPARE SPECIMEN LEXICAL ENTRIES

Although the analysis contained in Appendix A is largely self-explanatory, let us highlight certain aspects of these sublanguage lexemes in this section.

6.11.1 *Account* (n)

The most immediately noticeable feature is of course the extent to which the PROLEX and PROCOMPARE corpora are seen to complement each other with this type of analysis. This complementarity between the PROLEX and PROCOMPARE corpora is, for instance, seen in the range of collocates associated with *account*. While the PROLEX corpus uses a term such as *current account*, the equivalent term *checking account* which is present in the PROCOMPARE corpus indicates the British and American varieties respectively. A quick check with the EBD (Collin 1986: 47) and the LDBE (Adam 1989: 109) dictionaries confirms this to be the case.

Collocations form a very important aspect of the lexicon: indeed the sublanguage may be said to be defined, in part at least, by the choice of the collocations used. With *account*, the occurrence of such attributive terms as *brief* and *full* indicates a more general language in use (i.e. where *account* here has the sense of 'description') and invite the prediction that these collocations do not tend to co-occur with *account* in business English especially relating to banking. This is because, in the business world, a semblance of objectivity is maintained, and such subjective epithets would be inappropriate.

There are two main senses associated with this noun in the two business English corpora. The first relates to a detailed record of transactions between debtor and creditor, and the second is related to banking. The EBD dictionary (Collin 1986) lists both these senses under the single lexical entry *account*, but gives prominence to the second sense in a separate entry *bank account*; the LDBE dictionary (Adam 1989) lists the two senses under two separate entries. Taking into account both senses, however, the definition of *account* in these two corpora may be said to include a record of the transactions of the money paid or owed between an institution and a customer (the 'account-holder') which the two parties concerned agree to maintain in an equilibrium state. Although the data obliges the generalisation that it is the institution which maintains this equilibrium by communication with the holder of the account, there is no reason why the holder cannot initiate the discourse (as when one writes to one's bank manager).

A major difference between the related concepts of ACCOUNT and RECORD is that ACCOUNT obliges a strong sense of maintaining this equilibrium (hence the notion of semantic prosody in Chapter 3), whereas a RECORD is just documentary. Collocative terms such as *settle* and *maintain* point to a desire to reach an equilibrium; on the other hand, the adjectival collocations *outstanding, overdue, overdrawn*, the associated verb form *settle* and the set phrase *insufficient funds in* point to a state of disequilibrium, and the need for its resolution.

In terms of grammatical features, it is noticeable that both these corpora list *account* as a count noun only, unlike a general dictionary which lists *account* as having the possibility of both 'count' and 'uncount' features: a general dictionary would of course take into account general senses such as ones associated with the following: *The doctor is a man of some account in the village*, and *You must take into account the boy's long illness* (LDOCE, Procter 1978: 6). The point to note here is that the range of senses in a specialised dictionary are reduced dramatically in the sublanguage corpus, and this is reflected in corresponding grammatical restrictions.

Finally, it is significant that in Business English, the noun lemma *account* occurs much more frequently than its verb lemma counterpart. This is because *account* (v) has the different meaning of 'explaining' something, (and is almost always followed by the preposition *for*, which has no specialised use in business correspondence). Therefore, it does not always make good sense to adhere to the blanket principle that the noun is derived from the homonymic verb, as the morphological section of the CELEX database (see Chapter 5) suggests. The noun and verb senses of *account* are best treated on their own terms.

6.11.2 *Advise* (v)

It is not coincidence that the adverb which most often immediately precedes the verb *advise* is *please* (see Section 7.3.6). The data from the PROLEX corpus suggests that *advise* is a verb mostly found in the active, which has the function of not only informing but also directing or requesting the addressee to a particular course of action. As such, it is customary to add the courtesy subjunct. In the PROCOMPARE corpus, the more 'old-fashioned', formulaic form *Please be advised* is used more frequently: this form is itself difficult to analyse, as the surface form encourages the analysis of *advised* as adjectival, whereas the underlying structure is a verbal one in which *[Addresser] advises/ informs [Addressee]*. I have opted to treat *advised* mainly as the -ed (participle) form of the verb, as the CLAWS automatic tagging also indicates.

Because of the tendency of *advise* to be preceded by the adverb *please*, the base form is virtually obligatory. This partly explains why the singular -s form of the verb in both corpora hardly ever occurs. Another reason is that, in the PROLEX corpus, the instances realising 'subject' indicate that collective institutional responsibility is preferred, except for the two instances where the first person singular pronoun functions in subject position.

Unlike in the CELEX database, where *advise* is listed as being capable of subcategorisation into 'transitive, transitive & complementation, intransitive, ditransitive' elements, the verb in the present instance is ditransitive, obliging the pragmatic structure in which X informs Y concerning Z. (The circumstance under which this takes place is optional.) Under the semantics frame, the general case roles associated with X and Y respectively – Actor and Recipient – correspond to more specific pragmatic case roles such as Supplier/ Banker and Customer/Employee.

6.11.3 *Appreciate* (v)

As both corpora indicate, *appreciate* is a verb immediately preceded most often by the modal *would*, thus indicating a sense of future conditional gratitude for this routine courtesy marker. The <syn pred arg2 form> slot indicates that the most frequent pattern is *['your' + either NP or -ing clause]*: the addressee is invited to a particular course of action which would then invite thanks from the addresser, which in both corpora tends to be the collective *we* – although in the PROCOMPARE corpus, the more personal first-person pronoun *i* occurs as many as 28 times.

In the passive form, the pattern *['your' + either NP or -ing clause]* usually takes the subject position. The corresponding verb *appreciated* always indicates the past participle form in both corpora, but the two corpora do not contain any sentences where *appreciate* means 'to increase in value' (as in the possible sentence *The dollar has appreciated in terms of the yen*). Thus, correspondingly, only the (mono)transitive pattern is recorded in both corpora, unlike in the CELEX database which lists both transitive and intransitive patterns.

There are two senses of this verb present in both corpora. The first sense relates to the idea of 'recognising with gratitude' (in the semantics), with the extended notion of a 'polite request' (see Greenbaum and Whitcut 1988: 53), as indicated in the pragmatics section. The second sense has to do with the idea of 'realisation', as in the following clause from the PROLEX corpus: *we wish you will appreciate our choice and demonstrated restraint*. The PROCOMPARE corpus has a greater number of occurrences of this second sense. The relative frequencies of these senses are not indicated (although word-sense disambiguation techniques – applicable to large corpora – can make this explicit).

6.11.4 *Claim* (v,n)

The word *claim* is deverbal in its behaviour, i.e. it has both verb and noun properties. This is not indicated in the CELEX database, which merely lists the word as being either a 'noun' or a 'verb'.

However, while this word might be deverbal in its behaviour, its nature in both the PROLEX and PROCOMPARE corpora is to occur more often as a noun than as a verb (as indicated by the raw CLAWS frequency count in the morphology section). As a noun, the specificity of the claim is seen in the important presence of the postmodifier to the head element. As the PROLEX corpus indicates, within the postmodifier, the prepositional elements are not mere instantiations: they indicate the situational pragmatics, i.e. someone makes a claim *for* some settlement *against* some institution / some other person *concerning* the topic at hand.

Turning to the premodifier, it can be seen that such collocates as *personal accident and hospitalisation, reimbursement, public liabilities,* and *motor* indicate that the PROLEX corpus is more specialised (at least in this respect), whereas the PROCOMPARE corpus uses more general collocates such as *said, lawful, known, potential,* and *outstanding.* This situation is hardly surprising, since the pragmatics section (for the PROLEX corpus) also indicates that most of the instantiations of *claim* come from the insurance domain. While it is difficult to sustain the claim that the PROCOMPARE texts come from this domain (since the PROCOMPARE corpus is targeted at more general situations), *claim* in both corpora is nevertheless given two senses: one which reflects the insurance situation, and the other a more general situation where the claimant files a claim.

6.11.5 *Full* (adj)
The two corpora indicate that there are few instances in which *full* (adj) functions as the head element in a noun phrase, as *in full.* Most of the time, as expected, it functions as a premodifier to some noun which functions as the head element. Comparing the two corpora, it can be observed that the PROCOMPARE corpus contains more set and formulaic phrases, such as *full and exclusive, full and total,* and *full and final.* The PROLEX corpus is more 'staid' in this respect. Viewed in this manner, the CELEX entry for this adjective is the most staid, listing the adjective as merely 'ordinary', and taking either 'attributive' or 'predicative' positions, or both.

6.11.6 *Please* (adv)
Greenbaum and Whitcut (1988: 541) have this to say of *please,* as an adverb: 'The expressions *please find* (*Enclosed please find our latest report*) and *please be advised that* (*Please be advised that your order is now ready*) are old-fashioned business English. The first can be replaced by *Here is* or *I enclose,* and the second omitted together.' This is where a specialised corpus – especially one which is indisputably large – comes in handy in evaluating such statements. As it stands, the forms *please find* and *please be advised* occur 8 and 2 times (i.e. not including the other forms associated with *be advised*) respectively in the PROLEX corpus; the corresponding figures in the PROCOMPARE corpus are 4 and 10 times

respectively. So, it is difficult to evaluate such a statement. However the common occurrence of the pattern *Please advise* in the PROLEX and (to a lesser extent) PROCOMPARE corpora should suggest that this collocation with *please* is anything but 'old-fashioned'.

Nevertheless, despite the two corpora being small, a versatile range of verbs occurs immediately after the adverb *please* and which invites the lexicographer to structure them for use by a learner of Business English.

6.11.7 *Regret* (v)

It is significant that in both corpora, the verb *regret* occurs without any inflectional endings, i.e. the *-s*, *-ed*, and *-ing* forms are not present in the morphology frame. This is also reflected in the syntax frame, where there is an absence of the modal, perfective, progressive, and passive verb constructions. In this regard, the subject form is usually *we*, instead of the singular first-person pronoun (blank occurrences (*[]*) in the PROLEX corpus, i.e. where the subject position is not realised, are due to telexes which tend to economise. In this case, the institution which apologises is inevitably equated with the sender, so there is no need to make this explicit in telexes). On reflection, it is appropriate that the pattern *we regret* ... is the stereotype, for two reasons: 1. Collective responsibility appears preferable to personal responsibility, particularly when unfavourable news is concerned (hence, the role NEGATIVE_TOPIC); 2. Any other forms of the verb (i.e. *regretted, have regretted, will regret*) would indicate insincerity on the part of the addresser, whereas the present tense form is taken to mean an immediate sense of regret. It seems to be the case that the more such forms get used, the more formulaic – yet mandatory – they become in Business English.

6.11.8 *Shipment* (n)

Like the COBUILD (Sinclair 1987, 1995) and LDBE (Adam 1989) dictionaries, *shipment* (n) is listed here as a separate entry, although there is clearly some deverbal behaviour. The morphological information for this entry in CELEX, however, does not indicate that *shipment* (n) is derived from *ship* (v). Rather, it indicates that *shipment* contains 'one productive lemma' + an affix, i.e. *ship* (v) + the suffix *ment*.

In terms of meaning, *shipment* (n) can refer, admittedly, to the *process* of consigning goods. However, the word also refers to the *goods* being consigned. Thus, it merits being listed as a separate entry.

Comparing the two corpora, one notes that the PROLEX corpus gives a richer listing of the slot <syn post LEX adv_colloc real>, i.e. the adverbial collocates that follow *shipment* include *to singapore, on {date}, for onward journey to rangoon* etc. By contrast, the PROCOMPARE corpus has only one instance. This can be taken another indication of how the two corpora supplement each other.

6.11.9 The relatedness of information

While the preceding sections seem to suggest an apparent repetition of lexical information in the CELEX database (which is nevertheless an important lexical enterprise), the same concern might also be levelled at the LFA lexicon. At the *inter*-lexemic level, the LFA entries should share common information. For instance, the verbs *advise*, *regret*, and *appreciate* are related verbs which are transitive and take, in principle, the regular -s, -ed, and -ing inflectional endings. In the next section, I shall discuss emerging issues related to the computational organisation of the lexicon for the encoding of these entries in a more compact manner.

As each LFA entry stands, however, at the conceptual level of representation (i.e. in a format convenient for humans to read), the various parameters of information (i.e. morphology, syntax, semantics, pragmatics) have a fair degree of relatedness at the *intra*-lexemic level (i.e. within the lexeme itself).

Taking the verb entries for illustration, throughout the various parameters, the 'atoms' (using DATR terminology, Chapter 5) 'LEX' and 'pred0' – equatable with each other – link all these parameters together. Moreover, more specifically, in the case of, say, *appreciate* (v), notice that in the PROLEX pragmatics frame

<prag pred01 structure>= X (arg1) APPRECIATES/(requests) (pred01) Z (arg2) from Y (implicit in arg2) under C (arg3), where X= INITIATOR / CNAME1, Y= ADDRESSEE / CNAME2, Z= ACTION_REQUESTED, C= CIRCUMSTANCE

X, the INITIATOR / CNAME1 (i.e. the first institution to be named, which usually initiates the discourse), is identified with *arg1*. In the semantics section, *arg1* has the case role of 'Actor'. In turn, in the syntax section, *arg1* is usually realised by an NP in Subject position, instantiated explicitly by *we, you, i* etc. Thus, the information that the 'appreciator' comprises all of these elements is inheritable between the various parameters.

Correspondingly, Z, the ACTION_REQUESTED, is identified with *arg2*. In the semantics section, this takes the case role of 'Goal'. In turn, in the syntax section, *arg2* is realised by instances which take such forms as *your* + NPs, *your* + V-*ing* clauses, and *if*-clauses - all of which function in Direct Object position. In addition, frequency information contained here, as in elsewhere, gives the default information that the Direct Object tend to be realised, first and foremost, by the form *your* + NP. Equally important is the powerful rule that, in passive clauses where *appreciate* is the main verb, invariably the Subject position is realised by the form *your* + **V**ing/NP, i.e. in such clauses as *your arranging to send a sample package is appreciated* and *your co-operation is appreciated*.

Turning now to Y, which is rendered as 'implicit in arg2', within the element designated ACTION-REQUESTED / *arg2* / Goal / DO, the addressee (i.e. the person whom the communication is sent to) is recoverable from the instances of *you* or *your* embedded within the Direct Object.

Finally, as in the case of *arg1* and *arg2*, information regarding the optional element Circumstance, *arg3,* is recoverable in a similar way.

It is reasonable to say that the LFA lexicon does not yet indicate such associations as the following: the modal *would* preceding *advise* would be likely to be associated with a request type of speech act, i.e. such associations would make the relation between, say, the pragmatic and syntactic parameters closer. Similarly, the pragmatics parameter in the entry for *advise* does not yet indicate in some way that the collocate *please* (as in *Please advise*) occurs in requests for advice from the respondent, but that *wish to* (as in *We wish to advise...*) occurs in declaratives indicating that the Initiator is offering / giving advice. There is, then, as I have discussed in Chapter 5, a trade-off in the amount of detail using an approach which is more bottom-up but which requires a level of abstraction from the top-down aspect as well. However, other types of cross-associations do exist (however implicit they may be). At the inter-lexemic level, the slot **<syn pre LEX adv_colloc real>** where *please* occurs 36 times in the entry for *advise* corresponds to the **<syn post LEX verb_colloc real>** slot where *advise* occurs, also 36 times, in the entry for *please.*

In this section, I have thus dwelt at length on the inter-relatedness of information for the various parameters because, in practice, these types of information interact with each other in a closer way than the apparent distinction between these parameters would lead us to believe.

6.11.10 Making the LFA lexicon more compact

The LFA lexicon, at the conceptual level of representation (as represented by Appendix A), can map more efficiently to its computational level of representation. For this purpose, a more formal lexical representation language such as DATR (Evans and Gazdar 1990) might help in structuring the entries in terms of inheritance equations and those which achieve formalism_2. For a start, I follow Andry et al. (1992) in taking the path equations indicated by (a) – (e):

a. Node1: <> == Node2
b. Node1: Path1 == Value1
c. Node1:Path1 == "Path2"
d. Node1:Path1 == Node2:Path2
e. Node1:Path1 == Node2:<>

I interpret (a) as reading 'Node 1 is like Node2': this allows, as Andry et al. (1992: 249) say, for 'Node1 to inherit all equations available at Node2, except those incompatible with equations at Node1'. Path equation (b) is used to assign values to paths, e.g. in the case of PROLEX verbs, for <syn lex cat> == v (this reads as 'in terms of the syntax parameter, the lexeme inherits the properties of a verb'). Path equation (c) reads as 'Path 1 is assigned the value of Path2 which is evaluated globally'. Path equation (d) reads as 'Node1:Path1 inherits the value found at Node2:Path2'. Finally, path equation (e) is a variant of (d), in which extensions of Path1 are specified at Node2.

Taking the PROLEX verb entries *advise*, *appreciate*, and *regret* for illustration, these regular verbs share information at the morpho-syntactic parameters. In terms of inflectional morphology, while corpus processing through CLAWS (see Sections 6.4; 6.10.1) establishes the surface stem form and its suffixes *-s*, *-ed*, and *-ing* (when they occur), it is now necessary to reorganise these types of information beyond 'surface' morphology. The stem so far is identifiable as the root. For structuring purposes, let us equate the root, **F**, with LEX. In turn, the *-ed* and the *-ing* forms are grouped together as past and present participle respectively. The ending *-s* should be listed separately to form the third person singular, which also takes present tense. These types of information may be tentatively written as follows:

VERB: <mor form> ==VERB_MOR:<>
VERB_MOR: <base> == "<mor lex>"
                              <past_participle> == ("<mor lex>" ed)
                              <present_participle> == ("<mor lex>" ing>)
                              <present third singular> == ("<mor lex>"s>)

Of course, it is also possible to include information concerning finiteness (combining tense, number, person) and the present and past tense forms in a similar way (see Andry et al. 1992: 251). The more interesting point, however, is how to ensure that instances exemplifying ("<mor LEX>" ing>) will be inherited by the path <present_participle> in the case of *advising* (v) but which will also exclude *advising* (adj) at the same time. My solution is to make use of the fact that CLAWS will give both tags, *advise_VVG* and *advise_JJ*. Thus, the information for the inheritance of the present participle form can be replaced by the following:

<present_participle> == ("<mor lex>" _vvg>)

This says that the present participle form is copied from (inherits) the global application of the root form to CLAWS-generated tags which end in VVG.

Similarly, then, the past participle form is copied from the root form + the CLAWS-generated VVN tag, i.e.

<past_participle> == ("<mor lex>" _vvn)

This solution, which I have illustrated for relating CLAWS generated output to the inheritance of forms in DATR, can be extended to other forms in order to (morphologically) disambiguate between them. Another solution would be to construct a table of raw frequency counts, in which the ordering of the frequency figures would indicate a kind of 'prioritised' inheritance, where the first frequency count for a particular property 'wins' over the other, in cases where there is a conflict. Thus, in the case of *regret*, to ensure that *regret_VVO*

(35) is inherited (but not *regret_NN1 (1)*), we need something like the following:

Regret: <>VERB
                   <base> == <mor freq>
                   <mor freq> == ("<mor lex>"_(35))

This says in effect that the base form (of the verb) inherits from the table of frequency counts, which we can call <mor freq>. This table, in turn, contains the frequency count for only the verb form, but not that for the noun.

More generally, the various verb lexemes *advise*, *appreciate*, and *regret* can be ordered in the following manner:

VERB_MOR: <base> == ("<mor lex>"_vvo_(87) _vvo_(61) _vvo_(35))

Such frequency information in DATR, as I have just shown, should be integrated into a parser for which a PATR-like macro could be constructed which automatically compares frequency counts and prioritises the highest frequency, where appropriate.

Turning now to the forms listed in the LFA lexicon as <syn LEX modals>, <syn LEX perfective>, <syn LEX progressive> and <syn LEX passive>, these also share similar types of information with the morphological parameter and can be structured in the manner I have sketched. The program listing in Evans and Gazdar (1990), for instance, contains a lexical account of passive, clitic negation, and subject-auxiliary 'inversion'. It also includes representative main verbs and all the English auxiliaries. In the present context, such a listing can be extended by incorporating raw frequency counts in the manner I have indicated. Again, taking the modal auxiliary *would* in each of the three illustrative verbs, we can have the following path equations, specific to *would*:

Would: <> MODAL
                   <base> == <mor freq>
                   <mor freq> == ("<mor lex>"_(37) _(2) _(0))

This says in effect that *would* behaves like a modal auxiliary in such a way that its form is inherited from the three verbs (in descending order of frequency).

Again, in applying the nonmonotonic aspect of DATR, if sufficient instances of a verb such as *regret* warrant the generalisation in business English that it is always the case that only the root form occurs (i.e. no *regretting, regretted, regrets*), then the following exceptional forms should be stated explicitly:

Regret: <> ==VERB
          <mor LEX> == regret
          <mor form past_participle> == []   {i.e. recall [] signals "empty set"}
          <mor form present_participle> == []
          <mor form present third singular> == []

Let us now illustrate the structuring of verb complementation, lexical semantic and pragmatic information. For instance, *regret* and *appreciate* are monotransitive

verbs (taking subject and direct object), whereas *advise* is a ditransitive verb
(taking subject, direct object and indirect object). Using these facts, the inheritance hierarchy can be structured as follows:

VERB   <syn lex cat> == v
                  <syn v arg> == pred0
                  <syn pred0> == ARG1:<>

The top node is the VERB node, by default. So, any information concerning
the subject is associated with this top verb node, which functions as a predicate
taking the argument ARG1, which will be detailed in a moment. This verb
node, by default, is inherited also in the case of an intransitive verb.

If the verb is a transitive verb, it also inherits all the properties associated with
the top verb node, i.e. in the present context, it inherits information concerning the subject as well. This is expressed in the first of the following equations:

TRANS_V: <> == VERB
              <syn pred0> == ARG2:<>

By default, let us also take the transitive slot as being monotransitive, in which
the second equation allows the extension to be specified by the node ARG2
(again, this will be detailed in a moment).

So far, then, we have detailed the behaviour of the verbs *appreciate* and *regret*.
For *advise*, the following equation obtains:

TRANS_DI: <> == TRANS_V
              <syn pred0> == ARG3:<>

In effect, this says that a ditransitive verb such as *regret* inherits all the properties
of a transitive verb (which includes its defaulted monotransitive property).
However, while so doing, it assigns nonmonotonic priority to the ARG3 node.

What then do these ARG nodes look like? For ARG1 (corresponding to
the one for verbs in the LFA lexicon), the following obtains:

ARG1:<syn pred0 function> == s
                  <sem pred0 case> == (actor)
                  <prag pred0> == (supplier initiator banker employer cname1
                  cognisant)

This says, in effect, that the predicate verb takes an argument which
functions as a subject. Typically (i.e. notice the round brackets), this subject
takes the semantic case role of ACTOR, which at the same time can function as
SUPPLIER, INITIATOR, BANKER etc. at the pragmatic parameter for the
PROLEX and PROCOMPARE corpora.

In a similar way, ARG2 and ARG3 obtain:

ARG2:   <syn pred0 function> == do
                  <sem pred0 case> == (content)

                              <prag pred0> == (content action_requested cognized

negative_topic)

ARG3:   <syn pred0 function> == io

<sem pred0 case> == (recipient)

<prag pred0> == (respondent addressee customer employee

cname2)

From these equations can be seen the way the various levels of information relate to one another. This hierarchy has also been structured in such a manner that will provide maximum generalisation. This is seen in the case of passives, for instance. Using the usual John–Mary example, *John likes Mary* is realised as Subject + Verb + DO, with its corresponding semantic cases ACTOR + PROCESS + RECIPIENT and *Mary is liked by John*. But the passive form *Mary is liked by John* is of course one in which the grammatical functions change for the instantiated elements, but the semantic roles remain the same. Thus, the structuring of ARG1, ARG2, and ARG3 is such that they are always associated with the S, DO and IO elements respectively. The round brackets in the semantic and pragmatic parameters show that, while these elements are typically associated with the semantic and pragmatic roles listed above, these roles can change in the manner just illustrated.

Finally, the limitations mentioned in the preceding sections can be redressed by using DATR to organise the information contained in the LFA lexicon in various ways. For instance, while a verb such as *appreciate* is syntactically pre-ceded by the modal *would*, the pattern *would appreciate* also signals the speech act of REQUESTIVE. This can be structured in a manner such as the following:

Appreciate: <> == VERB

<mor lex> == appreciate

<mor pre aux> == (would_(37))

<prag pre aux mor lex> == REQUESTIVE_SA.

6.12 CONCLUSION

In this chapter, I have highlighted a case study involving the process of 'transforming' two corpora of business English into their respective lexicons which can be stored in a computational format. This process involves corpus lexical processing and acquiring the lexicons using a mix of a top-down and bottom-up approach. In terms of the top-down approach, it is necessary to use linguistically-motivated categories for structuring the lexicon; in terms of the bottom-up approach, the (sublanguage) corpus has been suggested as an important complement to the dictionary (MRD) as a lexical resource. Such a lexicon, structured using the tenets of the LFA framework sketched in this book, is in a format amenable to computational storage in a lexical data or knowledge base which has the right tractability and expressiveness.

6.13 STUDY QUESTIONS

1. Is a lexicon which is structured using the LFA framework, as detailed in Appendix A, very different from the one postulated by John Sinclair, as detailed in Chapter 3?
2. How does a sublanguage approach for the construction of lexicons help in natural language processing?

6.14 FURTHER READING

For a vocabulary of written business communication, read Ghadessy (1993). Aspects of sublanguage are dealt with in McEnery and Wilson (1996: Chapter 6).

NOTES

1. The texts do not provide sentence-initial capitals because these texts were stored in upper-case in the original PROLEX Collection file, and using the **tr** command in UNIX to transform them gets rid of the upper-case entirely.
2. I use the C2a tagset here. The grammatical tagset used for CLAWS has changed variously over time. C2a is now replaced by C7, which although smaller than C2a, irons out some of the inconsistencies in C2a. The tagset used to work with SGML texts is C6, which is almost identical to the C7 tagset. The C5 tagset is more restricted: it has approximately 57 tags and was used for the processing of the British National Corpus project (see also Black and Leech 1993).
3. i.e. 'Immediate Dominance/Linear Precedence': see Gazdar et al (1985). I am grateful to Richard Sharman for letting me try out his parser. At the time when I was engaged in this work, it was impossible to obtain a copy of the FIDDITCH parser (Hindle 1994), whose public release had been suspended.
4. The term 'mini-text' seems equivalent to the 'span position', or 'window' (in the sense of Church et al).
5. Sinclair & Coulthard (1975), among others, have developed the concept of the **exchange** as a unit of discourse analysis.
6. For Halliday (1981: 44), it is the 'clause' that makes it possible to create the semantic unit of 'text'. Here, I use the 'word' instead, bearing in mind that Hallidayan linguistics also recognises that it is lexis that is the 'most delicate grammar'.
7. 'Faux' = First Auxiliary

Conclusion: Towards a more adequate concept of the lexicon

In this book, I have been concerned with both lexical theory and lexical practice. In terms of lexical theory, this book has been concerned with introducing you, the reader, to the joint perspectives of computational linguistics, computational lexicography, and corpus linguistics for extending the notion of a lexicon. A greater regard for a richer lexicon as the central repository of linguistic knowledge is made not for its own sake (although this, in itself, is an excellent object to work towards) but because the lexicon is now generally agreed to be the 'bottleneck' of natural language processing systems. Unlike the days of old when toy systems (capable of analysing only a few sentences) needed very small lexicons, NLP systems nowadays must deal with unrestricted text (i.e. natural language text or 'real' text) and so need larger and richer lexicons.

Such lexicons may be achieved by using the two main lexical resources: machine-readable dictionaries (MRDs) and machine-readable texts (MRTs). Both types of lexical resources are necessary and complement each other. However, while the subject of MRDs is well-treated in the literature, the use of MRTs as a lexical resource needs to be considered from three computational perspectives jointly: CL1 (computational linguistics), CL2 (computational lexicography and lexicology), and CL3 (corpus lexicography). A consideration of these perspectives invariably leads one to be concerned with the processes of textual acquisition, lexical acquisition, and lexical representation. These processes form the basis of my framework, which I call a Lexical Frame Analysis (LFA), whose assumptions I have detailed in the course of this book. In terms of practical implementation, a case study or small-scale lexical project exemplifies the tenets of the framework in practice.

By means of the specimen lexical entries in Appendix A, aspects of the relationship between corpus data (functioning as a lexical resource) and the abstraction known as a lexical frame (using frame theory) are brought out. The corpus, via lexical processing, offers a more contemporary snapshot of the language at a given point in time; frame theory offers a uniform means for representing word and world knowledge. A lexicon derived by this means is to be stored in the computational lexical structure known as the lexical data / knowledge base (LDB/LDB). While the specimen entries illustrate what the lexicon can entail at the conceptual level of representation, this level of representation also corresponds to its computational structure, for which some issues related to the organisation of the lexicon in such a postulated data or knowledge base have been examined.

The results from the case study might be seen as a microcosm of the larger issues involved in building a large-scale lexicon using these principles, although the practical encoding of any lexicon will invariably depend on the purpose for which it was crafted.

Whichever method is used for crafting a lexicon, it is important to stress that there is increasingly a need to *automate* the processes of textual acquisition, lexical acquisition, and lexical representation leading to the creation of a multifunctional lexical data/knowledge base. As indicated in this book, there are already a number of such data or knowledge bases which are admirable in their implementation. The central motivation for these enterprises, simplistically put, takes the following form: 'If "dictionary making" has traditionally been done by hand, what insights and advantages can be gained by using the computer?' Or, to formulate this question in another manner: 'How can the linguist's dictionary be created and stored in a multifunctional lexical data/knowledge base so that, in turn, this represents the creation of knowledge which can be disseminated in various ways?'

In its very modest way, this book has attempted to provide such an answer. Again, although I have chosen to use the corpus as the main lexical resource, exemplifying it by a consideration of two business English corpora (PROLEX and PROCOMPARE), the principle used is that all relevant sources – be they MRDs or MRTs – have their own respective lexical contribution. Also, although the case study has used the sublanguage approach, the general language notion is no less important for the creation of this multifunctional LDB/LKB. For instance, lexical information gathered from both a database such as CELEX (exemplifying MRDs) and the two corpora of business English (exemplifying MRTs) can be integrated. Conceivably, however, such an integration could take place in the form of combining the frequency values for these three sources, thus rendering them valuable to those users of business English who need them. Arguably, then, a frequency-informed LKB would need to provide a way of *interpolating* an estimated value for the probability of some function, where the probabilities for general English (e.g. as provided by CELEX) are very different from the value for business English (exemplifying a sublanguage), as given by the respective PROLEX and/or PROCOMPARE frequencies. For instance, consider the two senses of *advise*, i.e. ADVISE1 and ADVISE2. Suppose ADVISE1 in the PROLEX Corpus has a probability of 0.2

and ADVISE2 a probability of 0.8. Suppose also that, correspondingly, ADVISE1 has a probability of 0.6 and ADVISE2 also a probability of 0.6 in the CELEX database. Then, the question becomes one of deciding on a value for the estimated probabilities of these verbs in a new corpus of business English. As a first guess, the intermediate value between general English and PROLEX should be taken (i.e. say, 0.4 for ADVISE1 and 0.7 for ADVISE2). Extending this rationale, there is then some kind of 'compromise' to be struck between the data supplied for general English and the data provided for sublanguage English.

This book has also stressed the importance of the exchange and reusability of lexicons (so that individual efforts will not be wasted), for which the Text Encoding Initative and others are actively involved in specifying such standards. A further boost in this direction comes from the computer technology offered nowadays by the World Wide Web in which the numerous efforts in lexical research may be recognised and brought closer together. The World Wide Web, as the book has stressed, is becoming indispensable for lexical research (as indeed it is for many types of research), which is evolving in a rapid manner. Newer and better lexicons continue to be created for use in various systems.

In conclusion, it is hoped that this book, in its own small way, has extended the notion of the lexicon and the significance of the term 'dictionary making', thereby providing a basis for a more adequate study and implementation of lexical knowledge.

Appendix A
The LFA Lexicon (Specimen entries based on the PROLEX and PROCOMPARE Corpora)

ACCOUNT (n)

Prolexnoun_LEX account (103):

MORPHOLOGY_FRAME:
<mor LEX F> = "account (91) [NN1 91]"
<mor LEX -S>= "accounts (12) [NN2 12]"
<mor LEX related_wordforms>= "accountant (1) [NN1 1], accountee (2) [NN1 2], accounting (2) [JB 1 VVG 1]"

SYNTAX_FRAME:
<syn LEX cat>= N [X]; Ndeverbal []
<syn LEX N class>= Count [X]; Mass []
SYN_NP_SUBFRAME:
LEX= H
<syn pre H det real>= "your (26), our (10), the (6), {cname's} (5), this (5), the beneficiary's (2), opener's (2), all (1), these (1), a (1), buyer's (1), seller's (1)"
<syn pre H premod real>= "current (8), (long) outstanding (5), (considerably) overdue (4), above (2), personal (2), following (2), new (1); posb (2), savings (1), bank (1); head office (1), singapore dollar (1), {cname} branch (1), {cname} osaka (1); issuing bank (1)"
<syn pre H premod form>= Adj+LEX (24); N+LEX (4); Ncompound (N+N) + LEX (4); Adj+N+LEX (1)
<syn post H postmod real>= "of {cname} (6), of openers (2), of beneficiary (1); with you (2), with the post office savings bank (1), with the sum of ${amt.} (1); which should have been settled a long time ago (1), which is now slightly past due (1), which is now considerably past due (1); represented by this invoice (2), rendered by our office in {place} and {city} (1); under advice to us (2); covering ${amt.} (1)"

<syn post H postmod form>= PP (of) (9) / PP (with) (4) / wh rel clause (3) / -ed clause (3) / PP (under) (2) / -ing clause (1)

SYN_LEX_COLLOCATE_SUBFRAME:

<syn pre LEX noun_colloc real>= "debit of (3),settlement of (2), balance of (2), funds in (2), credit of (2), statement of (1)"

<syn pre LEX noun_colloc form>= N+prep+LEX

<syn post LEX noun_colloc real>= "number (17), receivable (4), holders (1)"

<syn post LEX noun_colloc form>= Ncompound (LEX + N) (22)

<syn pre LEX verb_colloc real>= "debit (6), regarding (3), maintain (2), favouring (2), to credit (1), will be for (1), to debit (1), to settle (1), referring to (1), to clear (1), to close (1)"

<syn pre LEX verb_colloc form>= V(transitive)+LEX (20)

<syn post LEX verb_colloc real>= "has been debited (2), has been transferred (2), has become overdrawn (1); was credited (2); is (not) settled (2); can be operated (1); is (1)"

<syn post LEX verb_colloc form>= LEX+V(perfective) (5) / LEX+V(passive) (4) / LEX + V(modal) (1) / LEX + copula (1)

<syn post LEX adj_colloc real>= "((long) overdue) (1)"

<syn LEX zscore real>="debit (17.170), receivable (12.373), represented (10.357), debited (9.831), current (9.678)"

SEMANTICS_FRAME:

<sem LEX> = ACCOUNT (arg01), ACCOUNT2 (arg02)

PRAGMATICS_FRAME:

<prag arg01 structure>= X settles ACCOUNT (arg01) with Y, where X= SUPPLIER / CNAME1, Y= CUSTOMER / CNAME2;Y (Initiator)—>X (Respondent) permissible

 <prag arg02 structure>= X settles ACCOUNT (arg01) with Y, where X= BANKER, Y= CUSTOMER;Y (Initiator)—>X (Respondent) permissible

<prag arg0 typological_information>= <S C X A T P N E>

<prag arg0 S>= S0 (5) S1 (5) S2 (5) S3 (0) S4 (2) S5 (0) S6 (1) S7 (47) S8 (18) S9 (1) S10 (3) S11 (0) S12 (0) S13 (0) S14 (6) S15 (10)

<prag arg0 C>= C0 (4) C1 (2) C2 (6) C3 (12) C4 (0) C5 (0) C6 (2) C7 (24) C8 (9) C9 (14) C10 (13) C11 (10) C12 (9)

<prag arg0 X>= X1 (74) X2 (29)

<prag arg0 A>= A1 (13) A2 (62) A3 (28)

<prag arg0 T>= T1 (80) T2 (23) T3 (0)

<prag arg0 P>= P1 (0) P3 (0) P4 (13) P5 (0) P6 (1) P7 (0) P8 (0) P9 (5) P10 (8) P2/1/2 (11) P2/1/3 (7) P2/1/4 (5) P 2/1/14 (1) P2/2/3 (8) P2/2/4 (9) P2/2/5 (2) P2/2/6 (1) P2/3/4 (5) P2/3/5 (2) P2/3/6 (1) P2/4/5 (3) P2/4/6 (1) P2/5/6 (2) P 2/6/14 (1) P2/f/1 (3) P2/f/2 (7) P2/f/3 (6) P2/f/4 (1)

<prag arg0 N>= N013 (2) N019 (1) N020 (1) N021 (1) N022 (2) N035 (1) N047 (2) N050 (6) N051 (4) N073 (2) N112 (2) N122 (2) N133 (1) N137 (1) N140 (1) N142 (1) N149 (1) N152 (1) N182 (3) N200 (1) N201 (1) N202 (2) N203 (1) N208 (3) N217 (2) N218 (1) N219 (1) N221 (1) N222 (1) N223 (2) N230 (3) N240 (1) N246 (1) N249 (1) N251 (2) N285 (3) N287 (1) N301 (3) N302 (2) N316 (1) N332 (1) N333(2) N361 (1) N364 (1) N365 (2) N369 (1) N372 (2) N373 (2) N382 (1) N453 (1) N455 (2) N456 (3) N502 (2) N516 (1) N517 (1) N524 (1) N527 (1) N540 (1) N541 (2) N542 (2) N543 (1) N548 (1) N564 (2)
<prag arg0 E>= E- (103) E+ (0)

****
Procomparenoun_LEX account (211):

MORPHOLOGY_FRAME:
<mor LEX F> = "account (183) [NN1 183]"
<mor LEX -S>= "accounts (28) [NN2 28]"
<mor LEX related_wordforms>="account (2) [VV0 2]; accounts (3) [VVZ 3]; accountant (1) [NN1 1]; accountants (2) [NN2 2]; accounting (11) [JJ 8 NN1 2 VVG 1]"

SYNTAX_FRAME:
<syn LEX cat> = **N [X]; Ndeverbal []**
<syn LEX N class>= Count [X]; Mass []
SYN_NP_SUBFRAME:
LEX=H
<syn pre H det real>="your (80), the (13), our (11), an (9), my (7), a (5), the customer's (1), any (1), this (11), every (1), her (1), their (1)"
<syn pre H premod real>= "charge (9), (regular) open (8), new (6), overdue (4), (past) due (3), said (2), current (2), complete (1), checking (1), credit (1), valued (1), own (1), above captioned (1), aging (1), specific (1), disputed (1), valued (1); expense (3), savings (3), loan (2), claims (1), installment (1); following unpaid (1), above referenced (1)"
<syn pre H premod form>= adj+LEX(44); N+LEX(10); adj+adj+LEX(2)
<syn post H postmod real>="with us (5), with you (2), with our company (1), with our firm (1), with our store (1), with your establishment (1) with a substantial deposit i had made several days prior (1), with your company (1); in the amount of \${amt.} (4), in [locale] (1); of \${amt.} (2), of {name} (1); for you (1), for your company (1); which bears a similar name to yours (1), that has become seriously past due (1), held in the name of {name} with {cname} (1); closed (1); falling more than 30 days behind (1)"
<syn post H postmod form>= PP(with) (13) / PP(in) (5) / PP(of) (3) / PP(for) (2) / wh rel clause (3) / ed-clause (1) / -ing clause (1)

SYN_LEX_COLLOCATE_SUBFRAME:

<syn pre LEX noun_colloc real>="statement of (4), payment on (3), review of (3), payment of (3), credit limit on (2), assignment of (2), past due charges on (2), balance in (2), surcharge on (1), adjustment in (1), convenience of (1), credit limit on (1), name and address on (1), use of (1), information about (1), terms and conditions of (1), liens on (1), instructions on (1), payment from (1), credit to (1), credit on (1), record of (1), change in (1), past due balance on (1), extension of credit on (1), past due balance of (1), balance on (1), notice of (1), notice to (1), status of (1), type of (1), settlement of (1), amount (owed) on (1), placing of (1)"

<syn pre LEX noun_colloc form>= N+prep+LEX

<syn post LEX noun_colloc real>= "balance (6), receivable (5),payable (2), number (4), terms (3), name (3), status (3), statement (2), credit (1), debtor (1), basis (1), analysis (1), inventory (1), representatives (1)"

<syn post LEX noun_colloc form>= Ncompound (LEX +N)

<syn pre LEX verb_colloc real>="opening (5), regarding (5), credited to (3), handling (1), failed to credit (1), credit (4), open (5), use (1), have (1), have reviewed (1), to pay (1), failed to bring (1), turn...LEX...over (3), settle (3), refer (1), indicating (1), adjust (1), deposited to (1), service (1), crediting of (1), handle (1), glancing over (1), discuss (1), having (1), reevaluate (1), bring...LEX.....up (1), maintaining (1), cleared from (1), review (1), close (1), clear (1), deposit (1), maintain (1), to getting....LEX....back (1), welcome (1), to forward (1)"

<syn pre LEX verb_colloc form>= V(transitive)+LEX

<syn post LEX verb_colloc real>= " has been opened (2), has fallen (seriously behind) (2), had been paid (2), has been credited (1), has been approved (1), has reached (1), has been referred (1); is held (2), is paid (1), is renewed (1), is sold (1), be maintained (1), is evaluated (1); does not make (full payment) (1), may be retransferred (1); is (6), exceeds (1),carries (a past due balance) (1),"

<syn post LEX verb_colloc form>= V(perfective) (10) / V(passive) (7); V(modal) (2) / V (copula) (6) / V(finite) (2)

<syn post LEX adj_colloc real>= (seriously) past due (3), current (1), overdue (1)

<syn LEX zscore real>= "open (17.075), your (13.595), receivable (13.178), balance (13.001), credited (12.434)"

SEMANTICS_FRAME:

<sem LEX> = ACCOUNT (arg01), ACCOUNT2 (arg02)

PRAGMATICS_FRAME:

<prag arg01 structure>= X settles ACCOUNT (arg01) with Y, where X=SUPPLIER, Y=CUSTOMER; Y (Initiator)—>X (Respondent) permissible

<prag arg02 structure>= X settles ACCOUNT (arg01) with Y, where X=BANKER,Y=CUSTOMER;Y (Initiator)—>X (Respondent) permissible

****

<u>*ADVISE*</u> (v)

Prolexverb_LEX advise (109):

MORPHOLOGY_FRAME:
<mor LEX F> = "advise (87) [VV0 64 VVI 23]"
<mor LEX -S> = "advises (0)"
<mor LEX -ED>= "advised (19) [VVN 15 VVD 4]"
<mor LEX -ING>= "advising (3) [VVG 3]"
<mor LEX related_wordforms>:= "advice (29) [NN1 29]; advisable (1) [JJ 1]; advising (2) [JJ 2]; advisor (1) [NN1 1]"

SYNTAX_FRAME:
<syn LEX cat> = V
<syn LEX modals>= "will (10), could (2), would (2), shall (1), can (1)"
<syn LEX perfective>= " have **V**ed" (2), "have been **V**ed" (2)
<syn LEX progressive>= **V**ing (3)
<syn LEX passive>= "as **V**ed" (3), "[] (2) / shall (2) / can (1) / will (1) + be + **V**ed", "keep...**V**ed" (1), "would be kept **V**ed (1)"
SYN_LEX_COLLOCATE_SUBFRAME:
<syn pre LEX adv_colloc real>= "please (36), kindly(1), please kindly (1)"
<syn pre LEX adj_colloc real>:= "pleased to (5), happy to (1)"
<syn pre LEX verb_colloc real>= "regret to (5), wish to (4), is to (1) , would like to (1), keep you **V**ed (1), appreciate your **V**ing"
<syn LEX zscore real>= "please (15.779), acceptability (9.694), how **(7.966), preferred (7.833), accordingly (7.642), wish (4.543)"**
SYN_PRED_SUBFRAME:
LEX=pred0
<syn pred0 Copular= []
<syn pred0 Monotransitive>= []
<syn pred0 Ditransitive>= <arg1 arg2 arg3 arg4>
<syn pred0 Complex_Transitive>= []
<syn pred0 arg1 real>= "[] (45), we (31), you (6), {cname} (3), i (2)"
<syn pred0 arg1 form> = NP
<syn pred0 arg1 function>= S
<syn pred0 arg1 status> = implicit (45), explicit (42)
<syn pred0 arg2 real>= "date of payment (2), price, cost & freight (1), the names of your bankers (1), the name and address of the remitting bank (1),

{quotation/list} (1), your interest in making an offer (1), [the] following remittances from {cname} (1), {vessel's} expected time of arrival (1), your preferred date-range for {cname's} loading (1), any interest (1), preferred structure and any complications envisaged on {cname's} pricing (1), the following (1), the name of {cname's} negotiating bank in new york (1), documentation instructions (1), feasibility of vessel switch (1), cargo segregation and documentation instructions (1), full details (1), disemulsibility test method (1), any success of your fuel oil / kero sale opportunities (1), status of the captioned item (1), the following authenticated telex dated {date} received from the above-mentioned bank (1), that your company has been accepted in our corporate rate program (1), that we are accomplishing guest satisfaction (1), (that) our bid was received and reviewed but found uncompetitive (1), (that) your share in us${amt.} should correctly read (as follows) (1), that we do not appear to have received your payment of the abovementioned collection (1), that the bill described above has been dealt with as follows (1), that our records show that we have nor received your payment of ${amt.} (1), that the captioned bill has been accepted by drawees (1), that the above bill has been accepted by the drawee (1), that i will be leaving singapore (1), that we accept your quotation (1), that we are unable to accept your quote in this instance (1), that the above consignment was found to have sustained damage (1), that we are not able to entertain your claims (1), that we are unable to take advantage of them this time (1), that we are not able to utilize your background and qualification for this particular position (1), that we can only extend the validity of quoted delivered price of ${amt.}/lb (1), that this alteration may take place as follows (1), that your policy is standing as lapsed (1), that we will not be placing any advertisement in the directory (1), that we will not be purchasing any tickets (1), that we are unable to donate any prizes (1); when vessel is fixed (1),whether you wish to quote (1),why you wish to advance it to {date} (1), how access can be effected without a terminal (1), how and when effected (1), whether [the] sale of two consecutive cargoes can be considered as term sale (1), whether the request for taking up {no.} [of] metric tons ...is acceptable (1), whether {paragraph_referred_to} is workable (1), when you will start issuing proforma invoices on our behalf (1), when you are in a position to continue premium payments again (1); how your policy may be revived (1), when the invoice would be processed for payment (1), how we could avoid such inconvenience in future (1); of its acceptability (2), of name of opening bank (2), of the commencing date of the deduction (1); on size of photo required (1); on the following (1); on an advertising programme which will be implemented (1); if we should send this over to you (1), if {cname} [is] selling {cname_obj} to other rare earth extraction companies (1); having received the following cable dated {date} (1)"

<syn pred0 arg2 form> = NP (22) / that-clause (21) / wh-clause (13) / [] (9) / PP (of) (5) / PP(on) (3) / if-clause (2) / ing-clause (1)

<syn pred0 arg2 function>= DO
<syn pred0 arg2 feats>= IF <T2>, prep ("on") optional, determiner optional; IF <T2> PP(on) substituted by NP
<syn pred0 arg2 status> = explicit (65), implicit (9)
<syn pred0 arg3 real>= "[] (55), you (14), us (9), {cname} (2), beneficiary (1); your malaysian / singapore offices (1)"
<syn pred0 arg3 form> = NP
<syn pred0 arg3 function>= IO
<syn pred0 arg3 status> = implicit (55), explicit (14)
<syn pred0 arg4 real>= "by return [telex] (2), to date (2), on {date} (2), by telephone (1), vide telex (1), through the {cname} bank (1), in mid-{month} (1), in due course (1), within ten days (1), at the same time (1), from our end (1), notwithstanding discrepancies (1), with a view to avoiding possible involvement (1), in view of the anniversary date of your policy which is on {date} (1), for your staff party at this point of time (1), for this talk / demonstration (1), without any responsibility or engagement on our part (1), in this instance (1), in turn (1); accordingly (3), as soon as possible (2), soonest (1), therefore (1), urgently (1); as follows (1); as soon as departure date is known (1), if you have not yet received any response from them (1), since we are informed the beneficiary did not receive the funds (1), if you are making payment direct to our {cname} office (1)"
<syn pred0 arg4 form> = PP (22) / advp (9) / adv_clause (4)
<syn pred0 arg4 function>= A
<syn pred0 arg4 feats> = Temporal (12); Cause-Reason-Purpose (8); Condition-Contrast (6); Manner-Means-Instrument (6); Location (1)
<syn pred0 arg4 status> = optional

SEMANTICS_FRAME:
<sem LEX> = ADVISE1 (pred01), ADVISE2 (pred02)
<sem pred0 arg1 case> = Actor
<sem pred0 arg2 case> = Content
<sem pred0 arg3 case> = Recipient
<sem pred0 arg4 case> = Circumstance

PRAGMATICS_FRAME:
<prag pred01 structure>= Concerning Z (arg2), X (arg1) ADVISE/inform (pred01) Y (arg3), under C (arg4), where X=SUPPLIER / BANKER / EMPLOYER / CNAME1, Y= CUSTOMER/ EMPLOYEE / CNAME2, Z=CONTENT, C=CIRCUMSTANCE; Y (Initiator)—>X(respondent) permissible
<prag pred02 structure>= X (arg1) ADVISE/directs/requests (pred02) a course of action Z (arg2) to Y (arg3), under C (arg4), where X= SUPPLIER / BANKER / EMPLOYER / CNAME1, Y=CUSTOMER / EMPLOYEE /

CNAME2, Z= CONTENT, C= CIRCUMSTANCE; Y (Initiator)— >X(respondent) permissible

<prag pred0 typological_information>= <S C X A T P N E>

<prag pred0 S>= S0 (14) S1 (4) S2 (3) S3 (5) S4 (12) S5 (3) S6 (8) S7 (9) S8 (15) S9 (0) S10 (15) S11 (1) S12 (3) S13 (2) S14 (2) S15 (13)

<prag pred0 C>= C0 (10) C1 (0) C2 (2) C3 (1) C4 (0) C5 (2) C6 (0) C7 (13) C8 (8) C9 (12) C10 (48) C11 (6) C12 (7)

<prag pred0 X>= X1 (56) X2 (53)

<prag pred0 A>= A1 (2) A2 (54) A3 (53)

<prag pred0 T>= T1 (61) T2 (46) T3 (2)

<prag pred0 P>= P1 (0) P3 (0) P4 (0) P5 (0) P6 (0) P7 (0) P8 (0) P9 (2) P10 (3) P2/1/2 (11) P2/1/3 (10) P2/1/4 (5) P2/1/6 (1) P2/1/f (1) P2/2/3 (5) P2/ 2/4 (1) P2/2/5 (2) P2/2/6 (2) P2/2/7 (2) P2/3/5 (4) P2/3/6 (4) P2/4/5 (2) P2/4/6 (4) P2/5/6 (2) P2/5/7 (1) P2/5/11 (1) P2/6/7 (1) P2/f/1 (7) P2/f/2 (13) P2/f/3 (12) P2/f/4 (6) P2/f/5 (2) P2/f/6 (4) P2/f/7 (1)

<prag pred0 N>= N025 (1) N027 (1) N040 (1) N073 (1) N074 (1) N076 (1) N083 (1) N084 (1) N092 (1) N094 (1) N095 (1) N099 (1) N100 (1) N102 (1) N107 (1) N108 (1) N110 (1) N115 (1) N117 (1) N125 (1) N126 (1) N130 (5) N131 (1) N134 (2) N136 (6) N137 (4) N140 (1) N141 (2) N142 (1) N143 (2) N147 (1) N148 (1) N149 (1) N157 (2) N158 (1) N167 (1) N170 (1) N176 (1) N180 (1) N181 (4) N182 (3) N222 (1) N223 (1) N226 (1) N228 (1) N230 (3) N244 (2) N249 (1) N254 (1) N255 (1) N256 (1) N261 (1) N272 (1) N280 (1) N281 (1) N288 (1) N289 (1) N291 (1) N302 (1) N307 (1) N309 (1) N316 (1) N324 (1) N364 (1) N369 (1) N374 (1) N375 (1) N382 (1) N395 (1) N403 (1) N413 (1) N446 (2) N454 (1) N460 (1) N508 (1) N517 (1) N524 (1) N527 (1) N535 (1) N538 (1) N539 (1) N542 (1) N549 (1) N566 (1)

<prag pred0 E>= E- (109) E+ (0)

****

Procompareverb_LEX advise (46):

MORPHOLOGY_FRAME:

<mor LEX F> = "advise (26) [VV0 12 VVI 14]"

<mor LEX -S> = "advises (1) [VVZ 1]"

<mor LEX -ED>="advised (17) [VVN 15 VVD 2]"

<mor LEX -ING>="advising (2) [VVG 1]"

<mor LEX related_wordforms>= "advisable (2) [JJ 2]; advice (3) [NN1 3]"

SYNTAX_FRAME:

<syn LEX cat> = V

<syn LEX modals>= "must (2), will (1)"

<syn LEX perfective>= "has **V**ed (1)"

<syn LEX passive>= "be **V**ed (10), will be **V**ed (2), have been **V**ed (2), were **V**ed (1), has been **V**ed (1)"

SYN_LEX_COLLOCATE_SUBFRAME:

<syn pre LEX adv_colloc real>= "please (16)"

<syn pre LEX adj_colloc real>:= "pleased to (2)"

<syn pre LEX verb_colloc real>= "wish to (3), wanted to (1)"

<syn post LEX adv_colloc real>= "as soon as (1), fully (1), completely (1)"

<syn LEX zscore real>= "please (13.716), dangers (12.294), left (12.214), damaged (9.141), contrary (8.636), wish (7.424)"

SYN_PRED_SUBFRAME:

LEX=pred0

<syn pred0 Copular>= []

<syn pred0 Monotransitive>= []

<syn pred0 Ditransitive>= <arg1 arg2 arg3 arg4>

<syn pred0 Complex_Transitive>= []

<syn pred0 arg1 real>= "[] (23), we (5), the {cname journal} (1), i (3), you (1), the undersigned (1), one of our customers (1), your department head (1)"

<syn pred0 arg1 form> = NP

<syn pred0 arg1 function>= S

<syn pred0 arg1 status> = implicit (23), explicit (13)

<syn pred0 arg2 real>= "that you have the right under federal law to obtain full disclosure of the nature and substance (1), that your account has been credited in the amount of ${amt.} (1), that we have credited your account in the amount of ${amt.} (1), that payments on said debt are in default (1), that you are in default under our security agreement dated {date} (1), that the credit limit on the account will be S{amt.} (1), that you have made an inquiry regarding {cname_obj} (1), that this oversight on your part shall in no way accrue an earned premium or short rate (1), that you have left us no alternative but to file suit immediately (1), that the undersigned does hereby exercise its option to extend or renew said lease (1), that your medical certification must be renewed prior to {date} (1), that we are reducing prices on certain items in our catalog (1), that we have moved our office to {caddress} (1), that these matters have been attended to (1), that {date} will be my last day of employment (1), that the undersigned hereby resigns as {blank} (1), that on {date} the {firm} changed hands pursuant to a recorded bill of sale of the same date (1), that we will be submitting our proposal on or before {confirmation of deadline} (1); of all special sales (1), of our special customer needs (1), of a product defect in the following particulars (1), of a change in your account status (1), of your intent in this matter (1), of this (1), of the procedure you should follow (1);how you wish to handle the return of the broken merchandise (1), as to what you would like me to do at this point (1), whether your reference should be held confidential (1), as to whether or not this has been done (1); [] (2), this office (1), as to your intentions (1)"

\<syn pred0 arg2 form\> = that-clause (18) / PP(of) (7) / [] (2) / wh-clause (4) / [] (2) / NP (1) / PP(as to) (1)

\<syn pred0 arg2 function\>= DO

\<syn pred0 arg2 status\> = explicit (35), implicit (2)

\<syn pred0 arg3 real\>= "you (17), [] (13), us (4), we (2), i (1), my secretary (1), me (1), your office manager (1)"

\<syn pred0 arg3 form\> = NP

\<syn pred0 arg3 function\>= IO

\<syn pred0 arg3 feats\>= S in \<syn LEX passive\>

\<syn pred0 arg3 status\> = implicit (13), explicit (27)

\<syn pred0 arg4 real\>= "immediately (1), as follows (1), as soon as possible (1), otherwise (1); if any discrepancy exists (1), so as to provide you ample time to renew your license (1), so that we can have it prepared for you (1); at your earliest possible convenience (2)"

\<syn pred0 arg4 form\> = advp (4) / adv-clause (3) / PP (2)

\<syn pred0 arg4 function\>= A

\<syn pred0 arg4 feats\> = Temporal (4); Cause-Reason-Purpose (2); Condition-Contrast (2); Manner-Means-Instrument (1); Location []

\<syn pred0 arg4 status\> = optional

SEMANTICS_FRAME:

\<sem LEX\> = ADVISE1 (pred01), ADVISE2 (pred02)

\<sem pred0 arg1 case\> = Actor

\<sem pred0 arg2 case\> = Content

\<sem pred0 arg3 case\> = Recipient

\<sem pred0 arg4 case\> = Circumstance

PRAGMATICS_FRAME:

\<prag pred01 structure\>= Concerning Z (arg3), X (arg1) ADVISE/inform (pred01) Y (arg3), under C (arg4), where X=SUPPLIER / BANKER / EMPLOYER / CNAME1, Y= CUSTOMER/ EMPLOYEE / CNAME2, Z=CONTENT, C=CIRCUMSTANCE; Y (Initiator)—>X(respondent) permissible

\<prag pred02 structure\>= X (arg1) ADVISE/directs/requests (pred02) a course of action Z (arg2) to Y (arg3), under C (arg4), where X=SUPPLIER / BANKER / EMPLOYER / CNAME1, Y= CUSTOMER/ EMPLOYEE / CNAME2, Z=CONTENT, C=CIRCUMSTANCE; Y (Initiator)—>X(respondent) permissible

****

APPRECIATE (v)

Prolexverb_LEX appreciate (77):

MORPHOLOGY_FRAME:
<mor LEX F> = "appreciate (61) [VVI 51 VV0 10]"
<mor   LEX -S> = "appreciates (0)"
<mor LEX -ED>= "appreciated (16) [VVN 16]"
<mor LEX -ING>=[]
<mor LEX related_wordforms>= "appreciation (6) [NN1 6], appreciative (1) [JJ 1]"

SYNTAX_FRAME:
<syn LEX cat> = V
<syn LEX modals>= "would (37), shall (5), will (2), do (1)"
<syn LEX perfective>= []
<syn LEX progressive>= []
<syn LEX passive>= "will be **V**-ed (8), would be **V**-ed (3), is **V**-ed (2), **V**-ed (1), was **V**-ed (1), are **V**-ed (1)"
SYN_LEX_COLLOCATE_SUBFRAME:
<syn LEX zscore real>= "would (25.307), could (12.448), greatly (12.049), much (11.729), receiving (9.897)"
SYN_PRED_SUBFRAME:
LEX=pred0
<syn pred0 Copular>= []
<syn pred0 Monotransitive>= <arg1 arg2 arg3>
<syn pred0 Ditransitive>= []
<syn pred0 Complex_Transitive>= []
<syn pred0 arg1 real>= "we (39), [] (28), i (3), you (3), mr {name} (1)"
<syn pred0 arg1 form> =NP
<syn pred0 arg1 function>=S
<syn pred0 arg1 feats>= optional if T1
<syn pred0 arg1 status> = explicit (46), implicit (28)
<syn pred0 arg2 real>="your cooperation (2), your attention to the above mentioned (1), your gesture foregoing usual {commission} (1), your kind attention to this matter (1), your kind assistance and cooperation (1), your early response (1), your prompt response (1), your comments on this subject (1), your early attention to this (1), your cooperation in confirming his/her employment by your company (1), your correspondence (1), your soonest reply (1), your advice re status of our bid (1), your prompt action on the above (1), (that) you telex (1), your making known your {cname} requirements at this point in time (1), your prompt response (1), your fine co-operation (1), your interest in our company (1), your reimbursement of S${amt.} (1); if you could arrange to

remit us a cheque to clear this account at your earliest convenience (1), if you could supply us the following info (1), if you can confirm with me before {date} (1), if you could advise {cname} accordingly (1), if you can send 2 copies of the latest documentation manual to {cname} (1), if you could have the above information updated in your record and circulated to all concerned (1), if you could kindly retain the relative parcels for another 2 weeks from date hereof (1), if you give captain {lname} the normal courtesies and assistance during his stay (1), if an article could be submitted to {cname} by {date} (1), if you will kindly arrange for a store-size almond cake for the winner of the mini-bar competition (1), if you would kindly enclose the required amount for postage (1), if you would ascertain and inform us of his/her present address (1), if you would kindly arrange for S$\{amt.\}$ being outstanding premium due {date} to be forwarded to us immediately (1), if you could settle the long overdue notices immediately (1), if you could expedite payment of all your outstanding invoices (1), if you could advise us how we could avoid such inconvenience in future (1), if you could include these in your next publication (1); a telex reply sent to {caddress} (1), a personal call (1), sample (1), early despatch of the crude borrow/loan statement (1), advice on interest rate applicable for the period from {date} thru {date} (1), information on these institutions (1), the favour of an early settlement (1), a report from you (1), the favour of an early return of the accepted draft (1), the service he rendered (1), the interest you have shown in our organization (1), our choice and demonstrated restraint (1), the opportunity to clarify the above points (1), the luncheon which you so kindly arranged at {cname}(1), its services and staff (1); your signing below (2), your taking time off to inform us (1), your sending 2 sets of the binders (1), your reviewing your {cname_obj} requirements for {year} (1), your bringing this matter to our attention (1), your advising us by return name of a new york bank acceptable to {cname} (1), your amending name of seller (1), your arranging to send sample package (1), your contribution of a page in the form of a complimentary message (1), receiving instructions regarding renewal during the course of the repair (1), receiving your quotation (1), receiving your comments on this (1), receiving your payment within seven days (1); [that] you must have been very busy with your business (1), that this long delay has cost more than S$\{amt.\}$ in financing cost (1), that any delay beyond that point would not be our responsibility (1), that we have given you a two-month extension of price validity (1), (that) you pass on our best wishes for a happy and prosperous retirement to {name} on {date} (1), (that) you read the following message from his aussie friends (1)"

\<syn pred0 arg2 form\> = ("your" + NP) (21) / if-clause (17) / NP (15) / ing-clause (14) ("your"-ing clause (10)) / that-clause (6)

\<syn pred0 arg2 function\>= DO

\<syn pred0 arg2 feats\>= for ("your" + **V**ing clause) or ("your" + NP), S IF V=\<syn passive\>

<syn pred0 arg2 status> = if V=<syn passive>, S is realised usually by ("your" + NP) or ("your" + **Ving** clause) & is obligatory

<syn pred0 arg3 real>="[very] much (7), greatly (4), therefore (2), most (1), truly (1), well (1), also (1); should you require any assistance for special services (1), as it is only through such feedback that we would be able to improve ourselves (1), as it is by constructive comments such as yours that we are able to improve the quality of our services (1), for evaluation (1), before we send these copies to {cname} (1), to allow us to develop material locally (1), so as to enable the social committe to plan ahead for the souvenir programme (1), so that these accounts which should have been settled a long time ago are not delayed any further (1), as we have paid S${amt.} for the cost of repairs to your insured's vehicle (1), in view of this (1)"

<syn pred0 arg3 form> = advp (17) / adv-clause (6) / PP (4)

<syn pred0 arg3 function>=A

<syn pred0 arg3 feats> = Cause-Reason-Purpose (8); Temporal (1); Condition-Contrast (1); Manner-Means-Instrument (1); Location []

<syn pred0 arg3 status> = optional

SEMANTICS_FRAME:

<sem LEX> = APPRECIATE1 (pred01); APPRECIATE2 (pred02)

<sem pred0 arg1 case> = Actor

<sem pred0 arg2 case> = Goal

<sem pred0 arg3 case> = Circumstance

PRAGMATICS_FRAME:

<prag pred01 structure>= X (arg1) APPRECIATES/(requests) (pred01) Z (arg2) from Y (implicit in arg2) under C (arg3), where X= INITIATOR / CNAME1, Y= RESPONDENT / CNAME2, Z= ACTION_REQUESTED, C= CIRCUMSTANCE

<prag pred02 structure>= X (arg1) APPRECIATES/(realizes) (pred02) Z (arg2) under C, where X= COGNIZANT, Z= COGNIZED, C= CIRCUMSTANCE

<prag pred0 typological_information>= <S C X A T P N E>

<prag pred0 S>= S0 (5) S1 (4) S2 (2) S3 (3) S4 (8) S5 (1) S6 (9) S7 (13) S8 (3) S9 (1) S10 (2) S11 (3) S12 (2) S13 (6) S14 (0) S15 (5)

<prag pred0 C>= C0 (7) C1 (0) C2 (4) C3 (1) C4 (7) C5 (0) C6 (1) C7 (5) C8 (7) C9 (20) C10 (13) C11 (4) C12 (8)

<prag pred0 X>= X1 (52) X2 (25)

<prag pred0 A>= A1 (2) A2 (23) A3 (52)

<prag pred0 T>= T1 (52) T2 (23) T3 (2)

<prag pred0 P>= P1 (0) P3 (0) P4 (0) P5 (0) P6 (0) P7 (0) P8 (0) P9 (2) P10 (1) P2/1/2 (6) P2/1/3 (4) P2/1/4 (1) P2/1/f (1) P2/2/3 (15) P2/2/4 (3) P2/3/4 (6) P2/3/6 (1) P2/4/5 (1) P2/5/7 (1) P 2/9/10 (1) P2/f/1 (8) P2/f/2 (7)

P2/f/3 (13) P2/f/4 (2) P2/f/5(2) P2/f/6 (2)

<prag pred0 N>= N025 (1) N028 (1) N033 (1) N035 (1) N043 (1) N060
(1) N061 (1) N071 (1) N075 (1) N079 (1) N089 (1) N099 (1) N102 (1) N103
(1) N108 (1) N110 (1) N114 (1) N119 (1) N121 (1) N123 (1) N129 (1) N136
(1) N149 (1) N156 (1) N160 (1) N189 (1) N226 (1) N227 (1) N230 (1) N234
(2) N286 (1) N287 (1) N292 (1) N300 (2) N301 (1) N311 (1) N320 (1) N326
(1) N328 (2) N329 (1) N373 (1) N374 (1) N378 (1) N382 (1) N397 (1) N402
(1) N403 (1) N411 (1) N413 (1) N418 (1) N419 (1) N426 (2) N436 (1) N437
(1) N440 (1) N441 (1) N442 (1) N475 (1) N477 (1) n505 (1) N512 (1) N536
(1) N540 (1) N544 (1) N545 (1) N549 (1) N551 (1) N559 (1) N560 (1) N562
(1) N563 (1) N565 (1)

<prag pred0 E>= E- (77) E+ (0)

****

Procompareverb_LEX appreciate (82):

MORPHOLOGY_FRAME:
<mor LEX F> = "appreciate (70) [VV0 23 VVI 47]"
<mor LEX -S>= "appreciates (1) [VVZ 1]"
<mor LEX -ED>= "appreciated (10) [VVN 10]"
<mor LEX -ING>= []
<mor LEX related_wordforms>= "appreciation (6) [NN1 6]"

SYNTAX_FRAME:
<syn LEX cat> = V
<syn LEX modals>= "would (34), shall (4), will (4), can (3), do (3)"
<syn LEX perfective>= "have **V**ed (1)"
<syn LEX progressive>= []
<syn LEX passive>= "is **V**ed (5), will be **V**ed (4)"
SYN_LEX_COLLOCATE_SUBFRAME:
<syn LEX zscore real>= "would (28.030), greatly (18.234), patronage
(14.778), having (11.015), completing (10.276)"
SYN_PRED_SUBFRAME:
LEX=pred0
<syn pred0 Copular>= []
<syn pred0 Monotransitive>= <arg1 arg2 arg3>
<syn pred0 Ditransitive>= []
<syn pred0 Complex_Transitive>= []
<syn pred0 arg1 real>= "we (37), i (28), you (3), the company (1)"
<syn pred0 arg1 form> = NP
<syn pred0 arg1 function>= S
<syn pred0 arg1 feats>= []

\<syn pred0 arg1 status\>= obligatory if V(active)

\<syn pred0 arg2 real\>= "your cooperation in this matter (5), your (continued) patronage (5), your cooperation and prompt attention to this matter (2), your cooperation (2), your perseverance in settling this matter (1), your interest in being employed by our firm (1), your courtesies (1), your consideration in this matter (1), your understanding in waiting (1), your straightforwardness (1), your candidness (1), your candor (1), your providing me with an estimate of both time and costs (1), your prompt efforts in correcting this error in my account (1), your comments or suggestions about the service we provided (1), your offer to help us in our campaign to {objective} (1), your interest in submitting to us an idea (1), your business (1), your further comments on any personal or professional strength and weaknesses (1), your offer of help..at this time (1); your authorizing one to be sent to the address indicated above (1), your extending the date for our payment of the account until {date} (1), your completing the Employer's Verification below for their confidential use (1), your expeditious handling of this matter (1), your returning this record of purchase (1), your completing the Deposit Verification for their confidential use (1), your either informing me of same or forwarding this letter to him (1), your affording us the opportunity to serve you (1); having your firm as one of our valued customers (1), hearing from our customers (1), receiving a new charge card with the imprint reflecting this name change (1), hearing from you (1), having you as a customer (1), hearing your comments (1), having an opportunity to speak with you (1), having the opportunity to speak with you personally (1), knowing what happened (1), having the opportunity to show you these innovations (1), receiving a corrected statement of my account (1), receiving your release as soon as possible (1), having the opportunity to discuss any openings you may have in this area (1), receiving your wholesale price list and information terms and ordering policy (1), having had the opportunity of being a member of {name of firm} for so many years (1), having had the opportunity to speak with you about my experience in related fields and my future goals (1), having had the opportunity to clarify our policy with you (1); if you would bring this announcement to the attention of your accounts payable department (1), if you could forward any documentation that you may have to support this claim (1), if you would change the name and address on my account to the following (1), if you would arrange to have this document sent to counsel for {other party to litigation} (1), if you would arrange for the replacement of the damaged items (1), if you would arrange for the replacement of the damaged items (1), if you would fill my original order as quickly as possible (1), if you would rush the missing parts to us immediately (1), if you would reimburse this office for the duplicate payment (1), if you would credit my account accordingly (1), if someone would straighten out the problem that exists on your end (1), if you would provide us with the names of all the employees that are to be tested (1), if you would tend to this matter as quickly as possible (1), if you would bring this letter to their attention (1), if you will indicate the correctness of the following information (1), if you would encourage everyone to go (1); the demands that this position has placed on you (1), all of the fine contributions you have made as {position} (1), the fact that it has taken some time to find out exactly what occurred (1), the interest you have shown in our products (1), the convenience afforded by this book (1), all that you have pointed out in your letter (1), a reference on the individual (1), an order of this size (1), our position in this matter (1), a statement of your opinions and experiences as outlined below (1)"

\<syn pred0 arg2 form\> = ("your" +NP) (30) / ing-clause (25) ("your" + **V**ing clause (8)) / if-clause (16) / NP (10)

\<syn pred0 arg2 function\>= DO

\<syn pred0 arg2 status\> = if V=\<syn passive\>, S is realised usually by ("your" + NP) or ("your" + **V**ing clause) & is obligatory

\<syn pred0 arg3 real\>= "greatly (5), sincerely (2),certainly (1), always (1), truly (1)"

\<syn pred0 arg3 form\> = advp (10)

\<syn pred0 arg3 function\>= A

\<syn pred0 arg3 sem feats\> = Manner-Means-Instrument (10)

\<syn pred0 arg3 status\> = optional

SEMANTICS_FRAME:

\<sem LEX\> = APPRECIATE1 (pred01); APPRECIATE2 (pred02)

\<sem pred0 arg1 case\> = Actor

\<sem pred0 arg2 case\> = Goal

\<sem pred0 arg3 case\> = Circumstance

PRAGMATICS_FRAME:

\<prag pred01 structure\>= X (arg1) APPRECIATES/(requests) (pred01) Z (arg2) from Y (implicit in arg2) under C (arg3), where X= INITIATOR / CNAME1,Y= RESPONDENT / CNAME2, Z= ACTION_REQUESTED, C= CIRCUMSTANCE

\<prag pred02 structure\>= X (arg1) APPRECIATES/(realizes) (pred02) Z (arg2) under C, where X= COGNIZANT, Z= COGNIZED, C= CIRCUMSTANCE

****

CLAIM:

Prolexnoun_LEX word claim (68):

MORPHOLOGY_FRAME:
<mor LEX F> = "claim (47) [NN1 47]"
<mor LEX -S>= "claims (21) [NN2 21]"
<mor LEX related_wordforms>="claim (6) [VVI 6]; claimed (2) [VVN 2]"

SYNTAX_FRAME:
<syn LEX cat> = **N** [X]; **Ndeverbal** [X]
<syn LEX N class>= **Count** [X]; **Mass** []
SYN_NP_SUBFRAME:
LEX=H
<syn pre H det real>= "our (7), the (6), your (3), the assured's (2), {cname's}
(2), each and every (2), a (2), no (1), this (1),such (1), the insured's (1), any (1)"
<syn pre H premod real>= "personal accident and hospitalisation (4),
reimbursement (3), average (1), captioned (1), counter (1), general adverse
motor (1), necessary (1), public liabilities (1)"
<syn post H postmod real>= "for immediate settlement (1), for your
prompt settlement (1), for the sum of ${amt.} (1), for ${amt.} (1), for damage
to {blank} (1); against the carrier and the port of singapore authority (2),
against you (1); payable (2); concerning the contamination of one drum (1),
pertaining to the supply of {no} metric tons of {cname_obj} (1), up to
${amt.}(1)"
<syn post H postmod form>= PP(for) (5)/ PP(against) (3) / rel-clause (2)
/ PP(concerning) (2) / PP(up to) (1)
<syn post H postmod feats>= arg2 ("against"), arg3 ("for", "concerning")
implicit
SYN_LEX_COLLOCATE_SUBFRAME:
<syn pre LEX noun_colloc real>= "settlement of (2), notice of (1), forms
of (1), outcome of (1), estimate of (1)"
<syn pre LEX noun_colloc form>=N+prep+LEX
<syn post LEX noun_colloc real>= "bill (4),policy(1), schedule (1),
invoice (1), issue (1), matter (1), discount letter (1), experience (1), number (1),
documents (1)"
<syn post LEX noun_colloc form>= Ncompound (LEX +N)
<syn pre LEX verb_colloc real>= "drop (2), entertain (2), settle (2), study
(1), handle (1), repudiate (1), accept (2), waive (1), make (1), lodge (1), submit
(1), consider (1), redirect (1), enclosing (1), render (1)"
<syn post LEX verb_colloc real>= "are covered (1), is fully settled (1), was
reviewed (1), was filed (1), will be forwarded (1)"
<syn post LEX verb_colloc form>= LEX+V(passive)

\<syn pre LEX prep_colloc real\>= "in settlement of (6) in respect of (1), upon receipt of (1), in support of (1)"

\<syn pre LEX prep_colloc form\>= PP(complex)

\<syn LEX zscore real\>= "hospitalisation (16.364), settlement (12.921), lodge (11.571), carrier (9.874), against (9.580)"

SYN_PRED_SUBFRAME:

LEX=Ndeverbal

Ndeverbal=pred0

\<syn pred0 real\>= "claim (3), have (not) claimed (2), may claim (2), claims (1), will claim (1)"

\<syn pred0 arg1 real\>= "you (5),we (1),the negotiating bank (1), the guest (1)"

\<syn pred0 arg1 form\>= NP

\<syn pred0 arg1 function\>= S

\<syn pred0 arg1 status\>= obligatory

\<syn pred0 arg2 real\>= "this amount (2), the fifth progress payment amounting to \${amt.} (1), reimbursement (1),your brief case (1), the said item (1), such relief (1), the u.k. tax relief (1)"

\<syn pred0 arg2 form\>= NP

\<syn pred0 arg2 function\>= DO

\<syn pred0 arg2 status\> = obligatory

\<syn pred0 arg3 real\>= "from the party concerned (1), by writing to {cname& address}(1)"

\<syn pred0 arg3 form\>= PP

\<syn pred0 arg3 function\>= IO

\<syn pred0 arg3 status\>= optional, but necessary in semantic structure of pred0

\<syn pred0 arg4 real\>= "on date (1); for work done on items {nos.} (1), on our behalf (1); by airmail (1), yesterday afternoon (1)"

\<syn pred0 arg4 form\>= PP (4) / advp (1)

\<syn pred0 arg4 function\>= A

\<syn pred0 arg4 feats\>= Temporal (2), Cause-Reason-Purpose (2), Means-Manner-Instrument (1)

\<syn pred0 arg4 status\> = optional

SEMANTICS_FRAME:

\<sem LEX\> = CLAIM (arg01), CLAIM (arg02)

\<sem pred0 arg1 case\>= Actor

\<sem pred0 arg2 case\>= Content

\<sem pred0 arg3 case\>= Recipient

\<sem pred0 arg4 case\>= Circumstance

PRAGMATICS_FRAME:

\<prag arg01 structure\>= Concerning Z (arg2=arg01), X (arg1) writes to Y (arg3), under C (arg4), where X= INSURER,Y=INSURED, Z= CLAIMED,

C= CIRCUMSTANCE;Y (Initiator)—> X (Respondent) permissible

<prag arg02 structure>= X (arg1) files Z (arg2=arg02) against Y (arg3) under C (arg4), where X=CLAIMANT, Y=OWER, Z = CLAIMED, C= CIRCUMSTANCE,Y (Initiator)—>X (Respondent) impermissible

<prag arg0 typological_information>= <S C X A T P N E>

<prag arg0 S>= S0 (2) S1 (0) S2 (1) S3 (0) S4 (0) S5 (0) S6 (32) S7 (11) S8 (2) S9 (4) S10 (0) S11 (0) S12 (0) S13 (0) S14 (0) S15 (16)

<prag arg0 C>= C0 (12) C1 (0) C2 (0) C3 (0) C4 (0) C5 (0) C6 (0) C7 (5) C8 (0) C9 (25) C10 (2) C11 (19) C12 (5)

<prag arg0 X>= X1 (36) X2 (32)

<prag arg0 A>= A1 (11) A2 (44) A3 (13)

<prag arg0 T>= T1 (50) T2 (15) T3 (3)

<prag arg0 P>= P1 (0) P3 (0) P4 (10) P5 (0) P6 (1) P7 (0) P8 (0) P9 (6) P10 (4) P2/1/2 (4) P2/1/3 (7) P2/1/4 (1) P2/1/5 (1) P2/2/10 (5) P2/2/3 (10) P2/ 2/5 (1) P2/3/10 (1) P2/4/10 (1) P2/7/10 (2) P2/f/1 (4) P2/f/2 (1) P2/f/3 (7) P2/f/4 (2)

<prag arg0 N>= N096 (1) N097 (1) N150 (1) N174 (1) N175 (10) N217 (1) N219 (1) N245 (2) N250 (1) N306 (1) N307 (1) N308 (2) N309 (5) N310 (3) N311 (4) N312 (4) N331 (1) N335 (2) N339 (1) N371 (1) N452 (1) N475 (1) N488 (1) N489 (1) N490 (1) N491 (2) N492 (2) N497 (1) N498 (2) N499 (3) N500 (2) N501 (2) N525 (1) N528 (1) N550 (2) N551 (1)

<prag arg0 E>= E- (68) E+ (0)

★★★

Procomparenoun_LEX claim (58):

MORPHOLOGY_FRAME:
<mor LEX F> = "claim (31) [NN1 31]"
<mor LEX -S>="claims (27) [NN2 27]"
<mor LEX related_wordforms>= "claim (7) [VV0 6 VVI 1]; claims (4) [VVZ 4]; claimant (9) [NN1 9]; claimed (5) [VVD 3 VVN 2]"

SYNTAX_FRAME:
<syn LEX cat> = N [X]; Ndeverbal [X]
<syn LEX N class>= Count [X]; Mass []
SYN_NP_SUBFRAME:
N=H
<syn pre H det real>="any (16), all (13), the (4), his (4), a (3), our (2), its (2), this (1), landlord's (1), further (1), other (1), following (1), additional (1), all of (1), no (1)"
<syn pre H premod real>= "said (3), lawful (2), known (1), potential (1), type (1), outstanding (1), adverse (1), ownership (1)"

<syn post H postmod real>="of any kind (2), of every kind (2), of defective goods (1), of title hostile to his rights in the goods (1), of lessor (1); for damages (3), for personal injury, property damage or wrongful death (2), for lien (1), for the total debt due (1); against {name} (2), against you (1), against said copyright (1), against the company (1); that lessor had (1) paid to you on {date} (1), that {name of creditor} has or may have in the future against the estate (1), made (1), owed {name} (1); arising out of {subject} for which release was executed (1), arising out of the aforesaid accident (1), originating prior to that date (1), disputed or otherwise (1); in an amount not to exceed ${amt.} (1), in the amount of ${amt.} (1), with respect to said lease (1)"

<syn post H postmod form>= PP(of) (7) / PP(for) (7) / PP(against) (5) / rel-clause (5) / non-finite cl (4) / PP(in) (2) / PP(with respect to) (1)

<syn post H postmod feats>= arg3("of", "for", PP, rel clause, non-finite cl), arg2 ("against") implicit

SYN_LEX_COLLOCATE_SUBFRAME:

<syn pre LEX noun_colloc real>= "notice of (4), basis of (3), waiver of (2), assignment of (1), releases on (1), existence of (1), increase in (1), liability for (1), settlement of (1), release of (1)"

<syn pre LEX noun_colloc form>= N+prep+LEX

<syn post LEX noun_colloc real>= "account (1)"

<syn pre LEX verb_colloc real>="to prosecute (1), to support (1), waives (1), disputes (1), to know of (1), satisfy (1), handling (1), release (1), discharge (1), release from (1), present (1), perfect (1), subordinates (1), to settle (1), to cancel (1)"

<syn pre LEX verb_colloc form>=V(transitive)+LEX

<syn post LEX verb_colloc real>= "is paid (2), is secured (1)"

<syn post LEX verb_colloc form>= LEX+V(passive)

<syn pre LEX adj_colloc real>= "free of (1)"

<syn LEX zscore real>= "demands (26.218), damages (19.015), causes (17.863), executions (13.412), whatsoever (11.569)"

SYN_Ndeverbal_SUBFRAME:

Ndeverbal=pred0

<syn pred0 arg1 real>= "the undersigned claimant (1), you (1), the undersigned (1), he (1), {claimant} (1)"

<syn pred0 arg1 form>= NP

<syn pred0 arg1 function>= S

<syn pred0 arg1 status>= obligatory

<syn pred0 arg2 real>= "a mechanic's lien (2), an interest (1); that you stated that you were too busy to find the answer to his question (1)"

<syn pred0 arg2 form>= NP (2) / that-clause (1)

<syn pred0 arg2 function>=DO

<syn pred0 arg2 status> = obligatory

<syn pred0 arg3 real>= "firms (1), corporations (1), against the above described property (1)"

<syn pred0 arg3 form>= NP
<syn pred0 arg3 function>= IO
<syn pred0 arg3 status>= optional, but necessary in semantic structure of pred0

SEMANTICS_FRAME:
<sem LEX> = CLAIM (arg01), CLAIM (arg02)
<sem pred0 arg1 case>= Actor
<sem pred0 arg2 case>= Content
<sem pred0 arg3 case>= Recipient

PRAGMATICS_FRAME:
<prag arg01 structure>= Concerning Z (arg2=arg01), X (arg1) writes to Y (arg3), under C (arg4), where X= INSURER, Y=INSURED, Z= CLAIMED, C= CIRCUMSTANCE; Y (Initiator)—> X (Respondent) permissible
<prag arg02 structure>= X (arg1) files Z (arg2=arg02) against Y (arg3) under C (arg4), where X=CLAIMANT, Y=OWER, Z = CLAIMED, C= CIRCUMSTANCE, Y (Initiator)—>X (Respondent) impermissible

★★★

FULL (adj)

Prolex_adjective_LEX full (41):

MORPHOLOGY_FRAME:
<mor LEX F> = "full (40) [JJ 40]"
<mor LEX -ER>= []
<mor LEX -EST>= "fullest (1) [JJT 1]"
<mor LEX related_wordforms>= "fully (1) [RR 7]"

SYNTAX_FRAME:
<syn LEX cat> = Adj
SYN_NP_SUBFRAME:
LEX= H
<syn pre H prep real>= "in (2)"
LEX= premod
<syn pre H det real>= "a (6), the (2), its (1)"
<syn LEX attr H premod real>= "LEX & final (2)"
<syn LEX attr H real>= "set (8), details (4), settlement (3), interest (2), invoice (2), address (1), capacity (1), page (1), understanding (1), payment (1), recovery (1), time position (1), extent (1), range (1), discharge (1), force (1), use (1); telephone number (1), commitment rate (1)"
<syn LEX attr H form>= LEX+N (31); LEX+Ncompound (N + N) (2)

SYN_ADJ_LEX_COLLOC_SUBFRAME:
<syn LEX pred adj_colloc real>= "LEX & complete (1)"
<syn LEX zscore real>="clean (20.113), set (19.420), originals (15.932), ocean (13.690), admitted (12.957)"

SEMANTICS_FRAME:
<sem LEX>= FULL (pred0)

PRAGMATICS_FRAME:
<prag pred0 structure>= X intensifies/maximises quantity/quality required by Y in pred0, where X=supplier/CNAME1,Y=customer/CNAME2
<prag pred0 typological_information>= <S C X A T P N E>
<prag pred0 S>= S0 (2) S1 (2) S2 (2) S3 (0) S4 (2) S5 (0) S6 (4) S7 (6) S8 (8) S9 (1) S10 (2) S11 (0) S12 (2) S13 (0) S14 ( ) S15 (10)
<prag pred0 C>= C0 (9) C1 (0) C2 (2) C3 (0) C4 (1) C5 (0) C6 (0) C7 (5) C8 (2) C9 (12) C10 (5) C11 (5) C12 ( )
<prag pred0 X>= X1 (27) X2 (14)
<prag pred0 A>= A1 (1) A2 (29) A3 (11)
<prag pred0 T>= T1 (26) T2 (15) T3 (0)
<prag pred0 P>= P1 (0) P3 (0) P4 (0) P5 (0) P6 (0) P7 (0) P8 (0) P9 (9) P10 (1) P2/1/2 (2) P2/1/3 (2) P2/2/10 (1) P2/2/13 (1) P2/2/3 (4) P2/2/4 (3) P2/2/6 (2) P2/3/14 (1) P2/3/4 (1) P2/3/5 (2) P2/3/7 (1) P2/7/8 (1) P2/f/1 (3) P2/f/2 (2) P2/f/3 (3) P2/f/4 (2)
<prag pred0 N>= N020 (1) N021 (1) N060 (1) N137 (2) N148 (1) N166 (1) N167 (1) N175 (2) N182 (2) N218 (2) N219 (2) N230 (1) N288 (1) N299 (1) N309 (1) N310 (1) N311 (1) N312 (1) N316 (1) N328 (1) N331 (1) N364 (1) N370 (1) N384 (1) N396 (1) N409 (1) N455 (1) N461 (1) N497 (1) N513 (1) N514 (1) N562 (4) N566 (1)
<prag pred0 E>= E- (41) E+ (0)

****
Procompare_adjective_LEX full (75):

MORPHOLOGY_FRAME:
<mor LEX F> = "full (74) [JJ 74]"
<mor LEX -ER>= []
<mor LEX -EST>= "fullest (1) [JJT 1]"
<mor LEX related_wordforms>= "full (17) [RR22 16 RR 1]; fully (23) [RR 23]"

SYNTAX_FRAME:
<syn LEX cat> = Adj
SYN_NP_SUBFRAME:

LEX= H
<syn pre H prep real>= "in (2)"
LEX= premod
<syn pre H det real>= "the (9), a (4), our (2), all (1), your (1), my (1)"
<syn LEX attr H premod real>= "LEX & exclusive (1), LEX & total (1), LEX & undivided (1), LEX & final (1), LEX & free access (1)"
<syn LEX attr H premod form>= LEX & adj (4), LEX & adj+N (1)
<syn LEX attr H real>= "payment (11), amount (7), rights (6), authority (3), force (3), power (2), refund (2), line (2), service (2), responsibility (2), name (1), disclosure (1), orders (1), use (1), intent (1), reimbursement (1), possession (1), permission (1), ability (1), house (1), time (1), extent (1), credit (1), knowledge (1) attention (2), statement (1), judgments (1), adjustment (1), satisfaction (1); name & place (3), power & authority (2), force & effect (1); purchase price (1)"
<syn LEX attr H form>= LEX + N (60); LEX + N + & + N (6); Ncompound (LEX +N) (1)
<syn LEX attr H postmod real>= "(payment) in LEX (6)"
<syn LEX attr H postmod form>= (N("payment")) + prep+LEX(postpositive)
SYN_ADJ_LEX_COLLOC_SUBFRAME:
<syn LEX pred adj_colloc real>= "LEX & complete (1)"
<syn LEX zscore real>= "authority (12.544), rights (12.007), devote (11.965), payment (9.992), responsibility (9.702)"

SEMANTICS_FRAME:
<sem LEX>= FULL (pred0)

PRAGMATICS_FRAME:
<prag pred0 structure>= X intensifies/maximises quantity/quality required by Y in pred0, where X=supplier/CNAME1, Y=customer/CNAME2

****
PLEASE (adv)

Prolex_adverb_LEX please (275):

MORPHOLOGY_FRAME:
<mor LEX F> = "please (275) [RR 275]"
<mor LEX related_wordforms>= "pleased (82) [VVN 71 VVD 6 JJ 5]; pleasure (28) [NN1 28]; pleasant (5) [JJ 5]"

SYNTAX_FRAME:
<syn LEX cat> = Adv
<syn LEX adv class>= adjunct []; subjunct [X]; disjunct; conjunct []

SYN_POSN_SUBFRAME:
<syn LEX pre S V>= []
<syn LEX post S Faux>= []
<syn LEX post S copula>= []
<syn LEX pre Vfinite>=   Adv + V (269); Aux+S+Adv+Vfinite (6)
(interrogative)
<syn LEX pre Vfinite feats>= Aux in Aux+S+Adv+Vfinite realized by
"would (5)" and "could (1)"; S ellipted in Adv+V pattern, thus Adv initial
<syn LEX post S V>= []
SYN_ADV_LEX_COLLOC_SUBFRAME:
<syn pre LEX adj_colloc real>= "enclosed (5)"
<syn pre LEX PP_colloc real>= "in the meantime (1)"
<syn pre LEX adv_colloc real>= "herewith (1), kindly (1), also (1), so (1)"
<syn post LEX verb_colloc real>= "advise (36), note (25), confirm (16),
contact (12), find (8), arrange (7), remit (7), accept (5), complete (4), send (4),
convey (3), honour (3), refer (3), acknowledge (2), debit (2), ensure (2), include
(2), instruct (2), place (2), present (2), proceed (2), relay (2), send (2), telex (2),
write (2), airmail (1), attend (1), bring (1), cancel (1), carry (1), clarify (1), close
(1), congratulate (1), coordinate (1), direct (1), endorse (1), expedite (1), follow
(1), furnish (1), give (1), ignore (1), indicate (1), issue (1), investigate (1), liaise
(1), lodge (1),nominate (1), notify (1), prepare (1), provide (1), read (1), recall
(1), re-direct (1), release (1), reply (1), return (1),revert (1), revise (1), sand (1),
return (1), signify (1), sign (1), submit (1), supply (1), transfer (1); let...have (15),
let...know (8), pass on (3), attend to (3), take note (1), have ...done (1),
have...completed (1), rest [assured] (1), keep....informed (1), keep...appraised
(1), look...up (1), look out for (1), draw on (1), give...ring (1), deal..with (1); [do
not] hesitate to contact (8), [do] call (4), [do not] hesitate to call (2), [do not]
add (1), [do not] forget (1);be informed (6), be advised (6), be guided (2), be
assured (2), be reminded (1); investigate & arrange (1), check & advise (1),
arrange & advise (1), assist & advise (1), complete & return (1); feel [free] to
contact (2), continue to insure (1)"
<syn post LEX verb_colloc form>=V(finite) (196) /V(phrasal (prep)) (40)
/ Aux(do)+(not)+V(finite) (16) / Aux(be)+V(-ed)/Adj(-ed) (17) / V+&+V
(5) /V+to+V (3)
<syn LEX zscore real>= "advise (16.501), contact (15.038), note (13.519),
hesitate (12.339), let (10.053)"

SEMANTICS_FRAME:
<sem LEX>= PLEASE (pred0)

PRAGMATICS_FRAME:
<prag pred0 structure>= X requests Y to pred0 + V concerning Z, where
X=ADDRESSER, Y= ADDRESSEE, pred0= (ROUTINE) COURTESY

MARKER, V= PROCESS / ACTION, Z= (COMMUNICATIVE) CONTENT

\<prag pred0 typological_information\>= \<S C X A T P N E\>

\<prag pred0 S\>= S0 (21) S1 (28) S2 (11) S3 (13) S4 (33) S5 (11) S6 (14) S7 (35) S8 (21) S9 (7) S10 (29) S11 (1) S12 (7) S13 (3) S14 (5) S15 (36)

\<prag pred0 C\>= C0 (28) C1 (6) C2 (13) C3 (3) C4 (11) C5 (1) C6 (4) C7 (39) C8 (18) C9 (48) C10 (54) C11 (36) C12 (14)

\<prag pred0 X\>= X1 (165) X2 (110)

\<prag pred0 A\>= A1 (5) A2 (99) A3 (171)

\<prag pred0 T\>= T1 (172) T2 (96) T3 (7)

\<prag pred0 P\>= P1 (0) P3 (0) P4 (0) P5 (0) P6 (0) P7 (2) P8 (0) P9 (3) P10 (17) P2/1/2 (15) P2/1/3 (6) P2/1/4 (8) P2/1/5 (3) P2/1/8 (1) P2/1/f (4) P2/2/3 (30) P2/2/4 (8) P2/2/5 (4) P2/2/f (1) P2/3/4 (24) P2/3/5 (3) P2/3/6 (1) P2/3/7 (1) P2/4/5 (8) P2/4/6 (7) P2/4/7 (2) P2/5/6 (4) P2/5/7 (2) P2/6/7 (2) P2/6/8 (2) P2/11/14 (1) P2/f/1 (18) P2/f/2 (41) P2/f/3 (24) P2/f/4 (15) P2/f/5 (9) P2/f/6 (6) P2/f/7 (2) P2/f/14 (1)

\<prag pred0 N\>= N004 (1) N005 (1) N008 (1) N010 (1) N011 (1) N013 (1) N019 (1) N020 (1) N022 (1) N023 (3) N025 (2) N028 (1) N032 (2) N034 (1) N040 (1) N050 (1) N051 (1) N060 (1) N062 (2) N064 (1) N065 (1) N066 (1) N069 (1) N072 (1) N073 (2) N074 (1) N076 (1) N077 (1) N079 (2) N080 (1) N086 (1) N090 (1) N092 (3) N096 (1) N099 (1) N100 (1) N101 (1) N107 (1) N108 (1) N109 (1) N110 (1) N111 (1) N112 (1) N113 (1) N116 (2) N117 (1) N118 (1) N122 (2) N126 (1) N127 (2) N130 (4) N131 (1) N132 (1) N133 (1) N134 (3) N136 (3) N137 (1) N139 (1) N140 (1) N141 (1) N142 (1) N143 (1) N145 (1) N148 (2) N149 (2) N151 (1) N153 (1) N155 (2) N157 (1) N158 (1) N160 (1) N163 (1) N166 (1) N169 (1) N170 (1) N173 (1) N174 (1) N176 (5) N178 (1) N180 (2) N181 (2) N182 (1) N186 (2) N195 (1) N197 (1) N200 (2) N203 (1) N206 (2) N207 (1) N217 (2) N218 (2) N222 (1) N223 (1) N225 (2) N230 (8) N234 (1) N235 (5) N236 (1) N238 (1) N239 (1) N244 (1) N246 (1) N248 (1) N250 (2) N252 (2) N256 (1) N264 (1) N268 (1) N275 (2) N276 (1) N277 (1) N279 (1) N280 (1) N284 (1) N285 (1) N286 (1) N288 (2) N289 (1) N297 (1) N301 (1) N302 (1) N322 (1) N323 (1) N324 (1) N330 (1) N349 (1) N365 (2) N368 (1) N369 (1) N376 (3) N380 (1) N384 (3) N385 (2) N386 (2) N388 (1) N389 (1) N390 (3) N395 (2) N396 (4) N399 (2) N404 (1) N405 (1) N406 (1) N407 (1) N413 (1) N414 (1) N417 (2) N420 (1) N425 (1) N427 (1) N430 (2) N432 (2) N436 (1) N439 (1) N440 (1) N441 (1) N443 (1) N445 (1) N446 (1) N451 (1) N453 (2) N454 (2) N455 (3) N456 (2) N459 (1) N464 (2) N465 (2) N473 (1) N475 (2) N479 (1) N481 (2) N486 (2) N489 (1) N490 (1) N491 (1) N499 (1) N506 (1) N507 (2) N509 (1) N510 (1) N516 (1) N519 (1) N524 (2) N525 (1) N527 (2) N529 (1) N541 (2) N542 (2) N543 (1) N544 (1) N548 (1) N552 (1) N561 (1)

\<prag pred0 E\>= E- (271) E+ (1)

****

Procompare_adverb_LEX please (240):

MORPHOLOGY_FRAME:
<mor LEX F> = "please (247) [RR 240]
<mor LEX related_wordforms>= "please (9) [VV0 5VVI 2VVZ 2]; pleasant
(1) [JJ 1]; pleasantly (1) [RR 1]; pleased (40) [JJ 40]; pleasure (25) [NN1 25]"

SYNTAX_FRAME:
<syn LEX cat> = Adv
<syn LEX adv class>= adjunct []; subjunct [X]; disjunct; conjunct []
SYN_POSN_SUBFRAME:
<syn LEX pre S V>= []
<syn LEX post S Faux>= []
<syn LEX post S copula>= []
<syn LEX preVfinite>= Adv +V (231); Aux+S+Adv+Vfinite (9) (interrogative)
<syn LEX pre Vfinite feats>= in <Adv+Vfinite...>, only 1 instance of
S+Adv+Finite; Aux in Aux+S+Adv+Vfinite realized by "would (7), may (1),
could (1)"; S ellipted in Adv+V pattern, thus Adv initial
<syn LEX post S V>= []
SYN_ADV_LEX_COLLOC_SUBFRAME:
<syn pre LEX adj_colloc real>= "enclosed (1)"
<syn post LEX verb_colloc real>= "accept (30), call (21), contact (15),
advise (16), send (6), sign (5), find (4), forward (4), have (4), acknowledge (3),
mail (3), return (3), check (2), disregard (2), identify (2), include (2), indicate (2),
review (2), telephone (2), add (1), adjust (1), amend (1), authorize (1), be (1),
bring (1), cancel (1), come (1), complete (1),comply (1), confirm (1), consider
(1), detach (1), execute (1), give (1), govern (1), inform (1), issue (1), note (1),
provide (1), quote (1), remit (1), report (1), resubmit (1), see (1), ship (1), submit
(1), tell (1), take (1), use (1); let....know (15), give..a call (5), direct..to (3),
provide..with (3), let...hear (2), arrange for (1), bring....attention (1), call upon
(1), come up (1),give...attention (1), fill out (1), give...instructions (1),let...show
(1), make...payments (1), make...adjustments (1), make...corrections (1),
make...payable (1), turn over (1); attempt to effect (1), feel [free] to contact (5)/
to call upon (2)/to call (2)/to use (1)/to give...a call (1)/to either drop in or
make an appointment (1)/to bring (1)/to resubmit (1)/ to drop in (1)/to
write(1)/to include (1); be advised (10), be assured (3); don't hesitate to call (5),
do not hesitate to contact (3), do not hesitate to write (1)"
<syn post LEX verb_colloc form>=Vfinite (158) /V+to+V (18) /V(phrasal
(prep)) (41) / Aux(be)+Ved/Adj (ed) (13) / Aux (do)+(not)+V(finite) (9)
<syn LEX zscore real>="call (23.036), accept (18.570), contact (18.208),
hesitate (16.707), let (15.925)"

SEMANTICS_FRAME:

<sem LEX>= PLEASE (pred0)

PRAGMATICS_FRAME:
<prag pred0 structure>= X requests Y to pred0 + V concerning Z, where X=ADDRESSER, Y= ADDRESSEE, pred0= (ROUTINE) COURTESY MARKER, V= PROCESS/ ACTION, Z= (COMMUNICATIVE) CONTENT

****

REGRET (v)

Prolexverb_LEX regret (35):

MORPHOLOGY_FRAME:
<mor LEX F> = "regret (35) [VV0 35]"
<mor LEX -S>= []
<mor LEX -ED>= []
<mor LEX -ING>= []
<mor LEX related_wordforms>: "regret (1) [NN1 1]; regrets (1) [NN2 1]; regretably (1) [RR 1], regretfully (1) [RR 1]"

SYNTAX_FRAME:
<syn LEX cat> = V
<syn LEX modals>= []
<syn LEX perfective>= []
<syn LEX progressive>= []
<syn LEX passive>= []
SYN_LEX_COLLOCATE_SUBFRAME:
<syn post LEX verb_colloc real>="to advise (5), to inform (4), to know (1), to report (1), to note (1), to say (1)"
<syn post LEX verb_colloc form>= LEX+to+V(transitive)
<syn LEX zscore real>="that (13.363), unable (12.189), adverse (11.720), inform (11.133), we (9.712)"
LEX=Ndeverbal
<syn pre LEX prep>= "with (2)"
SYN_PRED_SUBFRAME:
LEX=pred0
<syn pred0 Copular>= []
<syn pred0 Monotransitive>= <arg1 arg2 arg3>
<syn pred0 Ditransitive>= []
<syn pred0 Complex_Transitive>= []
<syn pred0 arg1 real>= "we (24), [] (10), i (1)"

\<syn pred0 arg1 form\> = NP
\<syn pred0 arg1 function\>= S
\<syn pred0 arg1 status\> = explicit (21), implicit (9)
\<syn pred0 arg2 real\>= "that you still have not responded to our request for payment (2), that we are unable to give you information (1), that the said item has not been found, that we are unable to supply (1), our communication {ref.} was only relayed to you this morning (1), we are unable to entertain your claim (1), {cname} hostels are not available (1), your application [is] not successful (1), that miss {name}'s flight should have been marred in this way (1), that we are going to debit you for the loss of 1 drum of {cname_obj} (1), that we have to cancel our order (1), any inconvenience caused (1), that we are unable to assist you (1), that we cannot be with you in person to celebrate the occasion (1), that your policy had no value as at the date of lapse (1), that we are only prepared to continue your policy subject to a revised compulsory excess of ${amt.} (1), that it is not possible for the post office savings bank to credit us the premium due (1), that we can not agree to sponsor the project (1); to inform you that at this point of time we do not have any suitable vacancy for which you may be considered (1),to inform you that we do not appear to have received your disposal (1), to advise that we are unable to accept your quote in this instance (1), to know of the damages occurred to the above-stated two shipments (1), to advise you that we are not able to entertain your claims (1), to inform you that a great number of drums from our last two orders had been found to be defective (1), to report that all the 9 pieces were damaged during the shipping (1), to advise that we are unable to take advantage of them this time (1), to advise that we are not able to utilize your background and qualification for this particular position (1), to note that we have not so far received your remittance for ${amt.} (1), to inform you that it is not the practice of the company to issue duplicate receipts (1), to advise that we are unable to donate any prizes for your staff party (1), to say that we are not able to include cost of airfreight (1)"
\<syn pred0 arg2 form\> = that-clause (18) / to-clause (13)
\<syn pred0 arg2 function\>= DO
\<syn pred0 arg2 status\> = obligatory
\<syn pred0 arg3 real\>= "owing to transmission error (1), as we do not trade this item (1), much as we would like to (1), as we are not licensed to do export sales (1); very much (2), sincerely (1); despite a careful and thorough search (1), in view of the above (1), in view of your failure to comply with our procedures (1)"
\<syn pred0 arg3 form\> = adv_clause (4) / advp (3) / PP (3)
\<syn pred0 arg3 function\>= A
\<syn pred0 arg3 feats\> = Cause-Reason-Purpose (5); Manner-Means-Instrument (3); Condition-Contrast (2); Location [], Temporal []
\<syn pred0 arg3 status\> = optional

SEMANTICS_FRAME:
\<sem LEX> = REGRET (pred0)
\<sem pred0 arg1 case> = Actor
\<sem pred0 arg2 case> = Goal
\<sem pred0 arg3 case> = Circumstance

PRAGMATICS_FRAME:
\<prag pred0 structure>= X (arg1) APOLOGIZES (pred0) in informing Y (implicit in arg2) regarding Z (arg2) under C (arg3), where X= SUPPLIER / CNAME1, Z= ADDRESSEE / CNAME2, Z= NEGATIVE_TOPIC, C= (NEGATIVE)_CIRCUMSTANCE
\<prag pred0 typological_information>=\<S C X A T P N E>
\<prag pred0 S>= S0 (2) S1 (0) S2 (3) S3 (5) S4 (3) S5 (3) S6 (8) S7 (5) S8 (1) S9 (0) S10 (1) S11 (0) S12 (1) S13 (1) S14 ( ) S15 (2)
\<prag pred0 C>= C0 (0) C1 (0) C2 (3) C3 (1) C4 (1) C5 (0) C6 (3) C7 (1) C8 (2) C9 (12) C10 (3) C11 (5) C12 (4)
\<prag pred0 X>= X1 (15) X2 (20)
\<prag pred0 A>= A1 (2) A2 (33) A3 (0)
\<prag pred0 T>= T1 (25) T2 (10) T3 (0)
\<prag pred0 P>= P1 (0) P3 (0) P4 (0) P5 (0) P6 (0) P7 (0) P8 (0) P9 (0) P10 (0) P2/1/2 (4) P2/1/3 (6) P2/1/4 (1) P2/1/6 (1) P2/1/f (1) P2/2/3 (7) P2/2/5 (1) P2/3/4 (1) P2/f/1 (4) P2/f/2 (4) P2/f/3 (3) P2/f/4 (1) P2/f/5 (1)
\<prag pred0 N>= N021 (1) N022 (1) N031 (1) N041 (1) N064 (1) N105 (1) N136 (1) N150 (1) N183 (1) N188 (1) N190 (1) N238 (1) N281 (1) N290 (1) N309 (2) N334 (1) N337 (1) N338 (1) N340 (1) N342 (2) N374 (1) N375 (1) N412 (1) N425 (1) N446 (1) N474 (1) N488 (1) N510 (1) N513 (1) N536 (1) N537 (1) N539 (1) N557 (1)
\<prag pred0 E>= E- (35) E+ (0)

****

Procompareverb_LEX regret(20):

MORPHOLOGY_FRAME:
\<mor LEX F> = "regret (20) [VV0 20]"
\<mor LEX -S> = []
\<mor LEX -ED>= []
\<mor LEX -ING>= []
\<mor LEX related_wordforms>: "regret (3) [NN1 3]; regrettable (2) [JJ 2]"

SYNTAX_FRAME:
\<syn LEX cat> = V
\<syn LEX modals>= []
\<syn LEX perfective>= []

<syn LEX progressive>= []
<syn LEX passive>= []
SYN_LEX_COLLOCATE_SUBFRAME:
<syn post LEX verb_colloc real>="to inform (12), to say (1), having to (1)"
<syn post LEX verb_colloc form>= V(non-finite)
<syn LEX zscore real>="inform (31.723), deep (24.124), unintentional (17.058), necessity (15.179), we (12.285)"
SYN_PRED_SUBFRAME:
LEX= pred0
<syn pred0 Copular>= []
<syn pred0 Monotransitive>= <arg1 arg2 arg3>
<syn pred0 Ditransitive>= []
<syn pred0 Complex_Transitive>= []
<syn pred0 arg1 case> = Actor
<syn pred0 arg1 real>= "we (17), i (3)"
<syn pred0 arg1 form> = NP
<syn pred0 arg1 function>= S
<syn pred0 arg1 status> = explicit (20), obligatory
<syn pred0 arg2 case> = Goal
<syn pred0 arg2 real>= "to inform you..that the available position(s) has been filled (1), to inform you that i have been unable to locate another {item requested} for you (1), to inform you that we will be unable to ship the merchandise (1), to inform you that said order cannot be filled at this time (1), to inform you that there are no openings in our firm at this time (1), to inform you that we are unable to grant you any further extensions for the payment due (1), to inform you that your employment with the firm shall be terminated on {date} (1), to inform you that we are unable to extend any more time for payment of the above invoice (1), to inform you that we have awarded the contract to another firm (1), to inform you that the goods herein referred to are unavailable (1), to inform you that we are unable to open a charge account for you at present (1), to say that we do not have any of the discontinued models (1), to inform you that we cannot extend credit terms to you at the present time (1); this unintentional mistake on our part (1), the necessity of imposing this restriction (1), the unfortunate occurrence of these circumstances (1), the necessity of this action (1); having to take this action (1), having to withhold further deliveries (1); (that) this action is necessary (1)"
<syn pred0 arg2 form> = to-clause (13) / np (4) / ing-clause (2) / that-clause (1)
<syn pred0 arg2 function>= DO
<syn pred0 arg2 status> = obligatory
<syn pred0 arg3 case> = Circumstance
<syn pred0 arg3 real>= "due to the following reason (1), due to information obtained from the following consumer reporting agency (1), for the following

reason (s) (1), after checking with all of our other stores in the area (1), after careful review (1); because {reason set forth} (1), based on the report we received back from our credit bureau (1), therefore (1)"

<syn pred0 arg3 form> = PP (5) / adv_clause (2) / adv_p (1)
<syn pred0 arg3 function>= A
<syn pred0 arg3 sem feats> = Cause-Reason-Purpose (5); Temporal (2); Manner-Means-Instrument (1); Condition-Contrast []; Location []
<syn pred0 arg3 status> = optional
SYN_NP_SUBFRAME:
LEX= Ndeverbal
Ndeverbal=H
<syn pre H premod real>= "deep (2)"

SEMANTICS_FRAME:
<sem LEX> = REGRET (pred0)
<sem pred0 arg1 case> = Actor
<sem pred0 arg2 case> = Goal
<sem pred0 arg3 case> = Circumstance

PRAGMATICS_FRAME:
<prag pred0 structure>= X (arg1) APOLOGIZES (pred0) in informing Y (implicit in arg2) regarding Z (arg2) under C (arg3), where X= SUPPLIER / CNAME1, Z = ADDRESSEE / CNAME2, Z = NEGATIVE_TOPIC, C = (NEGATIVE)_CIRCUMSTANCE

★★

SHIPMENT (n)

Prolexnoun_LEX shipment (53):

MORPHOLOGY_FRAME:
<mor LEX F> = "shipment (42) [NN1 37]"
<mor LEX -S>= "shipments (11) [NN2 11]"
<mor LEX related_wordforms>= "ship (15) [NN1 14 VVI 1], shipping (23) [VVG 6 NN1 17], shipped (13) [VVN 7 VVD 6], shipowners (1) [NN2 1], ships (3) [NN2 3], shipyards (1) [NN2 1], shipper (1) [NN1 1], ship-chandler (1) [NN1 1]"

SYNTAX_FRAME:
<syn LEX cat> = N [X]; Ndeverbal []
<syn LEX N class>= Count [X]; Mass [X]
SYN_NP_SUBFRAME:

LEX=H
<syn pre H det real>= "the (6), our (2), both (2), a (2), such (1), these (1)"
<syn pre H premod real>= "partial (2), whole (1), next (1), above-stated two (1), two (1), previous (1), other (1), undermentioned (1), first experimental (1), prompt (1), immediate (1), inbound airfreight (1), entire (1), future (1)"
<syn post H postmod real>= "of {cname_obj} (4), of personal effects (1), in good condition (1), in containers (1), of 15 cases (1)"
<syn post H postmod form>= PP (8)
SYN_LEX_COLLOCATE_SUBFRAME:
<syn pre LEX noun_colloc real>= "notice of (2), port of (2), weight of (2), value of (1), receipt of (1), declaration of (1), packing of (1)"
<syn pre LEX noun_colloc form>= N+prep+LEX
<syn pre LEX verb_colloc real>= "covering (5), evidencing (3), occurred to (1), to make (1), received (1)"
<syn pre LEX verb_colloc form>= V(non-finite), V(ed)
<syn post LEX verb_colloc real>= "is allowed (2), were loaded (1), were insured (1), is prohibited (1); can be booked (1); is arriving (1)"
<syn post LEX verb_colloc form>= V(passive) (5) / V (modal) (1); V(progressive) (1)
<syn post LEX adv_colloc real>= "to singapore (2), at singapore (1), from japan to singapore (1), on {date} (1), onto the vessels concerned (1), to your company (1), to other customers (1), on {country} flag vessels (1), to {cvessel} (1), for onward journey to rangoon (1), from manila to rangoon (1), from u.s.a. (1)"
<syn post LEX adv_colloc form>= PP (15)
<syn LEX zscore real>= "covering (15.787), prohibited (15.119), evidencing (13.094), latest (11.846), prepaid (11.274)"

SEMANTICS_FRAME:
<sem LEX> = SHIPMENT1 (arg01) SHIPMENT2 (arg02)

PRAGMATICS_FRAME:
<prag arg01 structure>= X consigns goods (arg01) to Y, where X=SUPPLIER / CNAME1, Y=CUSTOMER / CNAME2
<prag arg02 structure>= The process of consigning goods (arg02) from X to Y, where X=SUPPLIER / CNAME1, Y=CUSTOMER / CNAME2
<prag arg0 typological_information>=<S C X A T P N E>
<prag arg0 S>= S0 (0) S1 (0) S2 (0) S3 (0) S4 (6) S5 (2) S6 (17) S7 (0) S8 (15) S9 (0) S10 (10) S11 (0) S12 (0) S13 (0) S14 (0) S15 (3)
<prag arg0 C>= C0 (3) C1 (0) C2 (0) C3 (0) C4 (0) C5 (0) C6 (0) C7 (12) C8 (5) C9 (27) C10 (1) C11 (0) C12 (5)
<prag arg0 X>= X1 (35) X2 (18)
<prag arg0 A>= A1 (5) A2 (47) A3 (1)
<prag arg0 T>= T1 (34) T2 (19) T3 (0)

<prag arg0 P>= P1 (0) P3 (1) P4 (7) P5 (0) P6 (0) P7 (0) P8 (0) P9 (18) P10 (0) P2/1/2 (2) P2/1/3 (2) P2/1/4 (1) P2/1/5 (1) P2/2/3 (6) P2/2/4 (3) P2/4/5 (1) P2/5/14 (5) P2/6/14 (1) P2/7/8 (1) P2/f/1 (2) P2/f/2 (1) P2/f/5 (1)
<prag arg0 N>= N096 (1) N173 (2) N182 (1) N218 (2) N219 (4) N221 (1) N222 (1) N252 (1) N253 (1) N254 (1) N255 (1) N280 (2) N288 (3) N309 (7) N316 (1) N339 (1) N344 (1) N346 (1) N360 (1) N361 (1) N364 (4) N365 (2) N366 (1) N393 (1) N397 (5) N402 (1) N529 (3) N549 (1) N551 (1)
<prag arg0 E>= E- (53) E+ (0)

****

Procomparenoun_LEX shipment (27):

MORPHOLOGY_FRAME:
<mor LEX F> = "shipment (23) [NN1 23]"
<mor LEX -S>= "shipments (4) [NN2 4]"
<mor LEX related_wordforms>= "ship (10) [VVI 8 VV0 2]; shipped (13) [VVN 6 JJ 2 VVD5]; shipping (14) [NN1 7 VVG 7]"

SYNTAX_FRAME:
<syn LEX cat> = N [X]; Ndeverbal []
<syn LEX N class>= Count [X]; Mass [X]
SYN_NP_SUBFRAME:
LEX=H
<syn pre H det real>= "the (6), a (3), our (1), all (1), that (1)"
<syn pre H premod real>= "new (2), partial (2), future (2), further (1), immediate (1)"
<syn post H postmod real>= "of the above referenced merchandise (2), of the aforementioned merchandise (1), of 60 cases (1), of your order (1), for 30 lbs (1), in single lot (1), from England (1), to {name of firm} (1), on credit (1); (which) we received on the above referenced purchase order (1)"
<syn post H postmod form>= PP (10) / rel-clause (1)
SYN_LEX_COLLOCATE_SUBFRAME:
<syn pre LEX noun_colloc real>= "method of (2), delay in (1), error in (1), form of (1), order number for (1)"
<syn pre LEX noun_colloc form>= N+prep+LEX; Ncompound (N + N) +prep+LEX
<syn pre LEX verb_colloc real>= "to cancel (2), to stagger (1), to attempt (1), replacing...with (1); have received (1), shall release (1)"
<syn pre LEX verb_colloc form>= V(non-finite) (5); V(finite) (2)
<syn post LEX verb_colloc real>= "can be made (2), will be made (1), must include (1); has been unloaded (1), has been delivered (1), has been dusted (1); is scheduled (1); was (1); left (1)"

\<syn post LEX verb_colloc form>= V(modal) (4) / V(perfective) (3) / V(passive) (1) / V(copula) (1) / V(finite) (1)

\<syn post LEX adj_colloc real>= "ready (1)"

\<syn post LEX adv_colloc real >= "for your review (1)"

\<syn LEX zscore real>= "method (18.375), unloaded (15.944), partial (15.882), cases (12.917), noticing (11.230)"

SEMANTICS_FRAME:

\<sem LEX> = SHIPMENT1 (arg01) SHIPMENT2 (arg02)

PRAGMATICS-FRAME:

\<prag arg01 structure>= X consigns goods (arg01) to Y, where X=SUPPLIER / CNAME1,Y=CUSTOMER / CNAME2

\<prag arg02 structure>= The process of consigning goods (arg02) from X to Y, where X=SUPPLIER / CNAME1,Y=CUSTOMER / CNAME2

Appendix B
Some World Wide Web Sites for CL1, CL2 and CL3

N.B.: Please note that, due to the current nature of the World Wide Web, the addresses listed here may (and probably will) change over time. The best way to address this potential problem is to use a search engine (e.g. Lycos or Magellan) offered by a browser such as Netscape. Type in the relevant keywords under the 'search' option: *computational linguistics, corpus, language, lexicography, lexicon, linguistics*, etc. The reader is also invited to access the author's homepage, currently at *http://www.nus.edu.sg/NUSinfo/FASS/ELL/Vincent/* for a list of regularly updated links. The following sites vary in their usefulness for textual and lexical material, as well as linguistic and lexicographic software:

- British National Corpus
  http://info.ox.ac.uk/bnc/
  [Details of the 100-million corpus of contemporary British English. Also, check out a list of English language corpora at: *http://sable.ox.ac.uk/bnc/corpora.html*]
- Centre for Lexical Information (CELEX)
  http://www.kun.nl/celex/
  [The Dutch Centre for Lexical Information; the CELEX database is also available on CD-ROM from the Linguistic Data Consortium]
- Computing in the Humanities and Social Sciences, Toronto
  http://www.chass.utoronto.ca:8080/cch/index.html
  [For useful linguistic information and textual software, in particular TACT – Textual Analysis Computing Tools – at *http://www.chass.utoronto.ca:8080/cch/software.html*]
- Centre for Computer Analysis of Language and Speech
  http://agora.leeds.ac.uk/ccalas
  [For some interesting language and computing projects at Leeds]
- Centre for Textual Studies:
  http://info.ox.ac.uk/ctitext

[Includes their Resource Guide and a list of Electronic Texts on the Web]
- Computation and Language E-Print Archive
  http://xxx.lanl.gov/cmp-lg
  [Search for CL1 articles on lexis and the lexicon by keying in the relevant words]
- Computational Linguistics
  http://www.cs.columbia.edu/~acl/home.html
  [The ACL's homepage]
- Consortium for Lexical Research
  http://crl.nmsu.edu/clr/CLRIntro.html
  [Lexical resources; includes membership subscription information]
- Corpus Linguistics
  http://www.ruf.rice.edu/~barlow
  [Check out Michael Barlow's homepage for relevant sites on corpus linguistics and useful software information; in particular *http://www.ruf.rice.edu/~barlow/mono.html* details the Monoconc concordancing program; check out ParaConc as well]
- Corpus Linguistics
  http://clg1.bham.ac.uk
  [Birmingham's Corpus Linguistics Group; also, check out COBUILD and subscription details to the Bank of English at *http://titania.cobuild. collins. co.uk*]
- International Computer Archive of Modern and Medieval English (ICAME)
  http://www.hd.uib.no/icame.html
  [The Association of 'corpus linguists'; relevant information on corpus linguistics software and hardware; see also the related Norwegian Computing Centre for the Humanities]
- Istituto di Linguistica Computazionale
  http://www.ilc.pi.cnr.it
  [Institute of Computational Linguistics, Pisa; check out relevant lexical projects like DELIS ('Descriptive Lexical Specifications')]
- Linguistic Data Consortium
  http://www.ldc.upenn.edu/
  [For data sharing; membership subscription available]
- Linguistics Resources on the Internet
  http://www.sil.org/linguistics/linguistics.html
  [Searchable index on linguistics and natural language processing; enter relevant keywords]
- Oxford Text Archive Home Page
  http://users.ox.ac.uk/~archive/ota.html
  [Information for language and literature texts, some shareware; also software and corpus information]

- Oxford University Publishing
  http://www1.oup.co.uk/oup/elt/software
  [Check out their range of software, including the concordancing software WordSmith]
- Special Interest Group on the Lexicon
  http://www.clres.com/siglex.html/
  [SIGLEX; sponsored by the Association for Computational Linguistics; check this out for electronic dictionaries, lexical databanks, and other relevant links]
- Text Encoding Initiative Home Page
  http://www-tei.uic.edu/orgs/tei/
  [For an update of the efforts of the TEI to standardise textual and lexical material]
  Also: look at *http://etext.virginia.edu/TEI.html*
- Unit for Computer Corpus Research on Language
  http://www.comp.lancs.ac.uk/computing/research/ucrel
  [Lancaster University's UCREL homepage; for updates and links on corpus linguistics, etc.]

Appendix C
Suggested solutions to exercises

CHAPTER 1

1. All definitions of what the **word** is continue to prove inadequate, although the notion is psychologically real: we all know what a word is, but cannot really define it. Aronoff (1992: 325) makes the useful observation that the term includes a number of theoretically distinct notions, the most important of these being the phonological word, the morphological or grammatical word, and the lexeme or 'dictionary entry'.

2. Different people have used these terms in different ways. In this book, I treat **word**, **lexical entry**, **lexeme**, and **lemma** as somewhat interchangeable terms. More precisely, of course, the term 'lemma' is used when one is concerned with inflectional variants; otherwise, the term lexeme is used for a dictionary/lexical entry: See Francis and Kucera (1982: 3). See also Mel'cuk (1992, 1996) for the related term **vocable** ('family of lexemes'). Some linguists do not make such a distinction between 'lexeme' and 'lemma' – Aronoff (1992) just uses the term 'lexeme'. Furthermore, Aronoff, in viewing the lexeme as 'dictionary entry', also makes the point that every lexeme 'must have a unitary meaning.' Of course, what constitutes 'unitary meaning' is another kettle of fish.

3. The preface to the LDEL dictionary (see Gay et al 1984) states that, 'inevitably, a dictionary partly overlaps an *encyclopedia*. In contrast to most dictionaries produced in America, France and other countries, British dictionaries of the nineteenth and twentieth centuries have generally eschewed what their compilers regarded as encyclopedic content. Theoretical distinctions suggest that the true province of a dictionary is words, not things; or purely lexical, not technical or factual, information; or generic, not specific, entries. In practice, however, no clear dividing line can be drawn between the two types of book. The dictionary definition of any entity must involve an account of its typical composition, attributes, and functions sufficiently detailed to distinguish it from other entities; the

modern reader can scarcely be content with such vague identifications as "*mackerel* a sea-fish" (Johnson) or "*laurel* the tree so called" (Dyche, 1768)'. With regard to proper names, the LDEL does not include them in the main text, but does include them in a 'biographical dictionary' and a 'gazetteer' section. With the publication of dictionaries such as the encyclopedic edition of the OALD (see Crowther 1992) and the *Longman Dictionary of English Language and Culture* (see Summers 1992), however, such distinctions are beginning to fade away.

5. This relates to Makkai (1980)'s distinction between HABIT and TRUE dictionaries.

6. In a fascinating experiment, Jackendoff (1992b, 1995) asked his daughter to collect expressions found in the 'Wheel of Fortune' programme for a period of several weeks. In his examination of this material, Jackendoff found the following percentages: 10% single words, 30% compounds, 10% idioms, 10% names, 10% meaningful names, 15% cliches, 5% titles, and 3% quotes. Thus, Jackendoff concludes that a speaker of [American] English must be carrying around thousands of [such] compounds, idioms, names, meaningful names, and cliches. These 'fixed expressions', he argues, hardly constitute a marginal part of our use of language. But how is all this material stored in the human memory? Is it like other more general-purpose parts of memory (along with facts of history, how to cook, etc.)? Unlike these latter abilities, the Wheel of Fortune material is made up of *words*, so it must be part of language. They have phonological, syntactic, and semantic structure and are integrated well into sentences and parts of sentences. So, we have no sense that a different activity is taking place. Jackendoff then makes the correct conclusion that the lexicon is (and should be) very much central in linguistic theory.

CHAPTER 2

2. Boguraev and Pustejovsky (1996: 3) rightly point out that, in CL1 research, 'it has become clear that, regardless of a system's sophistication or breadth, its performance must be measured in large part by the resources provided by the computational lexicon associated with it. The fundamental resources that go into a lexical item enable a wide range of morphological, lexical, syntactic, semantic and pragmatic processes to operate in the course of tasks such as language analysis, text processing, content extraction, document summarization, or machine translation.' In other words, a rich-enough lexicon enhances the performance of the CL1 system concerned.

CHAPTER 3

1. Depending on the variety of English represented by a person's mental lexicon, not all the expressions listed here will be apparent to speakers of other varieties of English (i.e. besides American English). Different socio-linguistic realities are expressed, so it does seem necessary to begin the

building of various regional Banks of English (for which the ICE project is a good start) in order to enable cross-comparisons of different varieties of English and so prevent miscommunication. For example, the word *stay* is used as a substitute for *live* in some varieties of English, e.g. Scottish English and informal Singapore English; in standard English, *stay* does not, of course, carry any sense of permanence.

2. The word *veritable* selects a semantic prosody that is 'dramatic', 'enormous', or 'extreme'. Being encountered for the first time, the object noun associated with *veritable* takes a colligation of 'a', not 'the' (since 'the' implies something already met before).

3. *Bright future* is usually said in the larger context of 'false optimism' (as John Sinclair notes). Although it is usually used in an immediate context which implies a matter of conviction, the larger context should show that this phrase is used when there is either a potential problem or slight worry that has to be dealt with.

CHAPTER 4

1. The advantages of corpora over 'human-oriented dictionary entries' include the fact that corpora provide experimental evidence of word uses, word associations, and such language phenomena as metaphors, idioms, and metonyms. According to Velardi et al, corpora are a genuine, 'naive' example of language use, whereas dictionaries can result from an effort of introspection performed by language experts, i.e. lexicographers.

2. *Bread and butter* and *drink and drive* are fixed expressions: in the Associated Press corpus, the two content words are always two words apart whenever they are found near each other, i.e. the mean separation is two, and the variance is zero. *Computer scientist* and *United States* are compounds which also have a very fixed word order (i.e. little variance), but the average separation is closer to one word rather than two. In contrast, 'relations such as *man/woman* are less fixed, as indicated by a larger variance in their separation. (The nearly zero value for the mean separation of *man/women* indicates that words appear about equally often in either order). Lexical relations come in several varieties. There are some like *refraining from* which are fairly fixed, and others like *keeping* (someone or something) *from* which are almost certain to be separated by a direct object' (Church et al. 1991: 34).

3. (i) The term 'lexical acquisition' is also used in the sense of a child's acquisition of his or her mental lexicon, which is of course not the primary sense intended in this book.

4. Mani and MacMillan (1996) use an algorithm which first segments the text into the appropriate units. A 'Mention Generator' (MS) then suggests certain sequences of words as candidate names, allowing various knowledge sources (KSs) to sift through these suggestions and consider which choice is best. Among other things, the MS sifts through the text using capitalised words as

candidate names; when it is sentence initial, the beginning word is excluded if it happens to be a function word. The KSs use heuristics such as looking for suffixes (like 'Inc'), prefixes followed by specific function words (e.g. 'bank of'), patterns involving '&' and exploiting lexicons containing names of organizations. The KSs also look for appositive phrases (e.g. 'X, a machine-tool supplier') and honorifics (like 'mr', 'His Holiness', 'Lt.Col') to make inferences about personhood, as well as gender and job occupation. There are also location KSs which use a lexicon of place names and geography-related headwords (e.g. 'the Bay of Fundy').

CHAPTER 5

1. See Miller (1990). A hyponym/hypernym is a semantic relation between word meanings, e.g. *maple* is a hyponym of *tree*, and *plant* is a hypernym of *tree*. A meronym/holonym is a part-whole (HASA) relation, e.g. *beak* and *wing* are meronyms of *bird*.

2. (i) Miller (1990) and his co-workers suggest *televangelist* as a possible example, since it takes the following levels: @ —> *evangelist* @ —> *preacher* @ —> *clergyman* @ —> *spiritual leader* @ —> *person*. [although a cursory examination of WordNet Version 1.5 seems to suggest that it is now listed as only => *evangelist, revivalist, gospeler, gospeller*].

   (ii) The repetition of generic information over and over in a redundant system suggests that each additional level means an increasingly severe burden on lexical memory.

3. *Beak* and *wing* must also be meronyms of *canary*.

CHAPTER 6

1. The lexicon detailed in Appendix A contains types of information very similar to the ones postulated by John Sinclair in his lexical framework. For instance, built into the use of *claim* is a prosody of 'resolution of someone's demand', controlling semantic preference verbs such as *drop, entertain, lodge, submit,* and *waive*.

2. It helps in the reduction of ambiguity for a particular domain. For instance, *tender* in business English (as in *It's time for us to submit the* tender) is never associated with the notion of tenderness in general English, as in the expression *Tender is the night*.

Bibliography

Aarts, J. and Meijs, W. (eds) (1984) *Corpus Linguistics: Recent Developments in the Use of Computer Corpora in English Language Research*, Amsterdam: Rodopi.

Aarts, J. and Meijs, W. (eds) (1986) *Corpus Linguistics II: New Studies in the Analysis and Exploitation of Computer Corpora*, Amsterdam: Rodopi.

Aarts, J. and Meijs, W. (eds) (1990) *Theory and Practice in Corpus Linguistics*, Amsterdam: Rodopi.

Aarts, J., de Haan, P. and Oostdijk, N. (eds) (1993) *English Language Corpora: Design, Analysis, and Exploitation*, Amsterdam: Rodopi.

Aarts, J. and van den Heuvel, T. (1985) 'Computational tools for the syntactic analysis of corpora', *Linguistics*, 23: 303–35.

Adam, J. H. (1989) *Longman Dictionary of Business English (2nd edition)*, Harlow, Longman and York Press.

Adriaens, G. and Small, S. L. (1988) 'Word Expert Parsing revisited in a cognitive science perspective', in Small et al. (eds), pp. 13–43.

Aijmer, K. and Altenberg, B. (eds) (1991) *English Corpus Linguistics: Studies in honour of Jan Svartvik*, Harlow: Longman.

Aitchison. J. (1987) *Words in the Mind: An Introduction to the Mental Lexicon (1st edition)*, Oxford: Blackwell.

Aitchison, J. (1994) *Words in the Mind: An Introduction to the Mental Lexicon (2nd edition)*, Oxford: Blackwell.

Akkerman, E. (1989) 'An independent analysis of the LDOCE grammar coding system', in Boguraev and Briscoe (eds), pp. 65–83.

Alonge, A. (1992) 'Machine-readable dictionaries and lexical information on verbs', in Tommola et al. (eds), I, pp. 195–202.

Amsler, R. A. (1982) 'Computational lexicology: A research program', *Proceedings of the National Computer Conference, Houston, May*, AFIPS: 657–63.

Amsler, R. A. (1984) 'Lexical knowledge bases', *COLING–84 (Proceedings of the 10th International Conference on Computational Linguistics, Stanford, California)*, Association for Computational Linguistics: 458–9.

Amsler, R. A. (1989) 'Words and worlds', in Wilks (ed.), pp. 11–5.

Andry, F., Fraser, N. M., McGlashan, S., Thornton, S. and Youd, N. J. (1992) 'Making *DATR* work for speech: Lexicon compilation in SUNDIAL', *Computational Linguistics (Special Issue on Inheritance: II)*, 18, 3: 245–67.

Anick, P. and Pustejovsky, J. (1990) 'An application of lexical semantics to knowledge acquisition from corpora', *COLING-90 (Proceedings of the 13th International Conference on Computational Linguistics, Helsinki)*, 2: 7–12.

Armstrong, S. (ed.) (1994) *Using Large Corpora*, Cambridge, MA: MIT Press.

Armstrong-Warwick, S. (1995) 'Automated lexical resources in Europe: a survey', in Walker et al. (eds), pp. 357–403.

Aronoff, M. (1992) 'Lexemes', in Bright (ed.) *International Encyclopedia of Linguistics*, 2, Oxford: OUP, p. 325.

Atkins, B. T. S. (1991) 'Building a lexicon: the contribution of lexicography', *International Journal of Lexicography*, 4, No. 3, pp. 167–204.

Atkins, B. T. S., Clear, J. and Ostler, N. (1992) 'Corpus design criteria', *Literary and Linguistic Computing, Journal of the Association for Literary and Linguistic Computing*, 7, 1: 1–16.

Atkins, B. T. S. and Levin, B. (1991) 'Admitting impediments', in Zernik (ed.), pp. 233–62.

Atkins, B. T. S., Levin, B. and Zampolli, A. (1994) 'Computational approaches to the lexicon: An overview', in Atkins and Zampolli (eds), pp. 17–45.

Atkins, B. T. S. and Zampolli, A. (eds) (1994) *Computational Approaches to the Lexicon*, Oxford: OUP.

Atwell, E. S. (1987) 'A parsing expert system which learns from corpus analysis', in Meijs (ed.) *Corpus Linguistics and Beyond (Proceedings of the Seventh International Conference on English Language Research on Computerized Corpora)*, Amsterdam: Rodopi, pp. 227–34.

Bailey, R. W. (1986) 'Dictionaries of the next century', in Ilson (ed.), pp. 123–137.

Bailey, R. W. (ed.) (1987) *Dictionaries of English: Prospects for the Record of Our Language*, Ann Arbor: The University of Michigan Press.

Baker, M., Francis, G. and Tognini-Bonelli, E. (eds) (1993) *Text and Technology: In Honour of John Sinclair*, Philadelphia: John Benjamins.

Ballard, B. W. and Jones, M. (1992) 'Computational linguistics', in Shapiro (ed.) *Encyclopedia of Artificial Intelligence (2nd ed.)*, New York: John Wiley, pp. 203–24.

Barnbrook, G. (1993) 'The automatic analysis of dictionaries: parsing COBUILD explanations', in Baker et al. (eds), pp. 312–31.

Barnbrook G. (1996) *Language and Computers: A Practical Introduction to the Computer Analysis of Language*, Edinburgh: Edinburgh University Press.

Barnett, B., Lehmann, H. and Zoeppritz, M. (1986) 'A word database for natural language processing', in *COLING-86, Bonn*, pp. 435–40.

Barry, R. E. (1989) *Business English for the 90's (3rd ed.)*, Englewood Cliffs, NJ: Prentice-Hall.

Barsalou, L. W. (1992) 'Frames, concepts, and conceptual fields', in Lehrer and Kittay (eds), pp. 21–74.

Basili, R. and Pazienza, M. T. (1992) 'Computational lexicons: The neat examples and the odd exemplars', *ANLP-92: Proceedings of the Third Conference on Applied Natural Language Processing, Trento, Italy*, Association for Computational Linguistics: 96–103.

Basili, R., Pazienza, M. T. and Velardi, P. (1992) 'A shallow syntactic analyser to extract word associations from corpora', *Literary and Linguistic Computing (Journal of the Association for Literary and Linguistic Computing)*, 7, 2: 113–23.

Basili, R., Pazienza, M. T. and Velardi, P (1996) 'A context driven conceptual clustering method for verb classification', in Boguraev and Pustejovsky (eds), pp. 117–42.

Beale, A. D. (1987) 'Towards a distributional lexicon', in Garside et al. (eds), pp. 149–62.

Beale, A. D. (1989) *The Development of a Distributional Lexicon: A Contribution to Computational Lexicography*, PhD thesis, Lancaster University.

Beaugrande, R. de, and Dressler, W. (1981) *Introduction to Text Linguistics*, New York: Longman.

Beckwith, R., Fellbaum, C., Gross, D. and Miller, G. A. (1991) 'WordNet: a lexical database organized on psycholinguistic principles', in Zernik (ed.), pp. 211–32.

Bennett, P. A., Johnson, R. L., McNaught, J., Pugh, J., Sager, J. C. and Somers, H. L. (1986) *Multilingual Aspects of Information Technology*, Hants: Gower.

Benson, M., Benson, E. and Ilson, R. (1986) *The BBI Combinatory Dictionary of English*, Amsterdam/Philadelphia: John Benjamins.

Biber, D. (1988) *Variation across Speech and Writing*, Cambridge: Cambridge University Press.

Biber, D. (1992) 'Using computer-based text corpora to analyze the referential strategies of spoken and written texts', in Svartvik (ed.), pp. 213–52.

Biber, D. (1993) 'Representativeness in corpus design', *Literary and Linguistic Computing (Journal of the Association for Literary and Linguistic Computing)*, 8, 4: 243–57.

Bindi, R., Calzolari, N., Monachini, M. and Pirelli, V. (1991) 'Lexical knowledge acquisition from textual corpora: a multivariate statistic approach as an integration to traditional methodologies', in *Using Corpora: Proceedings of the Seventh Annual Conference of the UW Centre for the New OED and Text Research, St Catherine's College, Oxford*, pp. 170–96.

Black, E. and Leech, G. (eds) (1993) *Statistically-driven Computer Grammars of English: The IBM/Lancaster Approach*, Amsterdam: Rodopi.

Bloomfield L (1933. *Language*, London: Allen and Unwin.

Boguraev, B. (1991) 'Building a lexicon: the contribution of computers', *International Journal of Lexicography*, 4, No. 3: 227–60.

Boguraev, B. and Briscoe, E. J. (1989) 'Utilising the LDOCE grammar codes', in Boguraev and Briscoe (eds), 85–116.

Boguraev, B. and Briscoe, E. J. (eds) (1989) *Computational Lexicography for Natural Language Processing*, London and New York: Longman.

Boguraev, B., Byrd, R. L., Klavans, J. L. and Neff, M. S. (1989) 'From structural analysis of lexical resources to semantics in a lexical knowledge base', in Zernik (ed.).

Boguraev, B. and Levin, B. (1993) 'Models for lexical knowledge bases', in Pustejovsky (ed.), pp. 325–40.

Boguraev, B. and Pustejovsky, J. (1996) 'Issues in text-based lexicon acquisition', in Boguraev and Pustejovsky (eds), pp. 3–17.

Boguraev, B. and Pustejovsky, J. (eds) (1996) *Corpus Processing for Lexical Acquisition*, Cambridge, MA: MIT Press.

Bradley, J. (1990) *TACT User's Guide (Version 1.2)*, University of Toronto.

Brent, M. R. (1994) 'From grammar to lexicon: unsupervised learning of lexical syntax', in Armstrong (ed.), pp. 203–22.

Bresnan, J. (ed.) (1982) *The Mental Representation of Grammatical Relation*, Cambridge, MA: MIT Press.

Brill, E. (1992) 'A simple rule-based part of speech tagger', *ANLP-92: Proceedings of the Third Conference on Applied Natural Language Processing, Trento, Italy*, Association for Computational Linguistics: 152–55.

Briscoe, T. (1992) 'Robust, simple parsers for naturally occurring input', in *Thirteenth ICAME Conference*, Plasmolen, pp. 15–22. (vademecum)

Briscoe, T., Copestake, A. and Boguraev, B. (1990) 'Enjoy the paper: lexical semantics via lexicology', *COLING-90 (Proceedings of the 13th International Conference on Computational Linguistics)*, 2: 42–7.

Briscoe, T., Copestake, A. and de Paiva, V. (eds) (1993) *Inheritance, Defaults, and the Lexicon*, Cambridge: CUP.

Bungarten, T. (1979) 'Das Korpus als empirische Grundlage in der Linguistik und Literaturwissenschaft', in Bergenholtz and Schaeder (eds) *Empirische Textwissenschaft: Aufbau und Auswertung von Text-Corpora*, Königstein: Scriptor Verlag, pp. 28–51.

Burchfield, R. (ed.) (1987) *Studies in Lexicography*, Oxford: OUP.

Burnard, L. (1992) 'Tools and techniques for computer-assisted text processing', in Butler (ed.), pp. 1–28.

Burnard, L. (1995) 'What is SGML and how does it help?' in Ide and Veronis (eds), pp. 41–50.

Butler, C. S. (1985) *Computers in Linguistics*, Oxford: Blackwell.

Butler, C. S. (1990) 'Language and computation', in Collinge (ed.) *Encyclopedia of Language*, London: Routledge, pp, 611–65.

Butler, C. S. (ed.) (1992) *Computers and Written Texts*, Oxford: Blackwell.

Calzolari, N. (1991a) 'Structure and access in an automated lexicon and related issues', in Cignoni and Peters (eds), pp. 139–61.

Calzolari, N. (1991b) 'Lexical databases and textual corpora: perspectives of integration for a lexical knowledge base', in Zernik (ed.), pp. 191–208.

Calzolari, N. and Bindi, R. (1990) 'Acquisition of lexical information from a large textual Italian corpus', *COLING-90 (Proceedings of the 13th International Conference on Computational Linguistics, Helsinki)*, 3: 54–59.

Calzolari, N. and Picchi, E. (1994) 'A lexical workstation: from textual data to structured database', in Atkins and Zampolli (eds), pp. 439–67.

Calzolari, N. and Zampolli, A. (1991) 'Lexical databases and textual corpora: a trend of convergence between Computational Linguistics and Literary and Linguistic Computing', in Lancashire (ed.) *Research in Humanities Computing, 1 (Selected Papers from the ALLC/ACH Conference, Toronto, June 1989)*, Oxford: Clarendon Press, pp. 273–307.

Carlson, L. and Nirenburg, S. (1992) 'Practical world modeling for NLP applications', in *Proceedings of the Third Conference on Applied Natural Language Processing, Trento, Italy*, Association for Computational Linguistics, pp. 235–36.

Carroll, J. and Grover, C. (1989) 'The derivation of a large computational lexicon for English from LDOCE', in Boguraev and Briscoe (eds), pp. 117–33.

Carter, R. (1987) *Vocabulary*, London: Allen and Unwin.

CELEX (1986) *CELEX News, December 1986, Newsletter No. 1.*, Centre for Lexical Information, Nijmegen University.

CELEX (1987) *CELEX News, October 1987, Newsletter No. 2.*, Centre for Lexical Information, Nijmegen University.

CELEX (1988a) *CELEX News, April 1988, Newsletter No. 3.*, Centre for Lexical Information, Nijmegen University.

CELEX (1988b) *CELEX News, December 1988, Newsletter No. 4.*, Centre for Lexical Information, Nijmegen University.

CELEX (1990) *CELEX News, August 1990, Newsletter No. 5.*, Centre for Lexical Information, Nijmegen University.

CELEX (1991) *User's Guide*, Centre for Lexical Information, Nijmegen University.

Chomsky, N. (1965) *Aspects of the Theory of Syntax*, Cambridge, MA: MIT Press.

Chomsky, N. (1970) 'Remarks on nominalization', in Jacobs and Rosenbaum (eds) *Readings in English Transformational Grammar*, London: Ginn, pp. 184–221.

Chomsky, N. (1986) *Knowledge of Language*, New York: Praeger.

Chomsky, N. (1995) *The Minimalist Program*, Cambridge, MA: MIT Press.

Chomsky, N. and Halle, M. (1968) *The Sound Pattern of English*, New York: Harper and Row.

Church, K. and Hanks, P. (1990) 'Word association norms, mutual information, and lexicography', *Computational Linguistics*, 16, 1: 22–9.

Church, K., Gale, W., Hanks, P. and Hindle, D. (1991) 'Using statistics in lexical analysis', in Zernik (ed.), pp. 115–64.

Church, K. and Mercer, R. L. (1994) 'Introduction to the special issue on computational linguistics using large corpora', in Armstrong (ed.), pp. 1–24.

Church, K. W., Gale, W., Hanks, P., Hindle, D. and Moon, R. (1994) 'Lexical substitutability', in Atkins and Zampolli (eds), pp. 153–77.

Cignoni, L. and Peters, C. (eds) (1991) *Linguistica Computazionale, 7, Nos. 1 and 2: Computational Lexicology and Lexicography (Special Issue Dedicated to Bernard Quemada)*, Pisa: Istituto di Linguistica Computazionale.

Clear, J. (1992) 'Corpus sampling', in Leitner (ed.), pp. 21–31.

Clear, J. (1993) 'From Firth principles: computational tools for the study of collocation', in Baker et al. (eds), pp. 271–92.

Clocksin, R. and Mellish, C. (1981) *Programming in Prolog*, Berlin: Springer-Verlag.

Collin, P. H. (1986) *English Business Dictionary*, Middlesex: Peter Collin.

Copestake, A. (1992) 'The ACQUILEX LKB: representation issues in semi-automatic acquisition of large lexicons', in *Proceedings of the Third Conference on Applied Natural Language Processing, Trento, Italy*, Association for Computational Linguistics, pp. 88–95.

Copestake, A. and Briscoe, T. (1991) 'Lexical operations in a unification-based framework', in Pustejovsky and Bergler (eds), pp. 88–101.

Copestake, A., Sanfilipp, A., Briscoe, T. and de Paiva, V. (1993) 'The ACQUILEX LKB: an introduction', in Briscoe et al. (eds), pp. 148–63.

Cowie, A. P. (ed.) (1989) *Oxford Advanced Learner's Dictionary of Current English (4th edition)*, Oxford: OUP.

Cowie, A. P. (1990) 'Language as words', in Collinge (ed.) *Encyclopedia of Language*, London: Routledge, pp. 671–700.

Crowther, J. (ed.) (1992) *Oxford Advanced Learner's Dictionary of Current English (Encyclopedic Edition)*, Oxford: OUP.

Crowther, J. (ed.) (1995) *Oxford Advanced Learner's Dictionary of Current English (5th edition)*, Oxford: OUP.

Cruse, D. A. (1986) *Lexical Semantics*, Cambridge: CUP.

Crystal, D. (1987) *Cambridge Encyclopedia of Language*, Cambridge: CUP.

Crystal, D. (1995) *Cambridge Encyclopedia of the English Language*, Cambridge: CUP.

Cutting, D., Kupiec, J., Pedersen, J. and Sibun, P. (1992) 'A practical part-of-speech-tagger', in *Proceedings of the Third Conference on Applied Natural Language Processing, Trento, Italy*, Association for Computational Linguistics, pp. 133–40.

Daelemans, W., Gazdar, G. and de Smedt, K. (1992a) 'Inheritance in natural language processing', *Computational Linguistics (Special Issue on Inheritance: I)*, 18, 2: 205–18.

Daelemans, W. and Powers, D. (eds) (1992b) *Background and Experiments in Machine Learning of Natural Language (Proceedings of the First SHOE Workshop)*, The Netherlands: Tilburg University.

de Haan, P. (1992) 'The optimum corpus sample size?' in Leitner (ed.), pp. 3–19.

Eisele, A. and Do'rre, J. (1986) 'A lexical functional grammar system in PROLOG', *COLING-86*: 551–3.

Ellison, P. (1990) 'Standard Generalized Markup Language'. 'Awareness'

Seminar Document: Manchester Computing Centre.

Estival, D. (1991) 'Declarativeness and linguistic theory', in Herin-Aime, Dieng, Regourd and Angoujard (eds), *Knowledge Modeling and Expertise Transfer*, Amsterdam: IOS Press, pp. 471–91.

Evans, R. (1990) 'An introduction to the Sussex PROLOG DATR system', in Evans and Gazdar (ed.), pp. 63–71.

Evans, R. and Cahill, L. (1990) 'An application of DATR: the TIC lexicon', in Evans and Gazdar (eds), pp. 31–9.

Evans, R. and Gazdar, G. (1989a) 'Inference in DATR', in *ACL Proceedings, Fourth European Conference*, pp. 66–71. Also in Evans and Gazdar (1990c), pp. 15–20.

Evans, R. and Gazdar, G. (1989b) 'The semantics of DATR', in Cohn (ed.) *Proceedings of the Seventh Conference of the Society for Artificial Intelligence and the Simulation of Behaviour*, London: Pitman/Morgan Kaufmann, 79–87. Also in Evans and Gazdar (eds) (1990), pp. 21–30.

Evans, R. and Gazdar, G. (1990) *The DATR papers*. Technical Report CSRP 139, School of Cognitive and Computing Sciences, University of Sussex, Falmer: Sussex.

Evans, R., Gazdar, G. and Moser, L. (1993) 'Prioritised multiple inheritance in DATR', in Briscoe et al. (eds), pp. 38–57.

Evens, M. (ed.) (1988) *Relational Models of the Lexicon: Representing Knowledge in Semantic Networks*, Cambridge: CUP.

Evens, M., Litowitz, B., Markowitz, J., Smith, R. and Werner, O. (1980) *Lexical-Semantic Relations: A Comparative Survey*, Alberta: Linguistic Research Inc.

Everaert, M., van der Linden, E., Schenk, A., and Schreuder, R. (eds) (1995) *Idioms: Structural and Psychological Perspectives*, Hillsdale, NJ: Lawrence Erlbaum.

Fass, D. (1993) 'Lexical semantic constraints', in Pustejovsky (ed.), pp. 263–89.

Fillmore, C. (1968) 'The case for case', in Bach and Harms (eds) *Universals in Linguistic Theory*, New York: Holt, Rinehart and Winston, pp. 1–88.

Fillmore, C. (1971) 'Types of lexical information', in Steinberg and Jakobivits (eds) *Semantics*, Cambridge: CUP, pp. 370–92.

Fillmore, C. (1977) 'Topics in lexical semantics', in Cole (ed.) *Current Issues in Linguistic Theory*, Bloomington: Indiana University Press, pp. 76–138.

Fillmore, C. (1985) 'Frames and the semantics of understanding', in *Quaderni di Semantica*, VI, 2, pp. 222–254.

Fillmore, C. (1992) '"Corpus linguistics" or "Computer-aided armchair linguistics"', in Svartvik (ed.), pp. 35–60.

Fillmore, C. and Atkins, B. T. (1992) 'Toward a frame-based lexicon: The semantics of RISK and its neighbours', in Lehrer and Kittay (eds), pp. 75–102.

Fillmore, C. and Atkins, B. T. (1994) 'Starting where the dictionaries stop: The challenge of corpus lexicography', in Atkins and Zampolli (eds), pp. 349–93.

Firth, J. R. (1957) 'A synopsis of linguistic theory, 1930–1955', in *Studies in Linguistic Analysis*, Special Volume, Philological Society, pp. 1–32.

Flickinger, D. P. (1992) 'Natural Language Processing: Lexical organization', in Bright (ed.) *International Encyclopedia of Linguistics,* 3, Oxford: OUP, pp. 66–7.

Fligelstone, S. (1992) 'Developing a scheme for annotating text to show anaphoric relations', in Leitner (ed.), pp. 153–70.

Francis, G. (1993) 'A corpus-driven approach to grammar: principles, methods and examples', in Baker et al. (eds), pp. 137–56.

Francis, W. N. and Kucera, H. (1982) *Frequency Analysis of English Usage: Lexicon and Grammar,* Boston: Houghton Mifflin.

Fraser, N. M. and Hudson, R. H. (1992) 'Inheritance in Word Grammar', *Computational Linguistics (Special Issue on Inheritance*: I), 18,2: 133–58.

Frawley, W. (1988) 'Relational models and metascience', in Evens (ed.), pp. 335–72.

Garside, R. (1987) 'The CLAWS word-tagging system', in Garside et al. (eds), pp. 30–41.

Garside, R., Leech, G. and McEnery, A. (eds) (1997) *Corpus Annotation: Linguistic Information from Computer Text Corpora,* Harlow: Addison Wesley Longman.

Garside, R., Leech, G. and Sampson, G. (eds) (1987) *The Computational Analysis of English: A Corpus-Based Approach,* Harlow: Longman.

Gay, H., O'Kill, B., Seed, K. and Whitcut, J. (1984) *Longman Dictionary of the English Language,* Harlow: Longman.

Gazdar, G. (1987) 'Linguistic applications of default inheritance mechanisms', in Whitelock et al. (eds), pp. 37–67.

Gazdar, G. (1988) 'The organization of computational lexicons', Cognitive Science Research Paper CSRP 99, University of Sussex: School of Cognitive and Computing Sciences.

Gazdar, G. (1990) 'An introduction to DATR', in Evans and Gazdar (ed.), pp. 1–14.

Gazdar, G. and Mellish, C. (1989) *Natural Language Processing in PROLOG: An Introduction to Computational Linguistics,* Wokingham, England: Addison-Wesley.

Ghadessy, M. (ed.) (1993) *Register Analysis: Theory and Practice,* London: Pinter.

Ghadessy, M. and Webster, J. (1988) 'Form and function in English business letters: implications for computer-based learning', in Ghadessy (ed.) *Registers of Written English: Situational Factors and Linguistic Features,* London: Pinter, pp. 110–27.

Gleason, H. A. (1975) 'The relation of lexicon and grammar', in Householder and Saporta (eds), pp. 85–102.

Greenbaum, S. (1991) 'The development of the International Corpus of English', Aijmer and Altenberg (eds), pp. 83–91.

Greenbaum, S. (ed.) (1996) *Comparing English Worldwide: The International Corpus of English,* Oxford: Clarendon Press.

Greenbaum, S. and Nelson, G. (1996) 'The International Corpus of English (ICE) Project', *World Englishes* 15, No. 1: pp. 3–15.

Grimes, J. E. (1988) 'Information dependencies in lexical subentries', in Evens (ed.), pp. 167–81.

Grishman, R. (1986) *Computational Linguistics: An Introduction*, Cambridge, CUP.

Gross, M. (1994) 'Constructing lexicon-grammars', in Atkins and Zampolli (eds), pp. 213–63.

Grover, C., Briscoe, T., Carroll, J. and Boguraev, B. (1988) 'The Alvey Natural Language Tools Project Grammar: A wide-coverage computational grammar of English', Lancaster Working Papers in Linguistics, No. 47.

Gruber, J. S. (1985) 'Lexical, conceptual, and encyclopedic meaning', *Quaderni di Semantica*, VI, 2, pp. 254–267.

Halliday, M. A. K. (1981) 'Text semantics and clause grammar: some patterns of realization', in Copeland and Davis (eds) *Seventh LACUS Forum 1980*, Columbia: Hornbeam Press, pp. 31–59.

Halliday, M. A. K. (1985) *An Introduction to Functional Grammar (1st edition)*, London: Edward Arnold.

Halliday, M. A. K. (1991) 'Corpus studies and probabilistic grammar', in Aijmer and Altenberg (eds), pp. 30–43.

Halliday, M. A. K. (1992) 'Language as system and language as instance: The corpus as a theoretical construct', in Svartvik (ed.), pp. 61–77.

Halliday, M. A. K. (1994) *An Introduction to Functional Grammar (2nd edition)*. London: Edward Arnold.

Halliday, M. A. K. and Hasan, R. (1985) *Language, Context, and Text: Aspects of Language in a Social-Semiotic Perspective*, Victoria: Deakin University Press.

Halteren, H. van, and Heuvel, T. van den (1990) *Linguistic Exploitation of Syntactic Databases: The Use of the Nijmegen Linguistic Database Program*, Amsterdam: Rodopi.

Halvorsen, P.-K. (1988) 'Computer applications of linguistic theory', in Newmeyer (ed.) *Linguistics: The Cambridge Survey*, 2 (*Linguistic Theory: Extensions and Implications*), Cambridge: CUP, pp. 198–219.

Harris, Z. S. (1991) *A Theory of Language and Information: A Mathematical Approach*, Oxford: Clarendon.

Hartmann, R. R. K. (ed.) (1983) *Lexicography: Principles and Practice*, London and New York: Academic Press.

Hasan, R. (1987) 'The grammarian's dream: Lexis as most delicate grammar', in Halliday and Fawcett (eds) *New Developments in Systemic Linguistics*, 1 (*Theory and Description*), London: Pinter, pp. 184–211.

Hearst, M. A. (1991) 'Noun homograph disambiguation using local context in large text corpora', in *Using Corpora: Proceedings of the Seventh Annual Conference of the UW Centre for the New OED and Text Research, St Catherine's College, Oxford*, pp. 1–22.

Hearst, M. and Schütze, H. (1996) 'Customizing a lexicon to better suit a computational task', in Boguraev and Pustejovsky (eds), pp. 77–96.

Heid, U. (1996) 'Using lexical functions for the extraction of collocations from dictionaries and corpora', in Wanner (ed.), pp. 115–46.

Heid, U. and McNaught, J. (1991) *EUROTRA-7 Study: Feasibility and Project Definition Study on the Reusability of Lexical and Terminological Resources in Computerized applications, Final Report*, Luxembourg: Commission of the European Communities.

Higgleton, E. and Seaton, A. (eds) (1995) *Times-Chambers Essential English Dictionary* (also published as *Harrap's Essential English Dictionary*, now *Chambers Essential English Dictionary*), Edinburgh and Singapore: Chambers and Federal Publications.

Hindle, D. (1994) 'A parser for text corpora', in Atkins and Zampolli (eds), pp. 103–51.

Hockey, S. (1988) *OCP Users' Manual (Version 2)*, Oxford: Oxford University Computing Service.

Hofland, K. and Johansson, S. (1982) *Word frequencies in British and American English*, Bergen: Norwegian Computing Centre for the Humanities; London: Longman.

Householder, F. W. and Saporta, S. (eds) (1975) *Problems in Lexicography*, Bloomington: Indiana University.

Hudson, R. A. (1984) *Word Grammar*, Oxford: Blackwell.

Hudson, R. A. (1988) 'The linguistic foundations for lexical research and dictionary design', *International Journal of Lexicography*, 1, No. 4: 287–312.

Hudson, R. A. (1990) *English Word Grammar*, Oxford: Blackwell.

Hudson, R. A. (1995) 'Identifying the linguistic foundations for lexical research and dictionary design', in Walker et al. (eds), pp. 21–51.

Hüllen, W. and Schulze, R. (eds) (1988) *Understanding the Lexicon: Meaning, Sense and World Knowledge in Lexical Semantics*, Tübingen: Max Niemeyer Verlag.

Hutchins, W. J. and Somers, H. L. (1992) *An Introduction to Machine Translation*, London: Academic Press.

Ide, N. (1992) 'What is computational linguistics?', *The Finite String (ACL newsletter)*, 18, 3, Association for Computational Linguistics: 65–8.

Ide, N. and Veronis, J. (1992) 'Outline of a model for lexical databases', *ALLC-ACH '92: Conference Abstracts and Programme (6–9 April 1992, Christ Church, Oxford)*, pp. 145–150.

Ide, N. and Sperberg-McQueen, C. M. (1995) 'The Text Encoding Initiative: Its history, goals, and future development', in Ide and Veronis (eds), pp. 5–15.

Ide, N. and Veronis, J. (1995) 'Encoding dictionaries', in Ide and Veronis (eds), pp. 167–79.

Ide N, and J. Veronis (eds) (1995) *Text Encoding Initiative: Background and Context*, Dordrecht: Kluwer.

Ilson, R. (ed.) (1985) *Dictionaries, Lexicography and Language Learning*, Oxford: Pergamon.

Ilson, R. (ed.) (1986) *Lexicography: An Emerging International Profession*, Manchester: Manchester University Press and Fulbright Commission.

Imlah, W. (1987) 'Lexical database requirements: LOKI deliverable NL2.a.' Technical Report, Scicon Ltd.

Imlah, W. G. and Demoen, B. (1988) 'A flexible Prolog-based lexical database system', in Gray and Lucas (eds) *Prolog and Databases: Implementations and New Directions*, Chichester: Ellis Horwood, pp. 332–9.

Ingria, R., Boguraev, B. and Pustejovsky, J. (1992) 'Dictionary/Lexicon', in Shapiro (ed.) *Encyclopedia of Artificial Intelligence* (2nd ed.), New York: John Wiley, pp. 341–65.

IPA (1987) *Journal of the International Phonetic Association*, 17, 22: 94–144.

Isoda, M., Aiso, H., Kamibayashi, N. and Matsunaga, Y. (1986) 'Model for lexical knowledge base', *COLING-86*: 451–3.

Jackendoff, R. (1975) 'Morphological and semantic regularities in the lexicon', *Language*, 51: 639–71.

Jackendoff, R. (1983) *Semantics and Cognition*, Cambridge, MA: MIT Press.

Jackendoff, R. (1992a) 'What is a concept?', in Lehrer and Kittay (eds), pp. 191–208.

Jackendoff, R. (1992b) 'The boundaries of the lexicon, or if it isn't lexical, what is it?' (Paper presented at the 9th Eastern States Conference on Linguistics, ESCOL), 24 November 1992.

Jackendoff, R. (1995) 'The boundaries of the lexicon', in Everaert et al. (eds), pp. 133–65.

Jackson, H. (1988) *Words and their Meanings*, Harlow: Longman.

Jacobs, P. S. (1991) 'Making sense of lexical acquisition', in Zernik (ed.), pp. 29–44.

Jacobs, P. S. (1992) 'Joining statistics with NLP for text categorization', *Proceedings of the Third Conference on Applied Natural Language Processing, Trento, Italy*, Association for Computational Linguistics: 178–85.

Jelinek, F. (1985) 'Self-organized language modeling for speech recognition' (Technical report), Yorktown Heights, N.Y.: Continuous Speech Recognition Group, IBM Thomas J. Watson Research Center. Reprinted in Waibel and Lee (eds) (1990) *Readings in Speech Recognition*, San Mateo: Morgan Kaufmann, pp. 450–506.

Jensen, K. and Binot, J.-L. (1988) 'Dictionary text entries as a source of knowledge for syntactic and other disambiguations', in *Second Conference on Applied Natural Language Processing* (ACL Proceedings), pp. 152–9.

Johansson, S. (ed.) (1982) *Computer Corpora in English Language Research*, Bergen: Norwegian Computing Centre for the Humanities.

Johansson, S. (1987) 'Machine-readable texts in English language research: Progress and prospects', in Lindblad and Ljung (eds), *Proceedings from the Third Nordic Conference for English Studies*, 1 (*Stockholm Studies in English 73*), Stockholm: Almqvist and Wiksell, pp. 125–37.

Johansson, S. and Hofland, K. (1989) *Frequency Analysis of English Vocabulary and Grammar: based on the LOB Corpus: 1 (Tag frequencies and word frequencies), and 2 (Tag combinations and word combinations)*, Oxford: Clarendon.

Johansson, S., Leech, G. N. and Goodluck, H. (1978) *Manual of Information to accompany the Lancaster-Oslo/Bergen Corpus of British English*, University of Oslo: Department of English.

Johansson, S. and Stenström, A. (eds) (1991) *English Computer Corpora: Selected Papers and Research guide*, Berlin: Mouton de Gruyter.

Johnson, S. (1755) *A Dictionary of the English Language*, Knapton and Others.

Kaplan, R. M. and Bresnan, J. (1982) 'Lexical functional grammar: a formal system for grammatical representation', in Bresnan (ed.), pp. 173–281.

Karlgren, H. (1990) 'Computational linguistics in 1990', *COLING-90: Proceedings of the 13th International Conference on Computational Linguistics, Helsinki, Finland*, 1, Association for Computational Linguistics: 97–9.

Kay, M. (1984a) 'Functional unification grammar: A formalism for machine translation', *COLING-84: Proceedings of the 10th International Conference on Computational Linguistics, Stanford, California*, Association for Computational Linguistics: 75–8.

Kay, M. (1984b) 'The dictionary server', *COLING-84: Proceedings of the 10th International Conference on Computational Linguistics, Stanford, California*, Association for Computational Linguistics: 461.

Kaye, G. (1988) 'The design of the database for the Survey of English Usage', in Kyto et al. (eds), pp. 145–68.

Kegl, J. (1989) 'The boundary between word knowledge and world knowledge', in Wilks (ed.), pp. 22–7.

Kilbury, J. (1990) 'Simulation of lexical acquisition', *ALLC-ACCH 90: The New Medium*, Siegen: Germany.

Kilbury, J., Naerger, P. and Renz, I. (1991) 'DATR as a lexical component for PATR', in *Proceedings of the 5th Conference of the European Chapter of the Association for Computational Linguistics*, pp. 137–42.

Kim, S. H. (1991) *Knowledge Systems through Prolog*, Oxford: OUP.

Klein, E. (1988) 'Grammar frameworks', Centre for Cognitive Science, University of Edinburgh. Research Paper.

Knight, K. (1992) 'Unification', in Shapiro (ed.) *Encyclopedia of Artificial Intelligence* (2nd ed.), New York: John Wiley, pp. 1628–37.

Knowles, F. E. (1982) 'The pivotal role of the various dictionaries in an MT system', in *Proceedings of the Conference on Practical Experience of Machine Translation*, Amsterdam: ASLIB, North-Holland, pp. 149–62.

Knowles, F. (1990) 'Language and IT: rivals or partners?', *Literary and Linguistic Computing*, 5, 1: 38–44.

Knowles, G. (1990) 'The use of spoken and written corpora in the teaching of language and linguistics', *Literary and Linguistic Computing*, 5, 1: 45–8.

Krishnamurthy, R. (1987) 'The process of compilation', in Sinclair (ed.), pp. 62–85.

Kucera, H. and Francis, W. N. (1967) *Computational Analysis of Present-Day American English*, Providence, RI: Brown University Press.

Kyto, M., Ihalainen, O. and Rissanen, M. (eds) (1988) *Corpus Linguistics, Hard and Soft: Proceedings of the Eighth International Conference on English Language Research on Computerized Corpora*, Amsterdam: Rodopi.

Lamb, S. (1973) 'Linguistic and cognitive networks', in Makkai and Lockwood (eds), *Readings in Stratificational Linguistics*, University of Alabama Press, pp. 60–83.

Leech, G (1981) *Semantics: The Study of Meaning*, London: Penguin.

Leech, G. (1987) 'General introduction', in Garside et al. (eds), pp. 1–15.

Leech, G. (ed.) (1990) *Proceedings of a Workshop on Corpus Resources*, Wadham College, Oxford: DTI/Speech and Language Technology Club.

Leech, G. (1991a) 'The state of the art in corpus linguistics', in Aijmer and Altenberg (eds), pp. 8–29.

Leech, G. (1991b) 'Corpora', in Malmkjær (ed.) *The Linguistics Encyclopedia*, London: Routledge, pp. 73–80.

Leech, G. (1992a) 'Corpora and theories of linguistic performance', in Svartvik (ed.), pp. 105–22.

Leech G (1992b) 'Corpus processing', in Bright (ed.) *International Encyclopedia of Linguistics*, 1, Oxford: OUP, pp. 313–4.

Leech, G. and Fligelstone, S. (1992) 'Computers and corpus analysis', in Butler (ed.), pp. 115–40.

Leech, G. and Garside, R. (1991) 'Running a grammar factory: The production of syntactically analysed corpora or "treebanks"', in Johansson and Stenström (eds), pp. 15–32.

Lehrer, A. and Kittay, E. F. (eds) (1992) *Frames, Fields and Contrasts: New Essays in Semantic and Lexical Organization*, Hillsdale, NJ: Lawrence Erlbaum.

Leitner, G. (1992) 'International corpus of English: Corpus design – problems and suggested solutions', in Leitner (ed.), pp. 33–64.

Leitner, G. (ed.) (1992) *New Directions in English Language Corpora: Methodology, Results, Software Developments*, Berlin: Mouton de Gruyter.

Lender, W. (1991) 'What's in a lexical entry? The contribution of computers to lexicography', in Cignoni and Peters (eds), *No. 2*, pp. 45–63.

Levin, B. (1991) 'Building a lexicon: the contribution of linguistics', *International Journal of Lexicography*, 4, No. 3: 205–6.

Lewis, D. (1992) 'Computers and translation', in Butler (ed.), pp. 75–113.

Louw, B. (1993) 'Irony in the text or insincerity in the writer?: the diagnostic potential of semantic prosodies', in Baker et al. (eds), pp. 157–76.

Maida, A. S. (1992) 'Frame theory', in Shapiro (ed.) *Encyclopedia of Artificial Intelligence (2nd ed.)*, New York: John Wiley, pp. 493–506.

Makkai, A. (1980) 'Theoretical and practical aspects of an associative lexicon for 20th century English', in Zgusta (ed.), pp. 125–46.

Makkai, A. and Webster, J. J. (1986) *LexECOgraphy: Towards a semiotically based structural linguistics in the age of microcomputers.* Manuscript.

Mani, I. and MacMillan, T. R. (1996) 'Identifying unknown proper names in newswire text', in Boguraev and Pustejovsky (eds), pp. 41–59.

Marcus, C. (1986) *Prolog Programming: Applications for Database Systems, Expert Systems and Natural Language Systems,* Reading, MA: Addison-Wesley.

Martin, W., Al, B. and van Sterkenburg, P. (1983) 'On the processing of a text corpus: from textual data to lexicographical information', in Hartmann (ed.), pp. 78–87.

McCawley, J. D. (1986) 'What linguists might contribute to dictionary making if they could get their act together', in Bjarkman and Raskin (eds) *The Real-World Linguist: Linguistic Applications in the 1980s,* Norwood, NJ: Ablex, pp. 1–18.

McEnery, A. (1992) *Computational Linguistics,* Wilmslow: Sigma Press.

McEnery, T. and Wilson, A. (1996) *Corpus Linguistics,* Edinburgh: Edinburgh University Press.

McNaught, J. (1988) 'Computational lexicography and computational linguistics', *Lexicographica, 4 (Special Issue on Computational Lexicography)*: 19–33.

McNaught, J. (1991) *Survey of existing reusable lexical and terminological resources: Japan, (EUROTRA-7 Study DOC-3),* Commission of the European Communities.

McNaught, J. (1992) 'Introduction to sublanguage: A tutorial', in Thompson (ed.), pp. 5–18.

McNaught, J. (1993) 'User needs for textual corpora in natural language processing', *Literary and Linguistic Computing,* 8, 4: 227–34.

McNaught, J., Nkwenti-Azeh, B., Martin, W. and ten Pas, E. (1991) *Feasibility of standards for terminological description of lexical items (EUROTRA-7 Study DOC-11),* Commission of the European Communities.

Meijs, W. (1986) 'Lexical organisation from three different angles', *Journal of the Association of Literary and Linguistic Computing,* 13, No.1.

Meijs, W. (ed.) (1987) *Corpus Linguistics and Beyond (Proceedings of the Seventh International Conference on English Language Research on Computerized Corpora),* Amsterdam: Rodopi.

Meijs, W. (1992a) 'Computers and dictionaries', in Butler (ed.), pp. 141–65.

Meijs, W. (1992b) 'Inferences and lexical relations', in Leitner (ed.), pp. 123–42.

Meijs, W. (1993) 'Exploring lexical knowledge', in Souter and Atwell (eds), pp. 249–60.

Mel'cuk, I. A. (1992) 'Lexicon: an overview', in Bright (ed.) *International Encyclopedia of Linguistics,* 2 , Oxford: OUP, pp. 332–5.

Mel'cuk, I. A. (1995) 'Phrasemes in language and phraseology in linguistics', in Everaert et al. (eds), pp. 167–232.

Mel'cuk, I. A. (1996) 'Lexical functions: a tool for the description of lexical relations in a lexicon', in Wanner (ed.), pp. 37–102.

Mel'cuk, I. A. and Zholkovsky, A. (1988) 'The explanatory–combinatorial dictionary', in Evens (ed.), pp. 41–74.

Mel'cuk, I. A. and Polguere, A. (1987) 'A formal lexicon in the Meaning-Text Theory (or How to do lexica with words)', *Computational Linguistics*, 13: 261–75.

Metzing, D. (1981) 'Frame representations and lexical semantics', in Eikmeyer and Rieser (eds) *Words, Worlds, and Contexts*, Berlin and New York: Walter de Gruyter, pp. 320–42.

Miller, G. A. (ed.) (1990) 'WordNet: An On-Line Lexical Database', *International Journal of Lexicography*, Volume 3, Number 4 (Special Issue).

Minsky, M. L. (1975) 'A framework for representing knowledge', in Winston (ed.) *The Psychology of Computer Vision*, NY: McGraw-Hill, pp. 211–80.

Moon, R. (1987) 'The analysis of meaning', in Sinclair (ed.), pp. 86–103.

Mylopoulos, J. and Brodie, M. (eds) (1989) *Readings in Artificial Intelligence and Databases*, California, San Mateo: Morgan Kaufmann.

Nakamura, J. (1993) 'Statistical methods and large corpora: a new tool for describing text types', in Baker et al. (eds), pp. 293–312.

Neff, M. S., Byrd, J. R. and Rizk, O. A. (1988) 'Creating and querying hierarchical lexical data bases', *Second Conference on Applied Natural Language Processing* (ACL Proceedings): 84–92.

Nirenburg, S. (1994) 'Lexicon acquisition for NLP: a consumer report', in Atkins and Zampolli (eds), pp. 313–47.

Nirenburg, S. and Defrise, C. (1993) 'Lexical and conceptual structure for knowledge-based machine translation', in Pustejovsky (ed.), pp. 291–323.

Nirenburg, S. and Raskin, V. (1987) 'The subworld concept lexicon and the lexicon management system', *Computational Linguistics*, 13, 3–4: 276–89.

Oakes, Michael P. (1998) *Statistics for Corpus Linguistics*, Edinburgh: Edinburgh University Press.

Ooi, V. B.Y. (1987) *Computational Lexicography: Constructing a Lexical Database in PROLOG*, M.A. dissertation, National University of Singapore.

Ooi, V. B. Y. (1993) *Computational Approaches to the Lexicon: A Lexical Frame Analysis of Business English*, PhD thesis, Lancaster University.

Ooi, V. B.Y. (1994a) 'Corpus linguistics', *SAAL Quarterly (Journal of the Singapore Association for Applied Linguistics)*, 28: 2–4.

Ooi, V. B.Y. (1994b) 'Using a sublanguage corpus (of business English) for the building of a lexical database', *Proceedings of the International Conference on Linguistic Applications (26–28 July 1994)*, Malaysia, Penang: Universiti Sains Malaysia: 145–56.

Ooi, V. B. Y. (1995) 'Corpus-based language modelling from a computational lexical perspective', *The Twenty-First LACUS Forum 1994*, North Carolina: Linguistic Association of Canada and the United States: 493–511.

Oostdijk, N. (1991) *Corpus Linguistics and the Automatic Analysis of English*, Amsterdam: Rodopi.

Palstra, R. (1988) *Telex English*, Hemel Hempstead: Prentice Hall.

Papegaaij, B. C., Sadler V. and Witkam, A. P. M. (eds) (1986) *Word Expert Semantics: An Interlingual Knowledge-Based Approach*, Dordrecht: Foris.

Paulussen, H. and Martin, W. (1992) 'DILEMMA-2: A lemmatizer-tagger for Medical Abstracts', *Proceedings of the Third Conference on Applied Natural Language Processing, Trento, Italy*, Association for Computational Linguistics: 141–46.

Piepenbrock, R. (1993) 'A longer-term view on the interaction between lexicons and text corpora in language investigation', in Souter and Atwell (eds), pp. 59–69.

Pike, K. L. (1983) 'On understanding people – an integrative philosophy', *Proceedings of the Ninth LACUS Forum*, Columbia: Hornbeam Press: 129–36.

Pike, K. L. and Pike, E. (1983) *Text and Tagmeme*, London: Frances Pinter.

Pitrat, J. (1987) 'Using declarative knowledge for understanding natural language', in Bolc (ed.) *Natural Language Parsing Systems*, Berlin: Springer-Verlag, pp. 93–135.

Pitrat, J. (1988) *An Artificial Intelligence Approach to Understanding Natural Language*, London: North Oxford Academic.

Pollard, C. and Sag, I. (1987) *Information-based Syntax and Semantics* (CSLI Lecture Notes, 13) Stanford, California: CSLI.

Popov, E.V. (1986) *Talking with Computers in Natural Language*, Berlin: Springer-Verlag.

Poznanski, V. and Sanfilippo, A. (1996) 'Detecting dependencies between semantic verb subclasses and subcategorization frames in text corpora', in Boguraev and Pustejovsky (eds), pp. 175–90.

Procter, P. (ed.) (1978) *Longman Dictionary of Contemporary English (1st edition)*, Harlow: Longman.

Procter, P. (ed.) (1995) *Cambridge International Dictionary of English*, Cambridge: CUP.

Pustejovsky, J. (1991) 'The generative lexicon', *Computational Linguistics*, 17, No. 4: 409–41.

Pustejovsky, J. (ed.) (1993) *Semantics and the Lexicon*, Dordrecht: Kluwer.

Pustejovsky, J. (1995) *The Generative Lexicon*, Cambridge, MA: MIT Press.

Pustejovsky, J. and Bergler, S. (eds) (1991) *Lexical Semantics and Knowledge Representation (Proceedings of a workshop sponsored by the special interest group on the lexicon of the Association for Computational Linguistics, 17 June 1991)*. California: University of California at Berkeley.

Pustejovsky, J., Bergler, S. and Anick, P. (1993) 'Lexical semantic techniques for corpus analysis', *Computational Linguistics*, 19, 2: 331–58.

Pustejovsky, J. and Boguraev, B. (1994) 'A richer characterization of dictionary entries: The role of knowledge representation', in Atkins and Zampolli (eds), pp. 295–311.

Quirk, R., Greenbaum, S., Leech, G. and Svartvik, J. (1985) *A Comprehensive Grammar of the English Language*, London: Longman.

Ramsay, A. M. (1991) 'Artificial Intelligence', in Malmkjær (ed.) *The Linguistics Encyclopedia*, London: Routledge, pp. 28–38.

Rayson, P. and Wilson, A. (1996) 'The ACAMRIT semantic tagging system: progress report', in Evett and Rose (eds), *Language Engineering for Document Analysis and Recognition, AISB 96 Workshop Proceedings*, Brighton, England.

Rich, E. and Knight, K. (1991) *Artificial Intelligence (2nd ed.)*, New York: McGraw-Hill.

Rieger, B. (1979) 'Repräsentivität: Von der Unangemessenheit eines Begriffs zur Kennzeichnung eines Problems linguistischer Korpusbildung', in Bergenholtz and Schaeder (eds) *Empirische Textwissenschaft: Aufbau und Auswertung von Text-Corpora*, Königstein: Scriptor Verlag, pp. 52–70.

Ritchie, G. D. (1987) 'The lexicon', in Whitelock (ed.), pp. 225–56.

Ritchie, G. D., Pulman, S. G., Black, A. W. and Russell, G. J. (1987) 'A computational framework for lexical description', *Computational Linguistics*, 13: 290–307.

Ritchie, G. D. and Thompson, H. S. (1984) 'Natural language processing', in O'Shea and Eisenstadt (eds) *Artificial Intelligence: Tools, Techniques, and Applications*, New York: Harper and Row, pp. 358–88.

Rowe, N. C. (1988) *Artificial Intelligence through Prolog*, Prentice-Hall.

Rumelhart, D. E. (1975) 'Notes on a schema for stories', in Bobrow and Collins (eds) *Representations and Understanding (Studies in Cognitive Science)*, New York: Longman, pp. 211–36.

Russell, G., Carroll, J., Ballim, A. and Warwick-Armstrong, S. (1992) 'A practical approach to multiple default inheritance for unification-based lexicons', *Computational Linguistics (Special Issue on Inheritance*: II), 18, 3: 311–37.

Sadock, J. (1991) *Autolexical Syntax: A Theory of Parallel Grammatical Representations*, Chicago: University of Chicago Press.

Sager, N. (1986) 'Sublanguage: linguistic phenomenon, computational tool', in Grishman and Kittredge (eds), pp. 1–17.

Sanfilippo, A. and Poznanski, V. (1992) 'The acquisition of lexical knowledge from combined machine-readable dictionary sources', *Proceedings of the Third Conference on Applied Natural Language Processing, Trento, Italy*, Association for Computational Linguistics: 80–7.

Schank, R. C. (1975) *Conceptual Information Processing*, Amsterdam: North Holland.

Schank, R. C. and Abelson, R. (1977) *Scripts, Plans, Goals and Understanding: An inquiry into human knowledge structures*, Hillsdale, NJ: Lawrence Erlbaum.

Schubert, L. K. (1992) 'Natural Language Processing: Semantics and knowledge representation', in Bright (ed.) *International Encyclopedia of Linguistics*, 3, Oxford: OUP, pp. 69–72.

Sebba, M. (1991) 'The adequacy of corpora in machine translation', in McEnery A (ed.) *Applied Computer Translation*, 1, 1, pp. 15–28.

Sekine, S., Carroll, J. J., Ananiadou, S. and Tsujii, J. (1992) 'Automatic learning for semantic collocation', *Proceedings of the Third Conference on Applied Natural Language Processing, Trento, Italy*, Association for Computational Linguistics:

104–10.

Sharman, R. A. (1989a) 'An Introduction to the Theory of Language Models', IBM UKSC Technical Report 204.

Sharman, R. A. (1989b) 'Probabilistic ID/LP Grammars for English', IBM UKSC Technical Report 217.

Sharman, R. A. (1990) 'The development and use of corpus-derived probabilistic language models', in Leech (ed.), pp. 16–20.

Shieber, S. M. (1984) 'The design of a computer language for linguistic information', *COLING-84: Proceedings of the 10th International Conference on Computational Linguistics, Stanford, California*, Association for Computational Linguistics: 362–66.

Shieber, S. M. (1986) *An Introduction to Unification-Based Approaches to Grammar*, Chicago: Chicago University Press.

Shieber, S. M. (1987) 'Separating linguistic analyses from linguistic theories', in Whitelock et al. (eds), pp. 1–36.

Shieber, S. (1992) 'Natural language processing: Grammar formalisms', in Bright (ed.) *International Encyclopedia of Linguistics*, 3, Oxford: OUP, pp. 61–4.

Sinclair, J. (1966) 'Beginning the study of lexis', in Bazell, Catford, Halliday and Robins (eds) *In Memory of J. R. Firth*, London: Longman, pp. 410–30.

Sinclair, J. (1972) *A Course in Spoken English Grammar*, London: OUP.

Sinclair, J. (1985) 'Lexicographic evidence', in Ilson (ed.), pp. 81–94.

Sinclair, J. (1987) 'Grammar in the dictionary', in Sinclair (ed.), pp. 104–15.

Sinclair, J. (ed.) (1987a) *Collins COBUILD English Dictionary (1st edition)*, London: HarperCollins.

Sinclair, J. (ed.) (1987b) *Looking up: An account of the COBUILD project in Lexical Computing*, London: Collins ELT.

Sinclair, J. (1991) *Corpus, Concordance, Collocation*, Oxford: OUP.

Sinclair, J. (1995) 'The search for units of meaning'. Manuscript.

Sinclair, J. (ed.) (1995) *Collins COBUILD English Dictionary (2nd Edition)*, London: HarperCollins.

Sinclair, J. (1996a) *Lexis and Lexicography*, Singapore: Unipress.

Sinclair, J. (1996b) Notes from video-conferencing sessions on lexicology, lexicography and computational linguistics for the Department of English Language and Literature, National University of Singapore, August to October. Manuscript.

Sinclair, J. and Coulthard, R. M. (1975) *Towards an Analysis of Discourse*, London: OUP.

Sinclair, J. and Kirby, D. M. (1991) 'Progress in computational lexicography', in Cignoni and Peters (eds), pp. 233–57.

Smadja, F. (1989) 'Lexical co-occurrence: the missing link', *Literary and Linguistic Computing*, 4, 3: 163–8.

Smadja, F. (1991) 'Macrocoding the lexicon with co-occurrence knowledge', in Zernik (ed.), pp. 165–89.

Smadja, F. (1994) 'Retrieving collocations from text: Xtract', in Armstrong (ed.), pp. 143–77.

Small, S. L. (1987) 'A distributed word-based approach to parsing', in Bolc (ed.) *Natural Language Parsing Systems.* Berlin: Springer-Verlag, 161–201.

Small, S. L., Cottrell, W. and Tanenhaus, M. K. (eds) (1988) *Lexical Ambiguity Resolution: Perspectives from Psycholinguistics, Neuropsychology, and Artificial Intelligence,* California, San Mateo: Morgan Kaufmann.

Smith, R. N. (1985) 'Conceptual primitives in the English lexicon', *International Journal of Human Communication,* 18, 1: *Advances in Lexicography (Special Section),* Canada: Boreal: 99–137.

Somers, H. (1990) 'Subcategorization frames and predicate types', in Schmitz, Schütz and Kunz (eds) *Linguistic Approaches to Artificial Intelligence,* Frankfurt: Verlag Peter Lang, pp. 461–88.

Souter, C. (1993) 'Harmonising a lexical database with a corpus-based grammar', in Souter and Atwell (eds), pp. 181–93.

Souter, C. and Atwell, E. (eds) (1993) *Corpus-based Computational Linguistics,* Amsterdam: Rodopi.

Sowa, J. F. (1984) *Conceptual Structures: Information Processing in Mind and Machine,* Reading, MA: Addison-Wesley.

Sowa, J. F. (ed.) (1991) *Principles of Semantic Networks: Explorations in the Representation of Knowledge,* California, San Mateo: Morgan Kaufmann.

Sowa, J. F. (1993) 'Lexical structure and conceptual structures', in Pustejovsky (ed.), pp. 223–62.

Sparck-Jones, K. (1992) 'Natural language processing: An overview', in Bright (ed.) *International Encyclopedia of Linguistics,* 3, Oxford: OUP, pp. 53–8.

Sproat, R. (1992) 'Lexicon in formal grammar', in Bright (ed.) *International Encyclopedia of Linguistics,* 2, Oxford: OUP, pp. 335–6.

Starosta, S. (1988) *The Case for Lexicase,* London: Pinter.

Stubbs, M. (1993) 'British traditions in text analysis', in Baker et al. (eds), pp. 1–33.

Stubbs, M. (1996) *Text and Corpus Analysis,* Oxford: Blackwell.

Summers, D. (ed.) (1987) *Longman Dictionary of Contemporary English (2nd edition),* Harlow: Longman.

Summers, D. (ed.) (1992) *Longman Dictionary of English Language and Culture,* London: Longman.

Summers, D. (1993) 'Longman Lancaster English Language Corpus: Criteria and design', *International Journal of Lexicography,* 6, 3: 181–208.

Summers, D. (ed.) (1995) *Longman Dictionary of Contemporary English (3rd edition),* Harlow: Longman.

Summers, D. (1996) 'Computer lexicography – the importance of representativeness in relation to frequency', in Thomas and Short (eds), pp. 260–6.

Sutton, S. (1992) *An Investigation into Statistically-based Lexical Ambiguity Resolution,* PhD thesis, Lancaster University.

Svartvik, J. (ed.) (1990) *The London-Lund Corpus of Spoken English: Description and Research*, Lund: Lund University Press.

Svartvik, J. (ed.) (1992) *Directions in Corpus Linguistics: Proceedings of Nobel Symposium No. 82, Stockholm, 4–8 August 1991*, Berlin: Mouton de Gruyter.

Svensén, B. (1993) *Practical Lexicography: Principles and Methods of Dictionary-Making*, Oxford: OUP.

Taylor, L. (1989) *Concordancing a Corpus: A guide to concordancing machine-readable corpora on the Sequent Symmetry computer*, University of Lancaster: Unit for Computer Research on the English Language.

Thomas, J. and Short, M. (eds) (1996) *Using Corpora for Language Research: Studies in the Honour of Geoffrey Leech*, London: Longman.

Thompson, H. (1989) 'Linguistic corpora for the language industry', Background paper, in Thompson (ed.).

Thompson, H. (ed.) (1992) *Record of the Workshop on Sublanguage Grammar and Lexicon Acquisition for Speech and Natural Language Processing, 7–8 January 1992*, Edinburgh.

Tommola, H., Varantola, K., Salmi-Tolonen, T. and Schopp, J. (eds) (1992) *Euralex '92 Proceedings (Parts I and II): Papers submitted to the 5th EURALEX International Congress on Lexicography in Tampere, Finland*, Finland: University of Tampere.

Trost, H. and Buchberger, E. (1986) 'Towards the automatic acquisition of lexical data', *COLING-86*: 387–9.

Velardi, P. (1991) 'Acquiring a semantic lexicon for natural language processing', in Zernik (ed.), pp. 341–67.

Velardi, P., Pazienza, M. T. and Fasolo, M. (1991) 'How to encode semantic knowledge: A method for meaning representation and computer-aided acquisition', *Computational Linguistics*, 17, 2: 153–70.

Vossen, P., Meijs, W. and den Broeder, M. (1989) 'Meaning and structure in dictionary definitions', in Boguraev and Briscoe (eds), pp. 171–92.

Vossen, P. and Copestake, A. (1993) 'Untangling definition structure into knowledge representation', in Briscoe et al. (eds), pp. 246–74.

Walker, A., McCord, M. C., Sowa, J. F. and Wilson, W. G. (1987) *Knowledge Systems and Prolog*, Reading, MA: Addison-Wesley.

Walker, D. E. (1992) 'Developing computational lexical resources', in Lehrer and Kittay (eds), pp. 421–42.

Walker, D. E., Zampolli, A. and Calzolari, N. (eds) (1995) *Automating the Lexicon: Research and Practice in a Multilingual Environment*. Oxford: OUP.

Wanner, L. (ed.) (1996) *Lexical Functions in Lexicography and Natural Language Processing*, Amsterdam: John Benjamins.

Webster, J. J. (1984) 'The Prolex Project', in *LEXeter '83 Proceedings (Papers from the International Conference on Lexicography at Exeter, 9–12 September 1983)*, Tubingen: Max Niemeyer Verlag: 435–40.

Webster, J. J. (1986) 'Project PROLEX: Operational procedures and objectives', in Makkai and Webster.

Wehrli, E. (1985) 'Design and implementation of a lexical data base', *Proceedings of the Second European Conference of the ACL*: 146–53.

White, J. (1991) 'Lexical and world knowledge: theoretical and applied viewpoints', in Pustejovsky and Bergler (eds), pp. 139–51.

White, J., Yeats, A. and Skipworth, G. (1979) *Tables for Statisticians* (3rd edition), Cheltenham: Stanley Thornes.

White J. (1991) 'Lexical and world knowledge: theoretical and applied viewpoints', in Pustejovsky and Bergler (eds), pp. 139–51.

Whitelock, P., McGee Wood, M., Somers, L. H., Johnson, R. and Bennett, P. (eds) (1987) *Linguistic Theory and Computer Applications*, London: Academic Press.

Wierzbicka, A. (1985) *Lexicography and Conceptual Analysis*, Ann Arbor: Karoma.

Wierzbicka, A. (1987) *English Speech Act Verbs: A Semantic Dictionary*, Sydney: Academic Press.

Wilks, Y. (ed.) (1989) *Theoretical Issues in Natural Language Processing*, New Jersey: Lawrence Erlbaum Associates.

Wilks, Y. A., Slator, B. M. and Guthrie, L. (1996) *Electric Words: Dictionaries, Computers, and Meanings*, Cambridge, MA: MIT Press.

Wilson. A. and Rayson, P. (1993) 'The automatic content analysis of spoken discourse: A report on work in progress', in Souter and Atwell (eds), pp. 215–26.

Winograd, T. (1975) 'Frame representations and the declarative-procedural controversy', in Bobrow and Collins (eds) *Representations and Understanding (Studies in Cognitive Science)*, New York: Longman, pp. 185–210.

Woods, A., Fletcher, P. and Hughes, A. (1986) *Statistics in Language Studies*, Cambridge: CUP.

Zeevat, H., Klein, E. and Calder, J. (1987) 'Unification Categorial Grammar', in *Working Papers in Cognitive Science*, 1, University of Edinburgh Centre for Cognitive Science, pp. 195–222.

Zernik, U. (ed.) (1989) *Proceedings of the First International Lexical Acquisition Workshop (August 21, 1989)*, Detroit, Michigan.

Zernik, U. (1991) 'Introduction', in Zernik (ed.), pp. 1–26.

Zernik, U. (ed.) (1991) *Lexical Acquisition: Exploiting On-Line Resources to Build a Lexicon*, Hillsdale, NJ: Lawrence Erlbaum.

Zgusta, L. (ed.) (1980) *Theory and Method in Lexicography: Western and Non-Western Perspectives*, Columbia, S. Carolina: Hornbeam Press.

Index

EU Authorised Representative: Easy Access System Europe Mustamäe tee 5

0, 10621 Tallinn, Estonia gpsr.requests@easproject.com

Printed and bound by CPI Group (UK) Ltd, Croydon, CR0 4YY

22/04/2025

01850386-0001